THE GOURMET PRESCRIPTION

For L., my Tamino

THE GOURMET PRESCRIPTION

DEBORAH FRIEDSON CHUD, M.D.

High Flavor Recipes for Lower Carbohydrate Diets

MANAGING EDITOR: JAIN LEMOS

FOOD PHOTOGRAPHS: TIM TURNER

AUTHOR PHOTOGRAPHS: RICK FRIEDMAN

BOOK DESIGN: MADELEINE CORSON

BAY BOOKS

QUESTIONS OR COMMENTS MAY BE SENT VIA E-MAIL TO DR. CHUD AT:
GOURMETPRESCRIPTION@KITCHENMD.COM

BAY BOOKS IS AN IMPRINT OF BAY BOOKS & TAPES, INC.
555 DE HARO ST., NO. 220, SAN FRANCISCO, CA 94107.

PUBLISHER: JAMES CONNOLLY
EDITOR: ANDREA CHESMAN
BOOK DESIGN: MADELEINE CORSON DESIGN
NUTRITIONAL ANALYSIS: MINDY HERMANN
CHEF/STYLIST: LYNNE GAGNÉ

LIBRARY OF CONGRESS CATALOGING-IN-PUBLICATION
DATA AVAILABLE
ISBN 0-912333-81-2

PRINTED IN CHINA
10 9 8 7 6 5 4 3 2 1
DISTRIBUTED BY PUBLISHERS GROUP WEST

CONTENTS

Foreword

I've only known Deborah Chud for a short time, but it feels like we've been friends a lifetime. | We're certainly kindred spirits in the kitchen. | We both share a passion for food—dreaming about it, talking about it, cooking, serving, and eating it. We both love the flavors of the Mediterranean, Latin America, North Africa, and the Far East. We both view cooking as an act of adventure, creativity, sharing, caring, and love. | We have another point in common: For health reasons we both had to make radical changes in the way we had cooked and eaten for years. In my case, the culprit was cholesterol. A decade of restaurant reviewing left me with high cholesterol levels that forced me to rethink my very notion of cooking. The result was a cookbook series—and culinary philosophy—I came to call High-Flavor, Low-Fat cooking. | For Deborah, the problem turned out to be excess insulin. Like many health conscious cooks of the 1980s, Deborah slashed the protein and fat in her diet, turning to pastas and grains of all kinds. Despite strict adherence to the nutritional wisdom of the day, she suffered from chronic pain, low energy, high cholesterol, and weight gain. | In 1996, a physician friend introduced her to the moderate protein, lower carbohydrate, low-fat food plan espoused by Dr. Barry Sears in his best-selling book, *The Zone*. Less than a month after trying the plan, she experienced a dramatic turnaround in her health. | Deborah is the sort of person who throws herself heart and soul into whatever she does. Within weeks, she was recrafting her favorite recipes to fit within the parameters of the Zone and other insulin modulating diets. She transformed her kitchen into a laboratory to develop new flavors and recipes that would revolutionize the field of lower carbohydrate cooking. | Deborah and I have yet another point in common. We both hate the word "diet." We believe that cooking should be a pleasure, not punishment, that food should make you celebrate life, not feel guilty. Of course, we want our recipes to be healthy, but above all, we want them to taste great. | Deborah Chud is a rarity among physicians who write about food: She actually puts her money where her mouth is. She doesn't just tell you what to eat. She takes you into her kitchen and shows you how to use global ingredients and cutting edge cooking techniques to make explosively flavorful food that's a pleasure to eat—regardless of your nutritional agenda. She is also one of the few in the field who develops, writes, and tests all her recipes herself in her own kitchen. She understands the main pitfall of most diets—monotony—and she shows you how to make restaurant-quality meals with such an astonishing range of flavors, you'll have a hard time believing they're good for you. Deborah also understands the time constraints under which most modern cooks operate. Her book includes more than 30 imaginative low fat, lower carbohydrate salad dressings and more than 40 intensely flavored, make-ahead sauces and condiments that can be used to jazz up simple entrees in a matter of minutes. Indeed, many of her recipes can be prepared in 30 minutes or less. You are about to embark on a culinary adventure, an adventure that will teach you new techniques, such as spice infusing and brining, high heat roasting, and the ultimate high-flavor, low-fat cooking method: stovetop smoking. You're about to discover new flavors: The soulful succulence of Smoked Allium Paste; the tongue-tingling tang of Charred Tomato Ketchup; the gentle sweetness of fructose (which sweetens without spiking your insulin levels); and the sybaritic sparkle of oven dried Tiny Tomato Jewels. You're about to take a journey that will bring you to flavor hot spots all over the planet, from Indian style Curried Ostrich Patties to Mexican Smoked Shrimp "Fajitas" (wrapped in lettuce leaves instead of tortillas), from Italian Lovers' Artichokes alla Romana and Filet Mignons with Porcini "Butter" to Not Exactly Peking Duck from the Far East. You'll also find updated versions of some of your American favorites, from Turkey Patties with Apples and Smoked Leeks to Turnip "Fries" to Smothered Pork Tenderloin with Vidalia Onions and Grapes. You'll even enjoy down-home Black-Eyed Peas and Collard Greens—dressed up in a quick sauté perfumed with white truffle oil. In short, you'll experience some awesome eating that just happens to be good for your health. When I asked Deborah to sum up her philosophy in a single sentence, she told me: "Eat as though your life depends on it." It certainly does. I can only add "Amen!" *–Steven Raichlen*

Preface I grew up in an atmosphere of serious food, serious eating, and—ultimately—serious medical consequences. My grandmother was a professional chef and caterer on Miami Beach in the '40s and '50s and a truly great Jewish cook. She made delicate, fluffy matzoh balls, quenelle-like gefilte fish, and unforgettably sweet, schmaltzy chopped liver. She used three types of bones in her stocks and deglazed her pans with wine before Julia Child ever appeared on PBS. Twenty years after her death, people still yearn for her savory stuffed breast of veal. As a baker, she was half artist, half magician. She made the moistest honey cake and the mellowest, translucent strudel. Her teglach, rugalach, and buttery polymorphous cookies sweetened Jewish celebrations in South Florida for two generations.

Unfortunately, my grandmother was also morbidly obese and, from mid-adulthood on, she battled two life-threatening complications of obesity: cancer and cardiovascular disease. Although she lived for many years following breast cancer surgery, they were years of hypertension, angina, congestive heart failure, multiple medications, side effects, and declining activity.

My grandmother had three food-loving sons. Two became obese adults with significant cardiovascular disease. One of them required bypass surgery (as has one of his obese children). The third son, my father, is an exceptional cook (and loves his own cooking!), but he has kept himself healthy through moderation and regular exercise.

I am clearly his daughter in many ways, but in none so marked as my lifelong interest in food and health. Between college and medical school, I worked my way through both volumes of *Mastering the Art of French Cooking*. During medical school, I studied hard and ate well. Jogging kept me trim and fit.

When I married my husband (also a physician) in 1984, the prevailing nutritional wisdom supported a high-carbohydrate, low-fat diet for weight control and cardiovascular health. We lived on pasta of every color and shape, polenta, couscous, bulgur, tortillas, millet, barley, wheat berries, quinoa, potatoes, and rice. I made my own bread and pizza, gnocchi and spaetzle. I bought nonstick pots and cooked with as little fat as possible. Protein appeared only at dinner, usually in the form of fish or chicken. To limit cholesterol and saturated fat, we ate no butter, eggs, or cheese and little red meat. Following my father's example, I maintained a rigorous daily exercise program that combined running with stair climbing, stationary bicycle, and skiing and rowing equipment.

To my infinite disappointment and frustration, ten years of this disciplined lifestyle resulted in a slow and steady weight gain and a "borderline" serum cholesterol. I also developed an array of musculoskeletal aches and pains from exercise-induced overuse injuries. When anti-inflammatory medications failed to help, I spent a small fortune on alternative therapies. I felt tired all the time and found myself going to bed earlier and earlier. My productivity diminished. At 44, I thought I was sliding into the inevitable physical deterioration of middle age. I was desperate and ready to try anything.

At a party, I chatted with a friend and fellow physician who suffered from a debilitating chronic disease. When I remarked on his robust appearance, he told me about his recent improvement on the Zone diet. In particular, he noted a dramatic increase in energy and an enhanced sense of well-being. The very next day, I bought and read *The Zone* by Dr. Barry Sears. Two days later, my husband and I began the Zone diet—the quintessential insulin-modulating regimen. Almost immediately, I discovered some of the benefits of better insulin control (weight loss, increased energy, pain relief) and I wanted to enjoy them for the rest of my life.

I could face a future without grain and potatoes, but there was one thing I could not give up: my passionate interest in cooking and food. Instinctively, I drew away from mathematically precise food formulas that made me feel hemmed in and restless. Instead, I sought adventures in cooking and eating that would serve the goal of insulin modulation. This book presents the best of my three years of insulin-conscious cooking.

–*Deborah Friedson Chud, M.D.*

Cooking for Insulin Modulation and Flavor

What do *The Zone, Sugar Busters!, Dr. Atkins' New Diet Revolution, Dr. Bob Arnot's Revolutionary Weight Control Program, Protein Power,* and all other "modified carbohydrate" diets have in common? They share a hormonal strategy for weight loss, blood sugar control, enhanced athletic performance, and improved cardiovascular health. If you eat (or try to eat) according to one of these programs, you are using food to affect your levels of the hormone insulin. In other words, you are practicing insulin modulation. | This is not a diet book; it is a cookbook for exuberant health. It supports insulin modulation through bold, imaginative, flavorful food.

INSULIN MODULATION In recent years, research on insulin activity has become vigorous and controversial. Certainly many issues and mechanisms remain unclear. However, a growing body of evidence points to insulin as a major player in the failure of high-carbohydrate, low-fat diets to control obesity, cardiovascular disease, and type 2 (adult-onset) diabetes in this country. My perspective on insulin derives from the scientific literature on glycemic index and low-glycemic diets and the popular books by Drs. Sears, Arnot, Atkins, Eades, and the Sugar Busters! team of Steward, Bethea, Andrews, and Balart.

Insulin influences appetite. When the carbohydrates you eat enter the bloodstream in the form of glucose, blood sugar levels rise. In response, the pancreas secretes insulin, which sends blood sugar levels down again. This leads to the sensation of hunger. The faster the insulin response, the faster you feel hungry again after meals. "Carbohydrate craving" is the term some people use to describe this kind of rapid cycling. It commonly occurs after high-carbohydrate, low-fat meals.

Insulin also influences fat metabolism. It puts the body in the storage mode and prevents stored fat from being used as an energy source. No matter how much you exercise, you may find the fat-storing and fat-locking actions of insulin difficult to overcome. If you have had trouble losing fat on a high-carbohydrate, low-fat diet, it may be due to your response to so much carbohydrate. Scientific evidence suggests that cardiovascular complications follow from this as well. High insulin levels correlate with high levels of triglycerides and low levels of HDL (good cholesterol). This blood lipid configuration raises cardiovascular risk.

Insulin-modulating diets limit fat storage and promote fat burning by controlling the insulin response to food. They alter the insulin response by adjusting the macronutrient composition of meals (ratios of carbohydrate to protein to fat). They also control insulin by limiting the intake of certain carbohydrates (sugar and grains) and relying more on others (high-fiber fruits and vegetables).

Insulin-modulating meals contain less carbohydrate, more protein, and more fat than high-carbohydrate, low-fat meals. You eat less carbohydrate and more fat to slow down insulin secretion and lower average insulin levels. You eat more protein to enhance secretion of glucagon, a hormone whose actions oppose those of insulin. (Glucagon helps release stored fat for energy use.) These changes promote weight loss and fat loss by decreasing fat storage, increasing fat burning, and delaying the onset of hunger after meals.

Insulin-modulating diets emphasize certain types of carbohydrates. Some carbohydrates convert to glucose and enter the bloodstream more slowly than others. These carbohydrates produce a slower insulin response, less rapid cycling, and less subsequent carbohydrate craving. They minimize fat storage and maximize fat burning by lowering and stabilizing average insulin levels. They are known as "low-glycemic carbohydrates." Examples include fructose, grapefruit, cherries, lentils, and most high-fiber vegetables.

Insulin-modulating diets tend to be low-glycemic diets. The "glycemic index" of a food describes its rate of conversion to glucose and release into the bloodstream relative to other foods. Foods that convert and release quickly (for example, French bread) are fast insulin stimulators with a high glycemic index. Foods that convert and release slowly (for example, cherries) are slow insulin stimulators with a low glycemic index.

My approach to insulin control has two components. I improve the glycemic profile of meals by creating carbohydrate recipes that do not send blood sugar skyrocketing. Then I slow down insulin response even further by balancing those carbohydrates with protein and fat. The proportions of macronutrients in any meal can reflect any diet orientation, and this involves personal choice. You can follow a specific regimen strictly or loosely, or you might develop a wholly personal strategy (such as "more protein, less pasta").

The popular insulin-modulating diets differ substantially in the macronutrient ratios they recommend. Dr. Arnot's diet appears at the higher-carbohydrate, lower-protein, lower-fat end of the spectrum with 55 to 65 percent carbohydrate, 20 to 25 percent protein, and 15 to 20 percent fat. The Zone diet occupies the middle ground with a 40/30/30 allocation of calories from carbohydrates, protein, and fat. The Atkins, *Protein Power,* and *Sugar Busters!* programs are lower-carbohydrate, higher-protein, higher-fat diets. The path to the "right" balance involves a combination of faith and experimentation. If you have gained weight or failed to lose weight on a high-carbohydrate, low-fat regimen, insulin control might work dramatically for you.

Regardless of specific diet philosophy, insulin-conscious meal planning employs protein and fat to counter the hormonal effects of carbohydrates in every meal and snack. To help you with this, I have divided recipes into two major chapters: *Protein Dishes* and *Carbohydrate Dishes,* instead of the traditional categories of appetizers, main dishes, and side dishes. The special chapter entitled *Condiments and Flavor Enhancers* contains recipes for an array of low-glycemic carbohydrates that make food more delicious without causing insulin spikes.

Where's the fat? Even the leanest protein sources contain intrinsic fat. In addition, almost every recipe contains a small quantity of *added* fat—usually in the form of olive oil or nut butter. These ingredients consist primarily of monounsaturated fats, which have cardiovascular benefits and, in the quantities used here, do not affect insulin. My personal assessment of good culinary results (great flavor), rather than mathematics, determined the amount of fat used in each dish.

My cooking style evolved along parallel insulin-controlling and gourmet-satisfying tracks. You can cook healthfully from the recipes in this book, but—again—it is not a diet book, and I do not prescribe a specific program. The recipes help control insulin levels by employing those carbohydrates that convert to glucose more slowly than others. Meal planning then requires a personal decision about macronutrient ratios. If you need help tailoring a diet to your individual needs, you may need to consult a nutritionist or a diet book.

ABOUT YIELDS, SERVING SIZES, AND NUTRITIONAL ANALYSES Each recipe contains a yield expressed in servings to suggest the *number of people* the recipe may comfortably serve. Plating instructions (for example, "Distribute the chicken breasts among 4 plates . . .") refer to these "conventional yields." They do not reflect any specific diet program.

For calorie and gram counters, a standard nutritional analysis accompanies each recipe. These analyses are based on the idea that each person served will share equally in the food the recipe provides, including the sauces. Thus, if a recipe makes a cup of sauce, but the recipe instructions suggest drizzling only a tablespoon on each portion and passing the remainder at the table, it is assumed that each person will take more sauce. Taking more sauce may not conform to a Zone diet, but may be perfectly acceptable for other diet plans.

The standard nutrient analyses were generated by an independent registered dietitian using the Nutritionist IV nutrient analysis program, USDA nutrient analysis tables, and her own database generated from various sources, including product labels. You might expect that these yields match each Zone yield exactly, but, in fact, they do not. Some of these discrepancies reflect the fact that the standard analyses count protein contributions from plant-based foods, while the Zone yields do not. Some discrepancies are based on the assumption that each diner will eat a full measure of sauce, where Zone eaters might avoid that extra sauce. Other discrepancies reflect a difference based on the work of different researchers in terms of the exact amount of protein a particular cut of meat yields; some are based on differences among different brands of commercial ingredients. The important point to remember is that all analyses are *estimates of estimates* and different databases will yield different results. Although they look precise and accurate, nutrient analyses are just estimates. So, don't get too caught up in gram counting.

Please also keep in mind that the nutritional analyses do not include optional ingredients, garnishes, or suggested accompaniments unless specific amounts are given. Brines and marinades are not included in the analyses unless they are consumed. When there is a range of servings or a range in the amount of an

ingredient, an average is used, for example, five servings for a recipe that serves four to six. When a recipe lists a choice of ingredients (such as broth or water), the first is used. Salt is figured only if a recipe calls for a specific amount. Salt added to cooking water is not included. Unless specified otherwise in recipe directions, nutritional analyses assume that all recipe ingredients are consumed. Grams and milligrams are rounded to the nearest whole number.

ABOUT THE ZONE DIET The principles of the Zone diet inform my meals and satisfy my demand for balance, intense flavor, and variety. I do not, however, religiously measure ingredients to insure a precise 40/30/30 distribution of calories from carbohydrate, protein, and fat. I value insulin control and great taste equally, and I have *interpreted* Dr. Sears' program in a way that keeps me trim, healthy, energetic, and splendidly fed. As a result, the recipes in this book respect the *spirit* of the Zone, without obsessive attention to math or exact gram counts.

In the Zone system, macronutrients are measured in units called "blocks." One "protein block" equals 7 grams of absorbable protein. One "carbohydrate block" equals 9 grams of absorbable carbohydrate. One "fat block" (when cooking from scratch) equals 3 grams of fat. A Zone meal for an average male adult consists of 4 protein blocks (28 grams of absorbable protein), 4 carbohydrate blocks (36 grams of absorbable carbohydrate), and 4 fat blocks (12 grams fat). A Zone meal for an average female adult consists of 3 protein blocks (21 grams protein), 3 carbohydrate blocks (27 grams carbohydrate), and 3 fat blocks (9 grams fat).

Nutritionally speaking, my husband and I are typical Zone eaters: His meals consist of 4 blocks of each macronutrient, while mine fit the 3-block female model. In addition, we eat two snacks a day, one in the late afternoon and one before bed—consisting of 1 block each of protein, carbohydrate, and fat.

I have provided an estimated "Zone yield" for each recipe. The Zone yield indicates the *approximate* number of protein and carbohydrate blocks *per recipe*. This should enable you to portion out protein and carbohydrate blocks according to your individual requirements. Due to the insulin neutrality of small amounts of fat, fat blocks are not specified per se. However, almost every recipe contains some added fat.

Where possible, I have also calculated fractional Zone blocks for sauces and dressings based on one-tablespoon servings. If the protein or carbohydrate count is less than one tenth of a block, it is expressed as zero.

Do not expect the Zone yields to be mathematically accurate down to the last gram. Again, all food count data derive from estimates. As a result, Zone yields (and other nutritional analyses) inevitably become *estimates of estimates*. In addition, variables affecting protein and carbohydrate absorption influence Zone counts. Since a fiber matrix interferes with absorption of plant protein, the protein content of vegetables, fruits, and beans has been ignored in determining protein blocks. (Plant protein is included in the protein counts supplied by the conventional nutritional analyses.) In calculating carbohydrate blocks, dietary fiber has been subtracted from total carbohydrate to reflect only the absorbable carbohydrate—the hormonally relevant amount.

To figure out the Zone yields, I have based my analyses on Corinne T. Netzer's *Encyclopedia of Food Values* (Dell Books). Whereas the computer program that generated the nutrient analyses gives different values for some cuts of meat, I have assumed that 1 to 1½ ounces of most meats and fish yields 7 grams of protein or 1 Zone protein block. The Zone diet is designed to work in a real world of grocery shopping and kitchen preparation, where a little estimating makes more sense than obsessive gram counting.

Here's an example to illustrate the use of Zone yields in meal planning. Let's say I plan a meal of Filet Mignons with Porcini "Butter" (page 122), Roasted Garlic Asparagus (page 167), Skillet Cherry Tomatoes (page 180), and fresh fruit for dessert. The Zone yield for the filet mignons equals 16 protein blocks, the amount of protein in 1 pound of beef. My husband requires 4 protein blocks, so he eats about one-quarter of the total recipe. I require 3 protein blocks, so I eat slightly less than one-quarter of the recipe. (We eyeball our respective portions without burdening mealtime with weighing and measuring.) Therefore, a little less than half the total recipe (about 7 blocks) disappears at dinner. The remaining 9 protein blocks will provide my lucky husband with two 4-block portions for lunches during the week and a single protein block for a snack.

Almost all protein dishes contain some carbohydrates. For purposes of Zone yield, absorbable carbohydrate content of less than 4.5 grams per total recipe is noted as "less than one carbohydrate block"; quantities over 4.5 grams per recipe are listed in 1-block increments with fractional blocks rounded to the nearest whole block. The recipe in this example, Filet Mignons with Porcini "Butter," contains only 12 grams of absorbable carbohydrate, slightly more than 1 carbohydrate block. Therefore, the Zone yield indicates "1 carbohydrate block." My husband's portion contains a tiny amount of carbohydrate (about 3 grams). My 3-protein block serving will contain even less carbohydrate. In fact, in planning the carbohydrate portion of our meal, I disregard these fractional blocks altogether.

To complete this particular meal, we will need the requisite number of carbohydrate blocks (4 for my husband, 3 for me). Garlic Roasted Asparagus and Skillet Cherry Tomatoes have identical Zone yields: 4 carbohydrate blocks per recipe. We each eat 1 block (one-quarter of the recipe) of asparagus and 1 block (one-quarter of the recipe) of tomatoes. I need 1 additional block— perhaps 1/2 cup of blueberries—to complete my meal. My husband eats a whole cup of blueberries to reach his goal of 4 carbohydrate blocks.

Our fat blocks come from the intrinsic fat contained in the beef, plus a small quantity of added fat in the form of the oil used to prepare the porcini "butter," asparagus, and tomatoes. We might also have a few almonds with our fruit. The fat content of this meal might not add up to 30 percent of the calories *exactly*, but it is close enough for us.

Insulin-conscious meal construction based on Zone yields takes a little practice. But the payoff in energy and weight control makes it worth the effort.

COOKING FOR FLAVOR High-flavor ingredients form the cornerstone of my cooking technique. I liberally employ high-flavor sauces, smoked vegetables, and flavored or infused oils and vinegars to enliven many dishes. Some of these high-power ingredients are purchased, and some are made ahead and stocked in my refrigerator or freezer. The chapter entitled *Condiments and Flavor Enhancers* is filled with recipes for such flavor boosters. Some, like Roasted Garlic Paste (page 24), an intense puree of roasted garlic, compensate for reduced fat content. Others, such as Charred Tomato Ketchup (page 38), take the place of high-glycemic commercial products. Each of these recipes will repay the time and effort you invest in it by making food more interesting and satisfying. In addition, flavor enhancers can be made far enough in advance that they do not increase preparation time when the pressure is on.

As a confident cook with a busy life, I well know the temptation to take shortcuts and substitute or eliminate ingredients. Unfortunately, the strategies underlying the recipes in this book took years (and many trials) to develop in my kitchen "laboratory." They compensate for restrictions inherent in insulin-modulating diets. Some strategies involve techniques (for example, butterflying, smoking, brining, and marinating); others involve ingredients (for example, specific cuts of meat, infusion pastes, and specialty food items). If a recipe indicates marinating overnight and you marinate for 2 hours, your hopes for intense flavor are doomed to frustration. If you substitute a ½-inch-thick swordfish steak for a 1-inch-thick red snapper fillet, you cannot possibly achieve the desired result because unique characteristics of each animal protein determine cooking techniques and times. Of course, you might get lucky, but you take a certain risk. Every recipe detail increases the likelihood of your success in cooking and eating well for insulin control.

STOCKING THE PANTRY For high-flavor cooking, stock up on the special ingredients that can make food more vivid. Extra virgin olive oil imparts a fruity, full-bodied olive presence to Mediterranean dishes. I prefer it to refined olive oil for its low acidity and character. In recipes of Asian inspiration, I use toasted sesame oil to add depth to sauces. Chinese chili pastes and bean pastes intensify flavor and contribute authenticity as well.

For sweetness, I turn to fructose, a low-glycemic natural sweetener derived from fruits. It converts to glucose much more slowly than sugar and causes a slower rise in blood sugar. It is available in granulated form in supermarkets and health food stores. Package directions recommend decreasing recipe quantities by one-third when substituting fructose for sugar because fructose is more potent. I have not been able to detect this difference in the small quantities I use. As a result, I substitute fructose for sugar, teaspoon for teaspoon. I have noticed one difference between them: Fructose does not dissolve in cold liquids as readily as sugar, and vigorous stirring with a wire whisk is often necessary.

Over the last few years, rainbows of flavored oils and vinegars have brightened supermarket shelves. They have rescued me from food boredom and help me adhere to my insulin-modulating program. I am not ashamed to say that I have become an incorrigible collector of them.

Here's to vinegars! I love their flavors (ume plum, black currant, blueberry, raspberry, tarragon, champagne, white balsamic), and my cabinets are bursting with them. Must you buy dill vinegar to make Steamed Salmon with Cucumbers and Pickled Radishes (page 53)? Of course not. Either white wine vinegar or rice vinegar would be fine. However, if you've never tasted dill vinegar, it might be worth a few dollars for a new flavor experience. Vinegar keeps almost indefinitely and has many applications, including dressing salads and slaws, deglazing pans,

poaching fish, and marinating meat. In my view, the cost of a flavored vinegar constitutes a worthwhile investment. By relieving monotony, it helps me stay on track nutritionally.

I feel the same way about flavored oils: roasted pepper, basil, rosemary, roasted garlic, hot chili. Beautiful, fun to use, and exotic in flavor, infused oils keep well for long periods. They are economical because a little goes a long way. I firmly believe that food boredom is the slippery slope of dietary indiscretion. I avoid it at all costs—which just might be the cost of a tiny bottle of white truffle oil. For me, splurging does not mean a sugary dessert; it means new and exciting ingredients that intensify flavor and make food more interesting.

EQUIPMENT A few special items do come in handy for insulin-conscious cooking. A digital scale helps keep me honest in determining portion size. Because meat is less forgiving when fat is thoroughly removed, I recommend an instant-read thermometer for gauging doneness. Nonstick cookware makes it easier to cook with a minimum of added fat. I use nonstick skillets and woks for sautéing and stir-frying, a nonstick broiler pan for broiling, and a nonstick jelly-roll pan for roasting vegetables. If a protein dish requires stovetop searing followed by roasting in the oven, I use a cast-iron skillet.

I consider roasted garlic a staple, and I make it in large quantities in a terra-cotta garlic roaster. You can use a conventional roasting pan, but I prefer the terra-cotta roaster because it consistently yields a moist product with only ¼ teaspoon olive oil per bulb.

The Camerons Stovetop Smoker

A stick, or immersion, blender does a quick, effective job of emulsifying salad dressings containing very little fat. You immerse the blade end in the dressing in your measuring cup or bowl, let it whirl, and then remove it. There is no need to transfer ingredients to a traditional blender with multiple parts to clean. Be sure you place the ingredients in a measuring cup or bowl with a capacity twice the volume of your sauce to prevent splattering. To clean your stick blender, hold the blade end under running water. Use a bottle brush to clean inaccessible spots.

The stovetop smoker has revolutionized my cooking, and I cannot imagine life without it. I consider it the most efficient low-fat, flavor-enhancing device in the world. With the stovetop smoker I have revitalized classic recipes that I had set aside out of boredom or concerns about excess fat. The deep, satisfying flavors of many recipes in this book come from the smoked vegetables and garlic it produces.

Foods can be smoked outdoors in a covered grill or free-standing smoker, or indoors in a wok. The stovetop smoker offers the advantages of speed, compact size, convenience, easy clean-up, and year-round use, regardless of climate. It enables me to smoke food on top of my stove with a minimum of fuss and almost no fat. I own two stovetop smokers, and I use them constantly. (I use the Camerons stovetop smoker. To order, contact Healthy Adventures; 888-766-9974.)

The stovetop smoker resembles a fish poacher and it is just as easy to use. First, read the manufacturer's instructions. When you are ready to use your smoker, follow your recipe. Remove the lid and take out the rack and drip tray. Cover the inside of the drip tray with foil to permit easy cleaning. Place 1 tablespoon of wood smoking chips in the center of the base. Place the drip tray directly on the chips. If the recipe says to spray the rack with oil, do so away from the stove. Replace the rack and lay the food to be smoked on it. Close the lid halfway. If you are cooking on an electric stove, preheat the burner to medium. If you have a gas stove, turn the heat to medium-high. Center the smoker on the burner.

When the first wisps of smoke appear, close the lid. If you observe large quantities of smoke escaping, reduce the heat slightly. Similarly, subtle warping of the smoker or difficulty sliding the lid during use indicate the smoker is too hot. Simply turn down the heat; in a minute or two, the problem should disappear.

Do not be afraid to open the smoker during cooking to check for doneness. When your food is cooked, remove the smoker from the heat and remove the food from the smoker, unless instructed by the recipe to do otherwise. Allow the smoker to cool. Follow the manufacturer's instructions for the disposal of used wood chips and cleaning. Expect the smoker base to blacken with use.

All smoking times are approximate and vary with many factors: burner BTUs, exact heat setting, and food thickness and temperature. For any given recipe, it is nearly impossible to duplicate smoking conditions precisely. Do not be alarmed if swordfish, for example, requires eight minutes on one occasion and eighteen minutes the next. Keep notes on your experiments so that you can tailor future recipes to the specifics of your own stove.

CONDIMENTS AND
FLAVOR ENHANCERS

Medical school convinced me of the cardiovascular and carcinogenic perils of foods high in saturated fat, including such flavor-boosters as bacon, ham, and sausage. Later on, insulin awareness prevented me from using high-glycemic ingredients such as sugar, honey, barley malt, and dried fruits. In desperation, I started to develop insulin-modulating flavor enhancers. I quickly discovered that smoked vegetables could create the illusion of ham hocks, and that roasted vegetables could bring subtle ingredients to life. I learned that fructose could generate alternatives to commercial condiments, including ketchup, which would liberate flavor while conserving carbohydrates. Eventually, I evolved a way of cooking that supported insulin control without sacrificing great taste. The fundamentals of my strategy lie in this chapter.   Smoked Allium Paste (page 22), Roasted Garlic Paste (page 24), and Smoked Garlic Paste (page 25) form a secret flavor arsenal that will empower you to stay on your insulin-conscious diet. In themselves, they make delicious and unusual condiments for a variety of meats, poultry, and fish. They also serve as ingredients in other recipes such as Roast Chicken with Rosemary-Garlic Paste (page 87) and Baked Pesto Portobellos (page 177). These versatile, flavorful pastes will keep for up to 2 weeks in the refrigerator or for up to 6 months in the freezer, so they can be prepared well in advance.   The smoked and roasted vegetables in this chapter have transformed my cooking, and many recipes revolve around them. Since weekday life is hectic, I use weekends to roast batches of tomatoes, eggplant, and garlic and to smoke shallots, leeks, onions, and portobellos. Smoked or roasted vegetables will keep for up to 1 week in the refrigerator. Ready to your hand, they make short work of a tasty meal at the end of an exhausting day.

Smoked Allium Paste™

32 TABLESPOONS OR 2 CUPS Smoked allium paste is an astonishing vehicle for flavor, and I continue to marvel at its chameleon-like properties. Made from three prominent members of the onion family—onions, garlic, and shallots—this beguiling puree lends itself to all sorts of disguises. Find it in assertively flavored Spiced Ancho Sauce (page 126), Smoky Ranch Dressing (page 68), and mellow Asparagus-Basil Mayonnaise (page 84). Do not hesitate to develop your own uses for it. Pureed green beans and broccoli, for example, combined with this paste form elegant sauces. The paste contains 50 percent less carbohydrate per tablespoon than roasted or smoked garlic paste: 2.5 grams versus 5 grams. Seasoned with salt and pepper, it works as a simple condiment with beef and lamb.

NUTRITIONAL ANALYSIS PER TABLESPOON: 24 CALORIES, 0 G PROTEIN, 3 G CARBOHYDRATE, 1 G FAT (0 G SATURATED), 0 MG CHOLESTEROL, 2 MG SODIUM, 0 G FIBER

---

3   medium onions (about 10 ounces)

¾   cup unpeeled shallot cloves (about 4 ounces)

1¼   cups unpeeled garlic cloves (about 5 ounces)

3   teaspoons extra virgin olive oil

2   tablespoons water or more as needed

Salt and freshly ground black pepper

1. Cut the onions and shallots in half, but do not peel. Combine in a bowl with the garlic and drizzle with 1 teaspoon of the olive oil. Season with salt and pepper and toss to coat.

2. Prepare a stovetop smoker with 1 tablespoon apple or cherry smoking chips. Place the vegetables on the rack and half-close the lid. Place the smoker on an electric burner preheated to medium or on a gas burner turned to medium-high. When the first wisps of smoke appear, close the lid. Smoke for about 30 minutes, or until the onions are tender. Remove the vegetables from the smoker. Peel the garlic cloves while they are still warm. Cool all the vegetables to room temperature.

3. Remove the skin and any dry layers from the onions and shallots, trim the ends, and transfer the vegetables to a food processor. With the machine running, add the remaining 2 teaspoons oil and water and process to a smooth puree. Add a little more water, if necessary. Season to taste with salt and pepper.

4. Serve immediately or store in the refrigerator for up to 2 weeks or in the freezer for up to 6 months. The paste can be reheated in the microwave. Serve warm or at room temperature.

Zone yield per recipe: Less than one protein block, 9 carbohydrate blocks (1 tablespoon paste = 0 protein blocks, ⅓ carbohydrate block)

Smoked Allium Paste

Roasted Garlic 1/4 TO 1/3 CUP OR ABOUT 5 TABLESPOONS

Garlic bulbs with large, firm cloves relinquish their skins more easily after roasting. To expedite the process, slip off the skins while the cloves are warm.

NUTRITIONAL ANALYSIS PER TABLESPOON: 27 CALORIES, 1 G PROTEIN, 6 G CARBOHYDRATE, 0 G FAT (0 G SATURATED), 0 MG CHOLESTEROL, 3 MG SODIUM, 0 G FIBER

1 large garlic bulb

1/4 teaspoon extra virgin olive oil

Salt and freshly ground black pepper (optional)

1. Leaving the garlic bulb intact, remove the loose, papery outer skin. With a small paring knife, slice off the top 1/4 inch of each clove to expose it. (If you try to do this with a chef's knife, you will cut off too much of some cloves and miss others entirely.)

2. Place the bulb cut side up in the base of a terra-cotta roaster and drizzle the exposed cloves with the oil. Season with salt and pepper, if desired. Cover with the dome and place in a cold oven. If you don't have a terra-cotta roaster, place the bulbs on a 10-inch square of aluminum foil, drizzle the oil on the garlic, fold the foil to make a closed packet, and set in a baking dish.

3. Turn the oven to 300° F. Roast for 30 minutes. Remove the dome from the terra-cotta roaster or remove the garlic from the foil. Return the roaster or baking dish to the oven and roast for 45 minutes.

4. When the cloves are cool enough to handle, slip them out of their skins. Use at once or store in the refrigerator for up to 1 week.

Zone yield per recipe: Less than one protein block, 3 carbohydrate blocks (1 tablespoon cloves = 0 protein blocks, ½ carbohydrate block)

Roasted Garlic Paste *(Variation)* 1/4 TO 1/3 CUP OR ABOUT 5 TABLESPOONS

NUTRITIONAL ANALYSIS PER TABLESPOON: 33 CALORIES, 1 G PROTEIN, 6 G CARBOHYDRATE, 1 G FAT (0 G SATURATED), 0 MG CHOLESTEROL, 3 MG SODIUM, 0 G FIBER

1. Prepare the roasted garlic as above, and slip the cloves out of their skins. Place the peeled garlic cloves in a food processor. With the motor running, add 1 teaspoon extra virgin olive oil and 1 tablespoon water. Process until smooth, scraping down the sides as needed. Add a little more water if necessary. Season with salt and pepper to taste. The paste will keep for 2 weeks in an airtight container in the refrigerator or for up to 6 months in the freezer.

Zone yield per recipe: Less than one protein block, 3 carbohydrate blocks (1 tablespoon paste = 0 protein blocks, ½ carbohydrate block)

Smoked Garlic <small>1/4 TO 1/3 CUP OR ABOUT 5 TABLESPOONS</small> Smoked garlic is as versatile and rich-tasting as roasted garlic and takes less time to prepare. Like its roasted twin, it contains approximately 1 gram of carbohydrate per average clove. Fortunately, its intensity makes it effective in small quantities. In its simplest incarnation (seasoned only with salt and fresh pepper), it complements beef, lamb, chicken, and assertive fish. It marries well with herbs, vegetables, and even some fruits (pears, for example) and can serve as an instant base or enrichment for sauces and dressings.

NUTRITIONAL ANALYSIS PER TABLESPOON: 33 CALORIES, I G PROTEIN, 6 G CARBOHYDRATE, I G FAT (0 G SATURATED), 0 MG CHOLESTEROL, 3 MG SODIUM, 0 G FIBER

¾ cup large garlic cloves (about 3 ounces)

1 teaspoon extra-virgin olive oil

1. Remove the loose, papery outer layers from the garlic, but do not peel. Place the cloves in a small bowl and toss with the olive oil.

2. Prepare a stovetop smoker with 1 tablespoon apple or cherry smoking chips. Place the garlic cloves on the rack, taking care so they do not slip through the rungs. Half-close the lid. Place the smoker on an electric burner preheated to medium or on a gas burner turned to medium-high. When the first wisps of smoke appear, close the lid. Smoke for 20 to 25 minutes, or until tender. (Note: If you intend to slice the garlic cloves, as in Black-Eyed Peas with Collard Greens and Smoked Garlic on page 189, smoke them for about 15 minutes, until they yield to a fork but remain firm enough to slice.) Remove to a bowl.

3. When the cloves are cool enough to handle, slip them out of their skins. Use at once or store in the refrigerator for up to 1 week.

Zone yield per recipe: Less than one protein block, 3 carbohydrate blocks (1 tablespoon cloves = 0 protein blocks, ½ carbohydrate block)

Smoked Garlic Paste *(Variation)* <small>1/4 TO 1/3 CUP OR ABOUT 5 TABLESPOONS</small>

NUTRITIONAL ANALYSIS PER TABLESPOON: 29 CALORIES, I G PROTEIN, 6 G CARBOHYDRATE, I G FAT (0 G SATURATED), 0 MG CHOLESTEROL, 3 MG SODIUM, 0 G FIBER

1. Prepare the smoked garlic as above. Place the peeled garlic cloves in a food processor. With the motor running, add 1 teaspoon extra virgin olive oil and 1 tablespoon water. Process until smooth, scraping down the sides as needed. Add a little more water, if necessary. Season to taste with salt and freshly ground black pepper, if desired. Use at once or store in the refrigerator for up to 1 week or in the freezer for up to 6 months.

Zone yield per recipe: Less than one protein block, 3 carbohydrate blocks (1 tablespoon paste = 0 protein blocks, ½ carbohydrate block)

Smoked Shallots

1½ CUPS Like other members of the genus *Allium,* shallots have an impressive antioxidant profile with anti-carcinogenic activity. Raw or cooked, they also display concentrated flavor power. As a side dish, smoked shallots complement beef, lamb, veal, and ostrich. As an ingredient, they contribute a smoky sweetness to stews, salads, stuffed vegetables, omelets, and frittatas. The smoking procedure for shallots is identical to that for onions, so you can smoke them together. If the shallots become tender first, simply remove them from the smoker and leave the onions to continue smoking.

NUTRITIONAL ANALYSIS PER CUP: 135 CALORIES, 4 G PROTEIN, 25 G CARBOHYDRATE, 3 G FAT (0 G SATURATED), 0 MG CHOLESTEROL, 18 MG SODIUM, 0 G FIBER

1½ to 2 cups whole shallots (about 8 ounces), skin left on, halved if large

1 teaspoon extra virgin olive oil

Salt and freshly ground black pepper (optional)

1. Slice off the top ¼ inch of the tip ends of the shallots to expose the flesh of the bulb slightly. Combine the shallots and oil in a bowl and toss to coat. Season with salt and pepper, if desired.

2. Prepare a stovetop smoker with 1 tablespoon apple or cherry smoking chips. Place the shallots on the rack and half-close the lid. Place the smoker on an electric burner preheated to medium or a gas burner turned to medium-high.

When the first wisps of smoke appear, close the lid. Smoke for 20 to 30 minutes, or until the shallots are tender.

3. Remove skins, tips, and any dry layers before serving. Use immediately or store in the refrigerator for up to 1 week.

Zone yield per recipe: Less than one protein block, 4 carbohydrate blocks

Smoked Onions

4 CUPS Onions respond well to smoking. Sharp or sweet, they can be cooked in a stovetop smoker with much less oil than it would take to sauté them. Served hot, at room temperature, or chilled, they make a remarkable side dish that flatters grilled or roasted red meats. They also convey a smoky flavor to sautés, soups, stews, salads, omelets, and frittatas. In Smoked Allium Paste (page 22), they contribute an element of mellow sweetness while they dilute the carbohydrate density of the garlic.

NUTRITIONAL ANALYSIS PER CUP: 71 CALORIES, 2 G PROTEIN, 14 G CARBOHYDRATE,
1 G FAT (0 G SATURATED), 0 MG CHOLESTEROL, 5 MG SODIUM, 3 G FIBER

---

4   cups quartered or halved onions
    (any variety), skin on

1   *teaspoon extra virgin olive oil*

    *Salt and freshly ground black
    pepper (optional)*

1. Prepare a stovetop smoker with 1 tablespoon cherry or apple smoking chips. Place the onions in a bowl and drizzle with the oil. Season with salt and pepper, if desired, and toss to coat. Place on the rack and half-close the lid. Place the smoker on an electric burner preheated to medium or on a gas burner turned to medium-high. When the first wisps of smoke appear, close the lid. Smoke for approximately 30 minutes, until tender.

2. Remove the skins and any dry layers or tips and chop coarsely. Use immediately or store in the refrigerator for up to 1 week.

Zone yield per recipe: Less than one protein block, 4 carbohydrate blocks

Smoked Leeks

8 WHOLE OR 6 CUPS SLICED LEEKS I will never forget the first time I smoked leeks and discovered the astonishing—practically alchemical—transformation wrought by the smoking process: My pale green and white leeks emerged a radiant pink and gold! Dress them with a vinaigrette and serve as an appetizer, or present them as a simple side dish with beef, lamb, or ostrich. They also make a wonderfully mysterious addition to stews, sautés, sauces, omelets, and frittatas.

NUTRITIONAL ANALYSIS PER CUP: 158 CALORIES, 4 G PROTEIN, 35 G CARBOHYDRATE, 1 G FAT (0 G SATURATED), 0 MG CHOLESTEROL, 47 MG SODIUM, 4 G FIBER

---

8   large leeks

1   teaspoon extra virgin olive oil

   Salt and freshly ground black pepper (optional)

1. Cut the leeks in half lengthwise. Trim off the roots and discard the green parts. Rinse under cold running water, allowing the water to run between the layers to remove any dirt. Place the leeks, cut side down, between 2 kitchen towels and press to remove excess water.

2. Prepare a stovetop smoker with 1 tablespoon apple or cherry smoking chips. Place the leeks on the rack cut side up. Brush lightly with the oil and season with salt and pepper, if desired. Half-close the lid. Place the smoker on an electric burner preheated to medium or gas burner turned to medium-high. When the first wisps of smoke appear, close the lid. Smoke for 20 to 30 minutes, until tender.

3. Slice, if desired, or leave whole. Use immediately or store in the refrigerator for up to 1 week.

Zone yield per recipe: Less than one protein block, 5 carbohydrate blocks

Smoked Portobello Mushrooms 8 WHOLE MUSHROOMS OR 5 CUPS SLICED MUSHROOMS

This recipe derives from Ron Pickarski, prize-winning chef and author of *Eco-Cuisine,* a sophisticated approach to plant-based food. Ron serves as consultant executive chef to C.M. International, maker of the Camerons stovetop smoker. He regularly contributes to its newsletter, *Smoke Signals,* where I first saw his extraordinarily delicious and useful recipe for smoked portobello mushrooms. In *Eco-Cuisine,* Ron adds water to his smoking chips, as I have done in this adaptation. Smoked mushrooms will cast their spell over plain broiled steak or a salad with balsamic vinaigrette. They can also be served as a hearty side dish with beef, lamb, veal, or ostrich or added to sautés, stews, omelets, and frittatas.

NUTRITIONAL ANALYSIS PER MUSHROOM: 28 CALORIES, 2 G PROTEIN, 5 G CARBOHYDRATE, 0 G FAT (0 G SATURATED), 0 MG CHOLESTEROL, 5 MG SODIUM, I G FIBER

8   medium portobello mushroom
    caps, about 4 ounces each
    Salt and freshly ground black pepper

1. Prepare a stovetop smoker with 1 tablespoon hickory smoking chips sprinkled with 1 tablespoon water. Place the mushroom caps, gill side down, on the rack overlapping if necessary. Half-close the lid. Place the smoker on an electric burner preheated to medium or on a gas burner turned to medium-high. When the first wisps of smoke appear, close the lid. Smoke for 20 minutes. Remove the smoker from the heat, but keep the smoker closed for another 20 minutes.

2. Transfer the mushrooms to a platter and season with salt and pepper. Serve immediately or reserve for use in another recipe. Smoked portobellos will keep for up to 1 week in the refrigerator.

Zone yield per recipe: Less than one protein block, 4 carbohydrate blocks

Smoked Portobello Mushrooms

Roasted Eggplant 6 CUPS

I used to think eggplant required large quantities of fat for proper cooking, but I was wrong. Roasting an eggplant results in a delicious product that you can incorporate into other recipes or present on its own merits as an appetizer or side dish. Feel free to experiment with the many varieties of eggplant, but keep in mind that roasting time varies with thickness.

NUTRITIONAL ANALYSIS PER CUP: 46 CALORIES, 2 G PROTEIN, 9 G CARBOHYDRATE,
1 G FAT (0 G SATURATED), 0 MG CHOLESTEROL, 5 MG SODIUM, 4 G FIBER

2   *pounds eggplants, ends trimmed, and halved lengthwise*

1   *teaspoon extra virgin olive oil*

    Salt and freshly ground black pepper (optional)

1. Preheat the oven to 450° F. Using a two-tined carving fork, pierce the cut sides of the eggplant all over, down to but not through the skin. Season with salt and pepper, if desired. Brush a nonstick baking sheet with the oil and place the eggplants cut side down.

2. Roast long, narrow Asian eggplants and Italian baby eggplants for 10 to 15 minutes, or until tender; roast Western globe or purple eggplants for 20 to 30 minutes, or until tender. If the eggplants will be cooked further in another recipe, remove from the oven when they yield to a fork but are not completely soft.

3. Peel, if desired. Slice or cut into cubes and adjust the seasoning. Serve warm or at room temperature, or store in the refrigerator for up to 1 week.

Zone yield per recipe: Less than one protein block, 4 carbohydrate blocks

Smoked Eggplant

6 CUPS Smoked eggplant has almost infinite uses. It can stand alone as a hearty vegetable side dish or cooperate with other ingredients in stir-fries, sautés, and stews. It works as an "extender" of bean dishes by decreasing carbohydrate density. Although lower in fiber than the whole vegetable, pureed smoked eggplant makes a delicious and unusual accompaniment to beef, lamb, or chicken. It requires only salt, pepper, and a little minced parsley to brighten its appearance.

NUTRITIONAL ANALYSIS PER CUP: 46 CALORIES, 2 G PROTEIN, 9 G CARBOHYDRATE, I G FAT (0 G SATURATED), 0 MG CHOLESTEROL, 5 MG SODIUM, 4 G FIBER

2   *pounds eggplants, ends trimmed, and halved lengthwise*

Salt

1   *teaspoon extra virgin olive oil*

1. Prepare a stovetop smoker with 1 tablespoon apple or cherry smoking chips. Spray the rack with olive oil. With a two-tined carving fork, pierce the cut sides of the eggplants all over, down to but not through the skin. Season with salt. Place the eggplants, cut side down, on the rack; they need not fit in a single layer. Half-close the lid. Place the smoker on an electric burner preheated to medium or a gas burner turned to medium-high. When the first wisps of smoke appear, close the lid. Smoke long, narrow Asian and Italian baby eggplants for 10 to 20 minutes; smoke larger Western or purple globe eggplants for 40 minutes.

2. Meanwhile, preheat the oven to 450° F. If the eggplants are not sufficiently tender after smoking, brush a baking sheet with 1 teaspoon olive oil, and place the smoked eggplants on it, cut side down. Roast in the oven until tender usually no more than 15 minutes).

3. Peel, if desired. Cut into cubes. Serve immediately, use in a recipe, or store in the refrigerator for up to 1 week.

Zone yield per recipe: Less than one protein block, 4 carbohydrate blocks

Smoked Bell Peppers 8 SERVINGS If you have never tasted smoked peppers, you are in for a treat! They are delicious alone, stuffed, or added to salads, sautés, omelets, and frittatas. Pureed, they make an unusual base for, or addition to, a sauce. They are easier to prepare than roasted bell peppers because they do not have to be skinned.

NUTRITIONAL ANALYSIS PER SERVING: 37 CALORIES, 2 G PROTEIN, 8 G CARBOHYDRATE, 0 G FAT (0 G SATURATED), 0 MG CHOLESTEROL, 5 MG SODIUM, 3 G FIBER

---

4 large bell peppers of any color, halved, seeded, and membranes removed

1. Prepare a stovetop smoker with 1 tablespoon apple or cherry smoking chips. Place the peppers cut side down on the rack, making sure they do not touch the sides of the smoker because at any point of direct contact, they will burn. Half-close the lid. Place the smoker on an electric burner preheated to medium or on a gas burner turned to medium-high. When the first wisps of smoke appear, close the lid. For crisp-tender peppers that will be used in another recipe, smoke for 20 to 30 minutes. For softer, silkier peppers, smoke for 30 minutes. Then remove the smoker from the heat and leave the peppers in the closed smoker for an additional 20 minutes.

2. Use the peppers immediately or store in the refrigerator for up to 1 week.

Zone yield per recipe: Less than one protein block, 2 carbohydrate blocks

Smoked Bell Peppers

Slow-Roasted Plum Tomatoes 2 CUPS These roasted tomatoes contain twice as much carbohydrate per cup as fresh tomatoes, but much more than twice the flavor. Use them as a side dish with grilled chicken, lamb, beef, or fish or as a component in sautés, stews, omelets, and frittatas. Feel free to substitute them for fresh tomatoes, but remember to halve the quantity to keep carbohydrate counts the same.

NUTRITIONAL ANALYSIS PER CUP: 119 CALORIES, 5 G PROTEIN, 26 G CARBOHYDRATE,
2 G FAT (0 G SATURATED), 0 MG CHOLESTEROL, 51 MG SODIUM, 6 G FIBER

2½ pounds plum tomatoes, cored
and halved lengthwise

Kosher salt

Chopped fresh herbs (optional)

1. Preheat the oven to 200° F.
Spray a nonstick baking sheet with
olive oil. Place the tomatoes on the
baking sheet cut side up and season
generously with salt. Sprinkle with
fresh herbs, if desired. Roast for 4
to 6 hours, until the edges of the
tomatoes have shriveled, but they
remain juicy. They should lose
about 50 percent of their weight by
the end of roasting, but should not
become hard, dry, or blackened.

2. Use immediately, or store the
tomatoes in an airtight container
in the refrigerator for 5 to 6 days.

Zone yield per recipe: Less than
one protein block, 4 carbohydrate
blocks

Tiny Tomato Jewels 2 cups

These little gems will decorate any plate. They go particularly well with Mediterranean preparations, especially chicken, fish, and lamb. They keep well in the refrigerator and prove extremely versatile. Add them to salads, vegetable sautés, omelets, frittatas, and bean dishes. For variety, sprinkle them with a handful of your favorite fresh herb before roasting. If you can find vine cherry tomatoes, by all means use them here. They bring tremendous intensity to this straightforward dish.

NUTRITIONAL ANALYSIS PER CUP: 95 CALORIES, 3 G PROTEIN, 17 G CARBOHYDRATE, 3 G FAT (0 G SATURATED), 0 MG CHOLESTEROL, 32 MG SODIUM, 4 G FIBER

4   cups halved cherry tomatoes

1   teaspoon extra virgin olive oil
    Kosher salt

1. Preheat the oven to 200° F. Brush a nonstick jelly roll pan with the olive oil. Arrange the tomatoes cut side up. Season generously with salt. Roast for 1½ to 2 hours, until the tomatoes are slightly shriveled with curled edges, but still juicy.

2. Serve immediately or allow to cool to room temperature. If you want to serve these hot, they can be reheated in the microwave.

Zone yield per recipe: Less than one protein block, 4 carbohydrate blocks

Smoked Plum Tomatoes

4 CUPS Use smoked tomatoes to replace fresh or canned tomatoes in a few of your old recipes and experience their transforming power. In sauces and stews, they become a fat-free vehicle for smoky flavor, replacing fat-laden bacon, ham, and sausage. They pair well with dried beans and vegetables such as zucchini, eggplant, and summer squash, and they are receptive to garlic and herbs. They also form the basis of unusual condiments, including ketchup. You may wish to vary the smoking time depending on their intended use.

NUTRITIONAL ANALYSIS PER CUP: 59 CALORIES, 2 G PROTEIN, 13 G CARBOHYDRATE, 1 G FAT (0 G SATURATED), 0 MG CHOLESTEROL, 26 MG SODIUM, 3 G FIBER

2½ pounds large plum tomatoes, cored and halved lengthwise (about 5 cups)

1. Prepare a stovetop smoker with 1 tablespoon apple or cherry smoking chips. Place the tomato halves cut side down on the rack; they will not all fit in a single layer. Half-close the lid. Place the smoker on an electric burner preheated to medium or on a gas burner turned to medium-high. When the first wisps of smoke appear, close the lid. For crisp-tender tomatoes that will be used in another recipe, smoke for 15 minutes; for fork-tender tomatoes, smoke for 20 to 25 minutes.

2. Remove the tomatoes from the smoker and save any juice that has collected on the drip pan. Remove the skins, if desired (do not remove the skins if you are making Smoked Tomato Ketchup, page 39), and discard. Use immediately or store the tomatoes and any collected juice for up to 1 week in the refrigerator.

Zone yield per recipe: Less than one protein block, 4 carbohydrate blocks

Smoked Plum Tomato Puree *(Variation)* 2¹/2 CUPS OR 32 TABLESPOONS

NUTRITIONAL ANALYSIS PER TABLESPOON: 4 CALORIES, 0 G PROTEIN, 1 G CARBOHYDRATE,
0 G FAT (0 G SATURATED), 0 MG CHOLESTEROL, 2 MG SODIUM, 0 G FIBER

1. Prepare the Smoked Plum Tomatoes. Using your finger, push the seeds out of the tomatoes. Puree in a food processor or blender.

Zone yield per recipe: Less than one protein block, 4 carbohydrate blocks (1 tablespoon puree = 0 protein blocks, ¹/10 carbohydrate block)

Pseudo-Mirin 1³/4 CUPS OR 28 TABLESPOONS Mirin is a sweet rice wine used in Japanese cooking. Many commercial brands contain high-glycemic sweeteners, such as corn syrup and barley malt. This pretender tastes remarkably like the genuine article while deriving its sweetness from low-glycemic fructose.

NUTRITIONAL ANALYSIS PER TABLESPOON: 31 CALORIES, 0 G PROTEIN, 6 G CARBOHYDRATE,
0 G FAT (0 G SATURATED), 0 MG CHOLESTEROL, 1 MG SODIUM, 1 G FIBER

1½ cups dry sake

¾ cup fructose

1. Combine the sake and fructose in a small saucepan over medium-low heat. Heat, stirring, for 1 to 2 minutes, until the fructose dissolves. Remove from the heat. Allow to cool to room temperature. Transfer to a bottle and refrigerate. It will keep indefinitely in the refrigerator.

Zone yield per recipe: Less than one protein block, 17 carbohydrate blocks (1 tablespoon = 0 protein blocks, ⅔ carbohydrate block)

Charred Tomato Ketchup

2 TO 2½ CUPS OR 32 TO 36 TABLESPOONS Commercial ketchups have two disadvantages: uninteresting flavor and high-glycemic ingredients. Without the dumbing down required for mass-market distribution, ketchup can be an exciting, even exotic protein enhancer. Sweetened with fructose instead of cane sugar and corn syrup, it can improve rather than disturb blood sugar control. With 3 to 4 grams of low-glycemic carbohydrate per tablespoon, this grilled tomato version blows commercial brands off the shelf. | The ketchup need not be made start-to-finish in one session because the charred tomatoes will keep for 3 to 5 days in the refrigerator. Serve with grilled meats.

NUTRITIONAL ANALYSIS PER TABLESPOON: 22 CALORIES, 1 G PROTEIN, 5 G CARBOHYDRATE, 0 G FAT (0 G SATURATED), 0 MG CHOLESTEROL, 103 MG SODIUM, 1 G FIBER

8	large vine-ripe tomatoes, halved horizontally
1	cup finely chopped onions
½	cup malt vinegar
⅓	cup fructose
2	teaspoons bottled white horseradish
2	teaspoons minced garlic
2	teaspoons minced fresh ginger
1½	teaspoons kosher salt
1	teaspoon paprika
¼	teaspoon ground cinnamon
¼	teaspoon ground cloves
¼	teaspoon ground mace
¼	teaspoon ground allspice
¼	teaspoon freshly ground black pepper
⅛	teaspoon cayenne pepper or to taste

1. Prepare a hot fire in a charcoal grill. Place the tomatoes on a lightly oiled grill, cut side up. Grill for 2 to 3 minutes, until the skin is nicely charred. Turn and grill for another 1 to 2 minutes. Remove from heat and set aside to cool in a nonreactive container.

2. When the tomatoes are cool enough to handle, cut out the stems and discard. Do not remove the skins. Transfer the tomatoes and any collected juice to a deep, nonreactive saucepan. Add the onions, vinegar, fructose, horseradish, garlic, ginger, salt, and spices. Bring to a boil, reduce the heat, and simmer for 1 hour, stirring occasionally.

3. Puree the tomato mixture in a food mill and return the puree to the saucepan. Simmer slowly, stirring occasionally, until a thick ketchup consistency is reached, about 1 hour. Remove from the heat. Adjust the seasoning.

4. Use immediately or store in the refrigerator for up to 3 weeks or for up to 6 months in the freezer.

Zone yield per recipe: Less than one protein block, 16 carbohydrate blocks (1 tablespoon ketchup = 0 protein blocks, ⅓ carbohydrate block)

Smoked Tomato Ketchup

3 TO 3 1/2 CUPS OR 48 TO 52 TABLESPOONS Although homemade ketchup requires long simmering, the results justify the time investment. You end up with a savory sauce with unusual depth that spikes your food but not your insulin. One tablespoon contains about half the carbohydrate of bottled ketchup. Serve with grilled meats.

NUTRITIONAL ANALYSIS PER TABLESPOON: I4 CALORIES, 0 G PROTEIN, 3 G CARBOHYDRATE, 0 G FAT (0 G SATURATED), 0 MG CHOLESTEROL, 33 MG SODIUM, 0 G FIBER

4   cups *Smoked Plum Tomatoes (page 36), with skins left on*

1   *(6-ounce) can tomato paste*

1   *cup finely chopped onion*

1   *cup finely chopped red or yellow bell pepper*

¼   *cup fructose*

¼   *cup cider vinegar*

1   *teaspoon minced garlic*

1   *bay leaf*

¼   *teaspoon ground cloves*

¼   *teaspoon allspice*

¼   *teaspoon mace*

¼   *teaspoon dry mustard*

⅛   *teaspoon cinnamon*

Salt and freshly ground black pepper

1. Combine all the ingredients in a medium saucepan, adding salt and pepper to taste. Bring to a boil, reduce the heat to low, and simmer for approximately 1 hour, stirring occasionally.

2. Remove the bay leaf and puree the ketchup in a food mill. If a thicker ketchup is preferred, return the ketchup to the saucepan and simmer until the desired consistency is reached. Adjust the seasoning.

3. Serve immediately or store in the refrigerator for several weeks or in the freezer for up to 6 months. Freeze it in small containers so you only have to defrost what you need.

Zone yield per recipe: Less than one protein block, 15 carbohydrate blocks (1 tablespoon ketchup = 0 protein blocks, ¼ carbohydrate block)

PROTEIN DISHES

Dietary protein is essential for normal cell structure and function and for the maintenance of lean body mass. In addition, it supports insulin control by stimulating the secretion of the hormone glucagon, which releases stored fat for energy use. Glucagon makes fat-burning possible by countering insulin's fat-storing and fat-locking effects. | In *Protein Dishes*, you will find recipes for fish, shellfish, poultry, and lean meats. Protein recipes generally call for 4 ounces (raw weight) of poultry or meat or 5 to 6 ounces of fish or shellfish per serving. This provides about 28 grams of protein or 4 Zone protein blocks. Note that the weight of cooked meat or poultry is about 20 percent less than its raw weight for the same amount of protein. (For example, 3.6 ounces of cooked light meat chicken yields the same 28 grams of protein as 4.4 ounces of raw chicken.) | To limit the fat contribution from protein, you will need to trim away all visible fat whenever possible. Degreasing gravies and sauces constitutes the second most effective means of lowering the fat content of protein dishes. If you have all the time in the world, refrigerate the sauce. The fat will rise to the top and solidify. You can then use a slotted spoon or pass the sauce through a cheesecloth-lined sieve to remove the solid fat. If you are pressed for time, use a strainer to retrieve valuable solids and then use a bulb baster to remove the liquid from under the fat layer. Transfer it to a small saucepan or measuring cup and return the solids to the degreased sauce. Adjust the seasoning, reheat if necessary, and serve. | Roasting times in recipes represent gross approximations due to the tremendous variability in oven temperature accuracy and roast shape. An instant-read thermometer can narrow your margin of error. Unfortunately, thermometers are not foolproof either, so—to make sure I'm on target—I frequently resort to the cut-and-peek method. A sliced roast will never reveal the evidence.

Fish and Shellfish
If you seek variety in sources of healthful protein, start with fish and shellfish. Consider the sheer number of species available (70 to 80), the range of low-fat cooking techniques you can apply (grilling, broiling, smoking, roasting, stir-frying, sautéing, steaming, poaching, braising), and the ethnic costumes you can dress them in. You could probably eat seafood every day for the rest of your life without becoming bored.

Fish and shellfish contain a surprising array of vitamins (especially B vitamins) and minerals (copper, iodine, phosphorus, and selenium). In addition, fish and shellfish contain omega-3 fatty acids, which have a protective effect on the cardiovascular system through their triglyceride-lowering and anti-coagulant actions. These remarkable oils also decrease average insulin levels, through a beneficial effect on muscle cell membranes. As a result, even rich fish, such as salmon, are valued rather than scorned for their fat.

How often should you eat fish? Recommendations vary. In one study, consumption of 2 servings of fish per week reduced the risk of heart attack by 50 percent. For the Zone diet, Dr. Barry Sears recommends 1 serving of cold-water fish (for example, salmon, sardines, or mackerel) or 3 servings of tuna a week for an adequate intake of omega-3 fatty acids. Because I love seafood of all kinds, I eat fish every day. My standard breakfast includes 2 ounces of smoked fish (salmon, Arctic char, tuna, trout, or sturgeon) with whole grain rye bread and light cream cheese. In addition, I make sure we have fish or shellfish for dinner a couple of times each week. When I dine out, I invariably order fish to minimize fat in restaurant meals.

The recipes in this chapter barely scratch the surface of fish cooking; however, they do illustrate a number of techniques and ethnic orientations. To expand their reach, make the following substitutions: monkfish, pollock, or striped bass for red snapper; mahi mahi, mackerel, or pompano for bluefish; cod or tilefish for halibut; grouper for sea bass. Cooking times are comparable for fish of similar thickness, and protein counts remain approximately the same per ounce.

Raw clams in the shell are difficult to estimate for protein content because they vary so much in water weight. In my experience, 2 dozen *average* size littleneck clams provide 1 serving of protein (4 Zone blocks). If you are strict about analyzing protein counts, remove the clams from their shells, then weigh out the proper serving size. If you wish to preserve their impressive appearance in the shell, remove 1 clam from its shell, weight it and do a little math: 4 ounces of cooked clams provide 29 grams of protein (1 serving). So 4 ounces divided by the weight of 1 clam will give you the number of clams you need for 1 serving. The same holds true for mussels.

Lobster's on-again-off-again relationship with its shell makes hard and soft-shell lobsters differ in water and protein content. Soft-shells contain *more* water and less protein per ounce than hard-shells. For 28 grams of protein (1 serving), you will need a 1¼-pound hard-shell or a 1½-pound soft-shell lobster.

Chilean Sea Bass with Ragout of Smoked Vegetables and Spinach (page 44)

Chilean Sea Bass with Ragout of Smoked Vegetables and Spinach

4 SERVINGS Food writer Victoria Abbott Riccardi has contributed hours of pleasure, fascination, and excitement to my education as a cook through her work in the *Boston Globe*. This recipe represents an adaptation of her indescribably delicious "Seared Chilean Sea Bass over Spinach and Shiitake Mushroom Ragout." When I made it, my husband said he would eat nothing else for the rest of his life. Serve with fresh fruit for dessert. (Pictured on page 43.)

NUTRITIONAL ANALYSIS PER SERVING: 311 CALORIES, 33 G PROTEIN, 31 G CARBOHYDRATE, 8 G FAT (1 G SATURATED), 58 MG CHOLESTEROL, 203 MG SODIUM, 7 G FIBER

---

2   cups fresh shiitake mushroom caps, brushed clean

4   (5-ounce) Chilean sea bass fillets, 1½ to 2 inches thick

    Salt and freshly ground black pepper

3   teaspoons extra virgin olive oil

2   tablespoons minced garlic

2   cups sliced Smoked Leeks (page 28)

2   cups diced Smoked Plum Tomatoes with juice (page 36)

1   bunch fresh spinach (about 3/4 pound), stems removed and leaves coarsely chopped

1   tablespoon fresh lemon juice or to taste

1. Prepare a stovetop smoker with 1 tablespoon hickory smoking chips sprinkled with 1 tablespoon water. Place the mushroom caps on the rack (if they don't fit in a single layer, overlap them) and half-close the lid. Place the smoker on an electric burner preheated to medium or a gas burner turned to medium-high. When the first wisps of smoke appear, close the lid. Smoke for 10 minutes. Remove from the heat and keep the smoker closed for an additional 10 minutes. Remove the mushrooms from the smoker and halve them if small, quarter them if large. Set aside.

2. Generously season the fillets on both sides with salt and pepper. Place four ½-teaspoon oil droplets in a large nonstick skillet over medium-high heat. Using a spatula, spread each drop of oil to create a "footprint" in the shape of a fish fillet. Place the fillets on the footprints and sauté for 5 minutes per side, until just cooked through. Remove the fish to a platter and keep warm.

3. Heat the remaining 1 teaspoon oil in the skillet over medium heat. Add the garlic and sauté for 1 minute. Add the smoked mushrooms and leeks and sauté for 1 minute. Stir in the smoked tomatoes and their juice. Add the spinach, a handful at a time, and cook, stirring, until just wilted. Add the salt and pepper to taste.

4. To serve, spoon the vegetables onto 4 plates and top each portion with a piece of the fish. Drizzle with lemon juice and serve immediately.

Zone yield per recipe: 16 protein blocks, 10 carbohydrate blocks

Baked Bluefish with Smoked Tomato-Orange Sauce and Roasted Fennel

4 SERVINGS Juice extractors rode into many kitchens on the wave of the high-carbohydrate, low-fat craze. Fruit and vegetable extracts appeared in chic recipes as colorful low-calorie, nonfat foundations for soups, sauces, and salad dressings. Unfortunately, juicing robbed vegetables and fruits of their primary means of glycemic control—namely fiber. While not as fiber-filled as the whole fruit or vegetable, purees—such as the orange puree below—are glycemically superior to extracted juice. Their pulpy texture also helps to thicken sauces without the addition of fat and flour. So pack up the juice extractor, and bring out the blender. The possibilities are endless.

NUTRITIONAL ANALYSIS PER SERVING: 274 CALORIES, 31 G PROTEIN, 17 G CARBOHYDRATE, 9 G FAT (2 G SATURATED), 84 MG CHOLESTEROL, 468 MG SODIUM, 1 G FIBER

1½ pounds fresh fennel bulbs (about 2 large bulbs), stalks trimmed

1¼ pounds skinless bluefish fillets, 1 to 1½ inches thick

1½ teaspoons extra virgin olive oil

Salt and freshly ground black pepper

Smoked Tomato-Orange Sauce

1   teaspoon extra virgin olive oil

½   to 1 teaspoon fennel seed

½   cup Smoked Plum Tomato Puree (page 37) or fresh tomato puree

½   cup orange sections, seeded and pureed

½   teaspoon fructose

½   teaspoon salt or more to taste

Freshly ground pepper

1. Preheat the oven to 450° F. Halve the fennel bulbs lengthwise and remove the cores. Place the cut sides of each bulb together and wrap each bulb tightly in foil. Place on a baking sheet and roast for 30 to 40 minutes, until tender. (This may be done ahead or timed so that the fish bakes during the last 15 minutes of the fennel's roasting time.) Meanwhile, coarsely chop the fronds and set aside.

2. Brush a baking dish with ½ teaspoon of the oil. Place the fish, skinned side down, in the baking dish and brush with the remaining 1 teaspoon oil. Season generously with salt and pepper. Bake for 10 to 15 minutes, until cooked through. Transfer to a platter.

3. Meanwhile, to make the sauce, heat 1 teaspoon oil in a small non-stick skillet over medium heat. Add the fennel seeds and sauté for 1 minute. Add the pureed tomatoes and orange sections, fructose, and salt. Simmer for 5 minutes, stirring occasionally. Season with salt and pepper to taste.

4. Remove the fennel packets from the oven and carefully open them to avoid burns from the steam. Drain the fennel, slice lengthwise into slivers, and distribute over the fish. Spoon the sauce over the fennel, garnish with the chopped fronds, and serve immediately.

Zone yield per recipe: 16 protein blocks, 7 carbohydrate blocks (1 tablespoon sauce = 0 protein blocks, ⅛ carbohydrate block)

Smoked Red Snapper with Hot Yellow Pepper Sauce 4 SERVINGS

Yellow bell peppers are high in fiber and antioxidants and low in carbohydrate density. Roasted and pureed, they offer a luxurious, fat-free basis for an intense and beautiful sauce that is delicious served warm, at room temperature, or chilled. If red snapper is unavailable, try the sauce with smoked or broiled catfish, swordfish, or bluefish. It also works with grilled lamb and chicken.

NUTRITIONAL ANALYSIS PER SERVING: 212 CALORIES, 31 G PROTEIN, 11 G CARBOHYDRATE,
5 G FAT (1 G SATURATED), 52 MG CHOLESTEROL, 387 MG SODIUM, 3 G FIBER

Hot Yellow Pepper Sauce

2   large yellow bell peppers

1½ teaspoons extra virgin olive oil

1   tablespoon minced garlic

1   tablespoon cider vinegar

2   teaspoons fructose

½   teaspoon salt or to taste

¼   teaspoon cayenne pepper

1¼ pounds skinless red snapper
    fillets, about 1 inch thick

½   teaspoon extra virgin olive oil

    Salt and freshly ground black
    pepper

1. To make the sauce, roast the peppers by thoroughly charring the skins under the broiler. Transfer to a paper bag and allow to steam for 10 to 15 minutes to loosen the skins. Remove the stems, skins, seeds, and membranes. Puree the flesh in a blender or food processor and set aside.

2. In a small nonstick skillet, heat the oil over medium heat. Add the garlic and sauté for 1 minute. Stir in the pepper puree and the vinegar, fructose, salt, and cayenne. Reduce the heat to low and simmer for 3 minutes, stirring occasionally. Adjust the seasoning. (The sauce can be made in advance and refrigerated for up to 1 week or frozen for up to 6 months. It should be served at the same temperature as the fish. It can be reheated in a saucepan or in the microwave as needed.)

3. Prepare a stovetop smoker with 1 tablespoon alder smoking chips. Spray the rack with canola or olive oil. Place the fish on the rack, skin side down, and brush with the oil. Season generously with salt and pepper. Half-close the lid and place the smoker on an electric burner preheated to medium or a gas burner turned to medium-high. When the first wisps of smoke appear, close the lid. Smoke for 15 to 20 minutes, until cooked through. Remove from the smoker.

4. Serve the fish warm, at room temperature, or chilled, with 1 tablespoon of the sauce spooned over each portion. Pass the extra sauce on the side.

Note: Smoking times are highly variable.

Zone yield per recipe: 16 protein blocks, 3 carbohydrate blocks (1 tablespoon sauce = 0 protein blocks, ⅕ carbohydrate block)

Smoked Red Snapper with Pommery Mustard Sauce *(Variation)* 4 SERVINGS

NUTRITIONAL ANALYSIS PER SERVING: 192 CALORIES, 30 G PROTEIN, 6 G CARBOHYDRATE,
5 G FAT (1 G SATURATED), 54 MG CHOLESTEROL, 274 MG SODIUM, 0 G FIBER

1. To make the mustard sauce, combine ¼ cup low-fat mayonnaise, ¼ cup nonfat plain yogurt, 1 tablespoon Pommery mustard, 1 tablespoon prepared white horseradish, and 2 tablespoons minced flat-leaf parsley in a small bowl. (The sauce can be made in advance and refrigerated for up to 3 days.)

2. Prepare the fish as directed above. Serve the fish warm, at room temperature, or chilled, with 1 tablespoon of the sauce spooned over each portion. Pass the remaining sauce on the side.

Zone yield per recipe: 16 protein blocks, 2 carbohydrate blocks (1 tablespoon sauce = 0 protein blocks, ⅕ carbohydrate block)

Broiled Bluefish Fillets with Smoked Garlic-Tomato Sauce

4 SERVINGS Bluefish has its admirers and detractors, and I am among the former. I love its assertiveness, and I have always relished the challenge of balancing its strong flavor. In this recipe, broiled bluefish fillets receive a sauce of smoked garlic, sherry vinegar, and tomato. The tomato adds a nice acidic counterpoint to the richness of the garlic puree.

NUTRITIONAL ANALYSIS PER SERVING: 245 CALORIES, 30 G PROTEIN, 8 G CARBOHYDRATE,
10 G FAT (2 G SATURATED), 84 MG CHOLESTEROL, 94 MG SODIUM, 1 G FIBER

1¼ pounds skinless bluefish fillets, about 1 inch thick

Salt and freshly ground black pepper

2   teaspoons extra virgin olive oil

Smoked Garlic-Tomato Sauce

⅓   cup fresh or canned tomato puree

¼   cup Smoked Garlic Paste (page 25)

4   teaspoons sherry vinegar

1   teaspoon extra virgin olive oil

¼   cup minced flat-leaf parsley

Salt and freshly ground black pepper

1. Preheat the broiler. Season the fish on both sides with salt and pepper and brush both sides with the oil. Place on a nonstick broiler pan and broil the fish 4 inches from the heat for 4 to 5 minutes per side, until cooked through. Remove to a platter.

2. Meanwhile, to make the sauce, combine the tomato puree, smoked garlic paste, and vinegar in a small measuring cup and whisk to blend. Heat 1 teaspoon oil in a small nonreactive skillet over medium heat and add the puree mixture. Cook for 1 to 2 minutes, stirring. Remove from the heat and stir in the parsley. Season to taste with salt and pepper.

3. To serve, spoon 4 tablespoons of the sauce over the fish and serve immediately, passing the additional sauce at the table.

Zone yield per recipe: 16 protein blocks, 3 carbohydrate blocks (1 tablespoon sauce = 0 protein blocks, ⅕ carbohydrate block)

Baked Halibut with Anchovy-Tomato "Butter" 4 SERVINGS

Because cooked halibut tends toward dryness, halibut recipes frequently employ liquid-based techniques such as steaming, braising, or poaching. The rich "butter" in this dish keeps the fish moist as long as you do not overcook it, meanwhile investing it with intense flavor in the absence of significant fat. If you have both fish and "butter" left over, treat yourself to a cold variation the next day. Serve the halibut chilled with a flavored mayonnaise consisting of 2 parts leftover "butter" plus 1 part nonfat plain yogurt and 1 part low-fat mayonnaise. You may decide to live on leftovers forever!

NUTRITIONAL ANALYSIS PER SERVING: 198 CALORIES, 31 G PROTEIN, 5 G CARBOHYDRATE, 5 G FAT (1 G SATURATED), 47 MG CHOLESTEROL, 176 MG SODIUM, 1 G FIBER

Anchovy-Tomato "Butter"

2   tablespoons Roasted Garlic Paste (page 24)

6   tablespoons canned tomato puree

2   teaspoons anchovy paste

3   tablespoons minced flat-leaf parsley

1¼ pounds halibut steaks, 1 to 1½ inches thick

    Salt and freshly ground black pepper

1   teaspoon extra virgin olive oil

1. To make the "butter," combine the roasted garlic paste, tomato puree, anchovy paste, and parsley in a small measuring cup and whisk to blend. Set aside. (The "butter" can be made in advance and refrigerated for up to 3 days.)

2. Preheat the oven to 400° F. Spray a nonstick roasting pan with olive oil. Season the halibut generously with salt and pepper and place in the pan. Spread 3 tablespoons of the "butter" over the top of the fish.

Drizzle with 1 teaspoon olive oil. Bake for approximately 10 to 15 minutes, until just cooked through. Serve immediately, passing the extra "butter" on the side.

Zone yield per recipe: 16 protein blocks, 2 carbohydrate blocks (1 tablespoon "butter" = 0 protein blocks, ⅙ carbohydrate block)

Sautéed Ocean Catfish with Smoky Tartar Sauce 4 SERVINGS

Cheryl and Bill Jamison have elevated smoking to high art. I adore their books and I've spent many hours learning from them. Facing two pearly catfish fillets one afternoon, I flipped through *Sublime Smoke* for inspiration. They suggested adding smoked onions to tartar sauce. No sooner read than done!

NUTRITIONAL ANALYSIS PER SERVING: 288 CALORIES, 27 G PROTEIN, 6 G CARBOHYDRATE, 16 G FAT (3 G SATURATED), 80 MG CHOLESTEROL, 605 MG SODIUM, 0 G FIBER

Smoky Tartar Sauce

¼ cup low-fat mayonnaise

¼ cup nonfat plain yogurt

¼ cup finely chopped Smoked Onions (page 27) (red onion is recommended)

1½ tablespoons sherry vinegar or to taste

2 teaspoons chopped capers

2 teaspoons chopped cornichons

½ teaspoon salt

Tabasco sauce

1½ pounds ocean catfish fillets

Salt and freshly ground black pepper

2 teaspoons extra virgin olive or canola oil

1. To make the tartar sauce, combine the mayonnaise, yogurt, smoked onion, vinegar, capers, cornichons, and salt in a small measuring cup and whisk to blend. Adjust the seasoning, adding Tabasco sauce and vinegar to taste, and set aside. (The sauce can be made in advance and refrigerated for up to 3 days.)

2. Generously season the fish on both sides with salt and pepper. Heat the oil in a nonstick skillet over medium-high heat. Add the fillets and sauté for 4 to 5 minutes per side, until cooked through.

3. To serve, divide the fish among 4 plates. Top each portion with 1 tablespoon of tartar sauce. Serve immediately, passing the remaining sauce on the side.

Zone yield per recipe: 16 protein blocks, 3 carbohydrate blocks (1 tablespoon sauce = 0 protein blocks, ⅕ carbohydrate block)

Broiled Sesame Salmon

4 SERVINGS Compared to wild salmon, the farm-raised variety available in most markets is considerably less rich in heart-healthy omega-3 fatty acids. However, I prefer farm-raised salmon to no salmon at all. It may be the world's most accepting and forgiving fish, tolerating a dizzying range of cooking methods: sautéing, steaming, poaching, braising, roasting, baking, broiling, and grilling. Here salmon is briefly marinated in Japanese flavorings and broiled. If you serve it with a side dish containing sesame seeds and wish to avoid redundancy, simply eliminate them from this recipe.

NUTRITIONAL ANALYSIS PER SERVING: 230 CALORIES, 29 G PROTEIN, 3 G CARBOHYDRATE, 10 G FAT (2 G SATURATED), 78 MG CHOLESTEROL, 835 MG SODIUM, 0 G FIBER

Marinade

3 tablespoons Japanese soy sauce

1½ tablespoons brown rice vinegar

1 teaspoon fructose or maple syrup

1 tablespoon lemon juice

½ teaspoon grated fresh ginger or to taste

1¼ pounds skinless salmon fillet in 4 equal pieces, 1 inch at its thickest point

1 tablespoon unhulled sesame seeds, toasted

1 scallion, thinly sliced

1. To make the marinade, combine the soy sauce, vinegar, fructose, lemon juice, and ginger in a small bowl or measuring cup and whisk to blend. Place the salmon pieces in a nonreactive container. Pour the marinade over them and turn to coat. Refrigerate for 1 hour.

2. Preheat the broiler. Spray a nonstick broiler pan with olive oil. Place the salmon, skin side up, on the pan and transfer the marinade to a small saucepan. Broil the salmon 4 inches from the heat for 4 minutes. Meanwhile, bring the marinade to a boil and simmer for 2 minutes. Turn the salmon, baste with the marinade, sprinkle with the sesame seeds, and broil for another 4 minutes, or until just barely cooked through.

3. The fish and marinade can be served hot, at room temperature, or chilled. Spoon a tablespoon of the boiled marinade over each piece and garnish with the sliced scallion.

Zone yield per recipe: 16 protein blocks, 1 carbohydrate block

Broiled Sesame Salmon with steamed asparagus

Roasted Salmon with Fresh Herbs 4 SERVINGS

I do not change my diet when I entertain. Instead, I try to create a menu that will not shock my guests or leave them feeling deprived. Over the years, the Sunday *Boston Globe* column by Sheryl Julian and Julie Riven has served as a rich source of easy and elegant dinner party ideas, readily adaptable to insulin-controlling parameters. The following recipe, derived from their foolproof and beautiful "Roasted Red Trout with Sautéed Cherry Tomatoes" has been the star of many party menus.

NUTRITIONAL ANALYSIS PER SERVING: 217 CALORIES, 28 G PROTEIN, 0 G CARBOHYDRATE, 11 G FAT (2 G SATURATED), 78 MG CHOLESTEROL, 64 MG SODIUM, 0 G FIBER

1¼ pounds skinless salmon fillets

1½ teaspoons extra virgin olive oil

Salt and freshly ground black pepper

2 to 3 tablespoons chopped mixed fresh herbs (parsley, rosemary, and thyme, or parsley, tarragon, and chives)

1. Preheat the oven to 450° F. Brush a baking dish with ½ teaspoon olive oil and add the salmon. Brush the salmon with the remaining 1 teaspoon oil and season generously with salt and pepper.

2. Roast for 8 to 12 minutes, until just cooked through. Remove from the oven and sprinkle with the herbs. Serve hot, warm, or at room temperature.

Zone yield per recipe: 16 protein blocks, less than one carbohydrate block

Salmon Patties with Smoked Leeks and Garlic Chives 4 SERVINGS

Since his 1950s childhood, my husband has adored the comforting croquettes of that era. In the days before insulin awareness, I served them to him regularly. Unfortunately, when we began the Zone diet, I reclassified them as G.U. (Glycemically Undesirable) due to the type and quantity of carbohydrate they contained. In my ongoing attempt to take his preferences into account, I have trotted out a long line of croquette impostors in which flavor-bearing vegetables replace the bread crumbs of yesteryear. These salmon patties gratified three loves at once: his for croquettes and salmon, and mine for him.

NUTRITIONAL ANALYSIS PER SERVING: 245 CALORIES, 29 G PROTEIN, 7 G CARBOHYDRATE, 10 G FAT (2 G SATURATED), 78 MG CHOLESTEROL, 411 MG SODIUM, I G FIBER

1¼ pounds skinless salmon fillets, cut into 1-inch chunks

4 tablespoons minced garlic chives

½ cup finely chopped Smoked Leeks (page 28)

4 teaspoons Japanese soy sauce

4 teaspoons Pseudo-Mirin (page 37)

1 teaspoon extra virgin olive oil

Salmon Patties with Smoked Leeks and Garlic Chives (continued)

1. Place one-quarter of the salmon in a food processor and puree. Add the remaining salmon and pulse a few times to chop into ¼ -inch dice. Transfer to a bowl. Add the leeks, chives, soy sauce, and Pseudo-Mirin.

Blend well without overworking. Form into 4 patties, each about 1 inch thick. Refrigerate for at least 1 hour, or up to 8 hours.

2. Preheat the broiler. Place the patties on a nonstick broiler pan and brush lightly with oil. Broil 4 inches from the heat for 3 to

4 minutes. Turn, brush with the remaining oil, and broil for another 3 to 4 minutes, until barely cooked through. Serve immediately.

Zone yield per recipe: 16 protein blocks, 3 carbohydrate blocks

Steamed Salmon with Cucumbers and Pickled Radishes

4 SERVINGS Although it contains no Japanese ingredients, this dish reflects the lightness and clarity of Japanese cuisine, and its reverence for fish and pickled vegetables. It makes a marvelous lunch or summer supper.

NUTRITIONAL ANALYSIS PER SERVING: 268 CALORIES, 29 G PROTEIN, 14 G CARBOHYDRATE, 10 G FAT (2 G SATURATED), 78 MG CHOLESTEROL, 1239 MG SODIUM, 1 G FIBER

Pickling Brine

¼ cup water

3 tablespoons fructose

2 tablespoons dill vinegar

1 teaspoon salt

1 bunch red radishes, halved length-wise and thinly sliced (about 2 cups)

1 large English cucumber (about 1½ pounds), halved lengthwise, seeded, and thinly sliced (about 2 cups)

3 teaspoons salt

1¼ pounds skinless salmon fillets, about 1 inch thick

1 teaspoon extra virgin olive or canola oil

1 tablespoon chopped fresh dill

1. To make the brine, combine the water, fructose, vinegar, and salt in a small saucepan and bring to a boil. Reduce the heat and simmer to dissolve the fructose, 1 to 2 minutes. Pour the hot brine over the sliced radishes in a nonreactive bowl. Cool to room temperature; then refrigerate overnight. (The radishes will keep for several days in the refrigerator.)

2. In a colander, toss the cucumbers with 2 teaspoons of the salt. Allow to drain for 45 minutes. Do not rinse. Dry well between layers of paper towels and transfer to a bowl. Refrigerate until you are ready to serve (for up to 1 day).

3. Place the salmon, skin side down, in a steamer and brush with the oil. Sprinkle with the remaining 1 teaspoon salt. Steam the salmon for approximately 6 minutes, until just barely done. (It will continue to cook briefly after you remove it from the steamer.) Cool to room temperature.

4. To serve, add the pickled radishes (along with their brine) and dill to the cucumber slices and toss to combine. Adjust the seasoning and serve alongside the salmon or spooned over it.

Zone yield per recipe (includes all of the brine): 16 protein blocks, 5 carbohydrate blocks (1 tablespoon brine = 0 protein blocks, ½ carbo-hydrate block)

Broiled Swordfish with Red Pepper-Orange Sauce 4 SERVINGS

Roasted bell peppers possess many virtues: intense color, rich flavor, vitamin A, high fiber content, and low carbohydrate density. Their silky texture and mellow taste create an instant sauce base. Here they are pureed with roasted pepper oil, orange juice, and ume plum vinegar to enhance broiled swordfish steaks. The sauce works just as well with salmon, sea bass, halibut, and shrimp. It also complements poached or broiled chicken.

NUTRITIONAL ANALYSIS PER SERVING: 256 CALORIES, 30 G PROTEIN, 10 G CARBOHYDRATE, 11 G FAT (2 G SATURATED), 55 MG CHOLESTEROL, 133 MG SODIUM, 4 G FIBER

1¼ pounds swordfish steaks, about 1 inch thick, cut into 4 pieces

Salt and freshly ground black pepper

2 teaspoons roasted pepper oil or extra virgin olive oil

1 garlic clove, crushed

1 teaspoon grated orange zest

¼ cup coarsely chopped fresh basil

Red Pepper-Orange Sauce

2 large red bell peppers

2 teaspoons roasted pepper oil or extra virgin olive oil

¼ orange, peeled, seeds removed, and coarsely chopped

1 tablespoon ume plum or red wine vinegar

Salt and freshly ground black pepper

Pinch cayenne pepper (optional)

1. Season the fish generously on both sides with salt and pepper. In a small bowl or measuring cup, combine the 2 teaspoons oil with the garlic and orange zest. Brush the swordfish lightly with the mixture. Set aside.

2. To make the sauce, roast the peppers by thoroughly charring the skins under the broiler. Transfer to a paper bag and allow to steam for 10 to 15 minutes to loosen the skins. Remove the stems, skins, seeds, and membranes. Coarsely chop.

3. Combine the roasted peppers, pepper oil, chopped orange, and vinegar in a blender and puree. Season with salt and pepper, plus cayenne, if desired. Set aside.

4. Preheat the broiler. Place the fish on a nonstick broiler pan. Broil 4 inches from the heat for about 4 minutes per side, until barely cooked through.

5. Serve the fish hot, at room temperature, or chilled. Garnish each portion with a tablespoon of the sauce and the basil. Pass the remaining sauce on the side.

Zone yield per recipe: 16 protein blocks, 3 carbohydrate blocks (1 tablespoon sauce = 0 protein blocks, ⅙ carbohydrate block)

Smoked Swordfish Steaks 4 SERVINGS

Fruity, salty ume plum vinegar, derived from Japanese ume plums, defies comparison. No adequate substitutes exist. Look for it in health food stores under the Eden Foods label. In combination with oil, onion, and garlic, it generates an irresistible marinade for swordfish steaks. After approximately 10 minutes in the smoker, this exotic and minimalist fish is ready to eat.

NUTRITIONAL ANALYSIS PER SERVING: 223 CALORIES, 28 G PROTEIN, 2 G CARBOHYDRATE, 11 G FAT (2 G SATURATED), 55 MG CHOLESTEROL, 128 MG SODIUM, 0 G FIBER

Marinade

1½ tablespoons extra virgin olive oil

1½ tablespoons ume plum vinegar

1 large garlic clove, crushed

¼ cup finely chopped onion

1¼ pounds swordfish steaks, 1 inch thick

Salt and freshly ground black pepper

1. To make the marinade, combine the oil, vinegar, garlic, and onion in a small bowl or measuring cup and whisk to blend. Place the fish in a nonreactive container. Pour the marinade over the fish and turn to coat. Refrigerate for 1 hour, turning occasionally.

2. Prepare a stovetop smoker with 1 tablespoon alder smoking chips. Remove the fish from the marinade and place on the rack. Season with salt and pepper. Strain the marinade through a sieve; distribute the solids over the fish and discard the liquid. Half-close the lid and place the smoker on an electric burner preheated to medium or a gas burner turned to medium-high. When the first wisps of smoke appear, close the lid. Smoke for 8 to 10 minutes, until the fish is just cooked through. Serve the fish warm, at room temperature, or chilled.

Note: Smoking times are highly variable.

Zone yield per recipe: 16 protein blocks, 1 carbohydrate block

Smoked Tuna Steaks with Anchovy-Tomato Mayonnaise

4 SERVINGS If you are a novice in stovetop smoking, this recipe is for you. The simple mayonnaise can be prepared in advance, thus freeing you to focus on your new piece of equipment. Also, the uniform thickness of tuna steaks eliminates the timing conflict that might attend, say, a salmon fillet. Best of all, smoked tuna is indescribably delicious, with a luxurious texture far superior, in my opinion, to pan-seared or grilled tuna. If you avoid overcooking (cut into it and check!), your tuna will be pink in the middle and flavorful throughout. It can be served warm, at room temperature, or cold, and it keeps beautifully in the refrigerator for nearly a week.

NUTRITIONAL ANALYSIS PER SERVING: 201 CALORIES, 28 G PROTEIN, 4 G CARBOHYDRATE, 8 G FAT (2 G SATURATED), 44 MG CHOLESTEROL, 538 MG SODIUM, 0 G FIBER

Anchovy-Tomato Mayonnaise

2   tablespoons low-fat mayonnaise

2   tablespoons nonfat plain yogurt

2   tablespoons canned tomato puree

1½ tablespoons minced flat-leaf parsley

1   tablespoon capers

2   teaspoons Roasted Garlic Paste (page 24)

1   teaspoon anchovy paste

½   teaspoon salt or to taste

1   pound tuna steaks, 1 inch thick

1   teaspoon extra virgin olive oil

    Salt and freshly ground black pepper

1. To make the anchovy-tomato mayonnaise, combine the mayonnaise, yogurt, tomato puree, parsley, capers, roasted garlic paste, anchovy paste, and salt in a small measuring cup and whisk to blend. Set aside. (The sauce can be made up to 3 days in advance and refrigerated until you are ready to serve. Bring to room temperature, if needed, to match the serving temperature of the fish.)

2. Prepare a stovetop smoker with 1 tablespoon alder smoking chips. Brush the tuna on both sides with the oil and season well with salt and pepper. Place the fish on the rack and half-close the lid. Place the smoker on an electric burner preheated to medium or on a gas burner turned to medium-high. When the first wisps of smoke appear, close the lid. Smoke for 10 to 15 minutes, or until the tuna is rare to medium rare.

3. Serve at room temperature or chilled, spooning 1 tablespoon of the flavored mayonnaise beside each serving.

Note: Smoking times are highly variable.

Zone yield per recipe: 16 protein blocks, 2 carbohydrate blocks (1 tablespoon mayonnaise = 0 protein blocks, ⅕ carbohydrate block)

Smoked Tuna Salad with Cranberry Beans and Fennel 4 SERVINGS

The lovely speckled beans in this unusual and refreshing tuna salad are called variously cranberry, borlotti, or Roman. Their mild, sweet flavor and smooth texture make them popular inclusions in Italian pasta dishes and soups.

NUTRITIONAL ANALYSIS PER SERVING: 310 CALORIES, 33 G PROTEIN, 20 G CARBOHYDRATE, 11 G FAT (2 G SATURATED), 44 MG CHOLESTEROL, 218 MG SODIUM, 1 G FIBER

1	*pound tuna steaks, about 1 inch thick*
1	*teaspoon extra virgin olive oil*
	Salt and freshly ground black pepper
1	*cup cooked and drained cranberry beans*
1	*cup chopped fennel bulb*
½	*cup sliced scallions (white parts only)*
2	*cups quartered cherry tomatoes*
1	*tablespoon capers*
2	*tablespoons minced flat-leaf parsley*
2	*tablespoons chopped fennel fronds*
8	*cups arugula, coarse stems removed*
	Salt and freshly ground black pepper

Dressing

1	*tablespoon extra virgin olive oil*
2	*tablespoons red wine vinegar*
2	*teaspoons Dijon mustard*
1	*teaspoon anchovy paste*

1. Prepare a stovetop smoker with 1 tablespoon alder smoking chips. Brush the tuna on both sides with the oil and season well with salt and pepper. Place the tuna on the rack, half-close the lid, and place the smoker on an electric burner pre-heated to medium or on a gas burner turned to medium-high. When the first wisps of smoke appear, close the lid. Smoke for 10 to 15 minutes for rare to medium rare fish. Remove from the smoker and cool to room temperature. Cut the smoked tuna into ¾-inch chunks and set aside. (The tuna can be smoked in advance and refrigerated for up to 1 week.)

2. To make the dressing, combine the oil, vinegar, mustard, and anchovy paste in a small measuring cup. Whisk to blend.

3. Combine the tuna, beans, fennel, scallions, tomatoes, capers, parsley, and fennel fronds in a large bowl. Add the dressing and gently toss to coat.

4. Divide the arugula among 4 plates and mound the tuna mixture on top. Serve immediately.

Note: Smoking times are highly variable.

Zone yield per recipe: 16 protein blocks, 8 carbohydrate blocks (1 tablespoon dressing = 0 protein blocks, 0 carbohydrate blocks)

Smoked Tuna Salad with Cranberry Beans and Fennel

Clams in Black Bean Sauce

2 TO 3 SERVINGS For decades, my father traveled regularly to the Far East where, with dedicated Chinese partners, he built an innovative and successful business. Over the years, his culinary activities also turned toward China as he attempted to satisfy yearnings for lovingly remembered dishes. These clams, enveloped in the smoky sharpness of fermented black beans, evoke Hong Kong's Siu Lam Kung, his enduring favorite. If you have concerns about measuring for precise protein content, see page 42.

NUTRITIONAL ANALYSIS PER SERVING: 305 CALORIES, 29 G PROTEIN, 17 G CARBOHYDRATE, 8 G FAT (1 G SATURATED), 58 MG CHOLESTEROL, 455 MG SODIUM, 0 G FIBER

1 tablespoon extra virgin olive or canola oil

1 tablespoon minced garlic

1 tablespoon minced fresh ginger

1 tablespoon minced flat-leaf parsley

¼ teaspoon hot red pepper flakes

½ cup dry white wine

4 dozen littleneck clams, scrubbed

8 ounces bottled clam juice

¼ cup fermented black beans, rinsed, drained, and dried on paper towels

1. Heat the oil in a large Dutch oven over medium heat. Add the garlic, ginger, parsley, and red pepper flakes. Sauté for 2 minutes. Add the wine and cook for 5 minutes. Add the clams, clam juice, and black beans. Cover and cook for 4 to 8 minutes over medium-high heat. Remove the clams to a bowl as soon as they open and discard any clams remaining unopened after 8 minutes.

2. To serve, divide the clams among 2 to 3 large bowls and ladle the broth over them. Serve immediately.

Zone yield per recipe: 8 protein blocks, 3 carbohydrate blocks

Clams in Black Bean Sauce

Roasted Clams with Smoked Tomatoes 2 SERVINGS

Clams al Forno, a signature starter at the renowned restaurant of chef-owners Johanne Killeen and George Germon, is—in itself—worth the 2-hour round trip between Providence, Rhode Island and my Massachusetts home. When I came upon the recipe for it in Killeen and Germon's generous book, *Cucina Simpatica,* I knew I had found the right basis for a personal experiment with roasted clams and smoked tomatoes. | Unfortunately, raw clams in the shell are pigs in a poke, defying all attempts at protein estimation. To be on the safe side, buy more than you think you need. In this case, I suggest 4 dozen to allow for several rejects and runts. If your clams are meaty, you'll have a few ounces left over for lunch the next day. If you're strict about protein, remove the clams from their shells, weigh out 4 ounces per person, and then ladle the hot liquid over them. Otherwise, simply divide the clams between 2 bowls, bathe them in broth, and dig in!

NUTRITIONAL ANALYSIS PER SERVING: 334 CALORIES, 26 G PROTEIN, 29 G CARBOHYDRATE, 10 G FAT (1 G SATURATED), 58 MG CHOLESTEROL, 272 MG SODIUM, 5 G FIBER

---

4   dozen littleneck clams, scrubbed

1   cup thinly sliced onions

⅓   cup sliced scallions

1½ tablespoons minced garlic

¼   teaspoon hot red pepper flakes or to taste

2   cups chopped Smoked Plum Tomatoes (page 36), drained with juice reserved

½   cup dry white wine

½   cup bottled clam juice

1   tablespoon extra virgin olive oil
    Freshly ground black pepper

2   tablespoons minced flat-leaf parsley

1. Place the rack in the upper third of the oven and preheat the oven to 500° F. Place the clams in a roasting pan large enough to hold them in a single layer. Distribute the onions, scallions, garlic, and red pepper flakes over the clams. Add the tomatoes, wine, and clam juice. Add enough water to the reserved tomato juice to make ½ cup and add this to the pan.

2. Drizzle the clams with the olive oil and grind some black pepper over them. Roast for 20 minutes, turning the clams several times during roasting. Check the clams after 20 minutes and remove any clams that have opened. Continue roasting for another 10 minutes, checking every 3 to 5 minutes and removing the clams from the oven as they open. Discard any clams that have not opened after 30 minutes.

3. Divide the clams between 2 deep bowls and ladle the steaming broth over them. Garnish with the parsley. Serve immediately.

Zone yield per recipe: 8 protein blocks, 5 carbohydrate blocks

Smoked Clam and Chickpea Stew 2 TO 3 SERVINGS Raw clams in the shell vary

significantly in water content. If you wish to measure 2 servings of protein with precision, do so after smoking: 8 ounces of smoked clams (meat only) equals 2 servings. Depending on shell size, you may have to smoke the clams in 2 batches. Don't worry, this stew is so delicious you will not resent it. You can smoke the clams several days in advance and reheat them in the stew just before serving. Be sure you taste the stew before adding salt because clams contribute plenty of their own.

NUTRITIONAL ANALYSIS PER SERVING: 283 CALORIES, 29 G PROTEIN, 23 G CARBOHYDRATE, 8 G FAT (I G SATURATED), 58 MG CHOLESTEROL, 235 MG SODIUM, 6 G FIBER

---

4   dozen littleneck clams, scrubbed

1   cup cooked and drained chickpeas

2   teaspoons extra virgin olive oil

2   teaspoons minced garlic

2   teaspoons minced flat-leaf parsley plus 1 tablespoon for the garnish

¼   teaspoon hot red pepper flakes

½   cup julienned red bell pepper

   Salt and freshly ground black pepper

1. Prepare a stovetop smoker with 1 tablespoon alder smoking chips. Place the clams on the rack in a single layer and half-close the lid. Place the smoker on an electric burner preheated to medium or on a gas burner turned to medium-high. When the first wisps of smoke appear, close the lid. Smoke for 20 to 25 minutes.

2. Transfer the clams to a bowl as they open, taking care to save the juice. Discard any unopened clams. Do not discard the juice in the drip tray.

3. Remove the smoked clams from their shells over a bowl to catch the juice. Set the clams aside. Add the juice from the smoker drip tray to the juice in the bowl and strain through a cheesecloth-lined sieve into a clean bowl.

4. In a blender, combine ¼ cup of the chickpeas with ¼ cup of the reserved clam juice. Puree until smooth. Set aside.

5. Heat the oil in a nonstick skillet over medium heat. Add the garlic, 2 teaspoons of the parsley, and the pepper flakes. Sauté for 1 to 2 minutes. Add the bell pepper and sauté for 2 to 3 minutes. Add the pureed and whole chickpeas and simmer for 2 minutes. Stir in the reserved clams. Simmer for 1 to 2 minutes, adding more clam juice, if needed. Adjust the seasoning, adding pepper and salt, if needed.

6. Serve immediately in shallow bowls, garnished with the remaining 1 tablespoon parsley.

Note: Smoking times are highly variable.

Zone yield per recipe: 8 protein blocks, 4 carbohydrate blocks

Crab Bundles with Avocado-Ginger Sauce 4 SERVINGS In the absence

of tortillas and other flatbreads, lettuce leaves come in handy for wrapping. They're fragile, though, and lead

to rather messy meals, so make sure you're among friends when you serve this dish. If you're fastidious, or expect

fastidious guests, present this as a composed salad on a bed of romaine. It will be considerably less fun to eat, but

just as delicious. | The high fat content of avocados has scared away fat-restricting dieters for years. Actually,

the monounsaturated fats found in avocados benefit the heart and have no effect on insulin levels. Since crabmeat

contains little intrinsic fat, it provides an ideal opportunity for enjoying this luxurious source of healthy fat.

NUTRITIONAL ANALYSIS PER SERVING: 259 CALORIES, 28 G PROTEIN, 15 G CARBOHYDRATE,
10 G FAT (1 G SATURATED), 61 MG CHOLESTEROL, 1541 MG SODIUM, 3 G FIBER

Avocado-Ginger Sauce

1   cup nonfat plain yogurt

1   ripe Haas avocado, peeled and
     seeded

1   tablespoon brown rice vinegar

1   tablespoon Japanese soy sauce

2   tablespoons minced pickled
     ginger, drained

½   cup finely chopped red onion
     Salt and freshly ground black
     pepper

16   ounces lump crabmeat, picked over

2   cups finely chopped English
     cucumbers (peeling is optional)

2   cups finely chopped red radishes

2   heads Boston lettuce, leaves
     separated

1. To make the sauce, combine the yogurt, avocado, vinegar, and soy sauce in a food processor. Pulse to a slightly chunky consistency, scraping down the sides as needed. Transfer to a bowl and stir in the pickled ginger and red onion. Blend well. Season to taste with salt and pepper. (The dressing can be made up to 24 hours in advance and refrigerated.)

2. Divide the crabmeat, cucumbers, and radishes among 4 plates. Arrange the lettuce leaves on a platter. Divide the sauce among 4 small bowls. To eat: Take a lettuce leaf or two. Spoon a little sauce into the center. Add some crab, cucumber, and radish. Top with a little more sauce. Roll and eat.

Zone yield per recipe: 16 protein blocks, 5 carbohydrate blocks (1 tablespoon sauce = 0 protein blocks, ¹⁄₁₀ carbohydrate block)

Lobster Salad with Avocado-Horseradish Dressing 4 SERVINGS

Ounce for ounce, smooth, thin-skinned Florida (Fuerte) avocados contain slightly more carbohydrate and significantly less fat than their pebbly-skinned California (Haas) cousins. This gives them a nutritional advantage in situations where aromatic smokiness, the hallmark of the Haas variety, is not critical. In this salad, horseradish and ume plum vinegar supply the depth and mystery that the unadorned Florida avocado lacks. They contribute a subtle, unidentifiable bite to the dressing that contrasts beautifully with lobster's natural sweetness. If you can't find ume plum vinegar, use red wine vinegar instead. | Four 1½-pound soft-shell or 1¼-pound hard-shell lobsters will provide enough meat for this recipe. Steam, boil, or microwave them; then remove the meat from the shell, and chill. You might also enjoy this salad with cooked shrimp, crabmeat, or cold poached scallops. Serve it as an appetizer or main course.

NUTRITIONAL ANALYSIS PER SERVING: 312 CALORIES, 36 G PROTEIN, 24 G CARBOHYDRATE, 9 G FAT (2 G SATURATED), 104 MG CHOLESTEROL, 1194 MG SODIUM, 7 G FIBER

Avocado-Horseradish Dressing

1   *ripe Florida avocado, peeled and seeded*

1   *cup plain nonfat yogurt*

1   *tablespoon prepared white horseradish*

1   *tablespoon red wine vinegar*

1   *tablespoon ume plum vinegar*

1   *teaspoon salt or to taste*

   Freshly ground black pepper

1   *head Boston lettuce, leaves separated*

20 *ounces cooked lobster meat in bite-sized chunks, chilled*

4   *cups sliced English cucumbers (peeling is optional)*

3   *cups halved cherry tomatoes*

1. To make the dressing, combine the avocado, yogurt, horseradish, vinegars, and salt and pepper to taste in a food processor or blender. Puree until smooth. Refrigerate until you are ready to serve. (The dressing can be made up to 24 hours in advance.)

2. To serve, arrange the lettuce leaves on 4 plates. Divide the lobster among the plates, mounding it in the center of each plate. Arrange the cucumber slices and tomatoes around the lobster. Spoon a tablespoon of dressing over each salad and serve immediately, passing the extra dressing on the side.

Zone yield per recipe: 17 protein blocks, 8 carbohydrate blocks (1 tablespoon dressing = 0 protein blocks, ¹⁄₁₀ carbohydrate block)

Lobster and Jicama Salad with Chipotle-Orange Dressing

4 SERVINGS A twist on the conventional pairing of jicama and orange, this salad offers a creamy, crunchy, hot, cool, tart, and sweet experience. It contains chipotle chiles in adobo, which add a little fire and smoke. Be sure to wear gloves when handling the chiles and adjust the heat level by increasing or decreasing the amount. Four lobsters—steamed, boiled, or microwaved—will provide enough meat for this recipe.

NUTRITIONAL ANALYSIS PER SERVING: 245 CALORIES, 32 G PROTEIN, 24 G CARBOHYDRATE, 2 G FAT (0 G SATURATED), 102 MG CHOLESTEROL, 1039 MG SODIUM, 5 G FIBER

Chipotle-Orange Dressing

¼ cup low-fat mayonnaise

¼ cup nonfat plain yogurt

2 tablespoons fresh lime juice

1 teaspoon minced canned chipotle chiles in adobo, seeds and membranes removed

2 teaspoons adobo sauce or to taste

2 teaspoons grated orange zest

1 to 2 teaspoons fructose

½ teaspoon salt or to taste

1½ cups julienned jicama

2 teaspoons fresh lime juice

20 ounces cooked lobster meat in bite-sized chunks, chilled

2 bunches watercress, chopped into 1½-inch lengths (about 4 cups packed)

1½ cups peeled sliced oranges, seeds removed

1. To make the dressing, combine the mayonnaise, yogurt, lime juice, chipotle, adobo sauce, orange zest, fructose, and ½ teaspoon salt in a small measuring cup. Whisk to blend. Taste and adjust the seasoning. Set aside. (The dressing can be made up to 24 hours in advance and refrigerated.)

2. Place the jicama in a bowl and toss with 2 teaspoons lime juice.

Combine the lobster with the jicama and add enough dressing to moisten well. Toss to coat.

3. Divide the watercress among 4 plates. Arrange the orange slices on top of the watercress. Mound the jicama-lobster mixture on top of the orange slices on each plate. Serve immediately, passing any extra dressing on the side.

Zone yield per recipe: 16 protein blocks, 8 carbohydrate blocks (1 tablespoon dressing = 0 protein blocks, ⅓ carbohydrate block)

Jicama Salad with Chipotle-Orange Dressing *(Variation)* 4 SERVINGS

NUTRITIONAL ANALYSIS PER SERVING: 106 CALORIES, 3 G PROTEIN, 22 G CARBOHYDRATE, 1 G FAT (0 G SATURATED), 0 MG CHOLESTEROL, 501 MG SODIUM, 5 G FIBER

1. Make the salad as above, omitting the lobster.

Zone yield per recipe: Less than one protein block, 8 carbohydrate blocks (1 tablespoon dressing – less than one protein block, ⅓ carbohydrate block)

Lobster and Jicama Salad with Chipotle-Orange Dressing

Smoked Scallops with Red Pepper Ketchup 4 SERVINGS I considered

calling the sauce below "*instant* red pepper ketchup" because it is, relatively speaking. Ketchup usually takes time to make. Luckily, pureed roasted red peppers form a naturally thick base. A few small directional shifts toward salty, sweet, and tart bring their flavors sufficiently in line with their texture to balance smoked scallops. For variety, substitute grilled or smoked swordfish.

NUTRITIONAL ANALYSIS PER SERVING: 214 CALORIES, 31 G PROTEIN, 14 G CARBOHYDRATE, 4 G FAT (0 G SATURATED), 56 MG CHOLESTEROL, 570 MG SODIUM, 3 G FIBER

Red Pepper Ketchup

2   large red bell peppers

1   teaspoon extra virgin olive oil

2   teaspoons minced garlic

1   tablespoon cider vinegar

1   teaspoon fructose

½   teaspoon salt or to taste

    Tabasco sauce

1½ pounds large sea scallops, rinsed
    and dried well on paper towels

1   teaspoon extra virgin olive oil

    Salt and freshly ground black
    pepper

1. To make the ketchup, roast the peppers by thoroughly charring the skins under the broiler. Transfer to a paper bag and allow to steam for 10 to 15 minutes to loosen the skins. Remove stems, skins, seeds, and membranes. Puree the flesh in a blender or food processor and set aside.

2. Heat the oil in a small nonstick skillet over medium heat. Add the garlic and sauté for 1 minute. Add the pureed peppers, vinegar, fructose, salt, and Tabasco sauce to taste. Simmer for 2 minutes, stirring occasionally. Remove from the heat and cool to room temperature. (This ketchup can be made ahead and refrigerated for up to 1 week or frozen for up to 6 months. Bring to room temperature before serving.)

3. Place the scallops in a bowl and drizzle with the oil. Season generously with salt and pepper and toss to coat. Prepare a stovetop smoker with 1 tablespoon apple smoking chips. Place the scallops on the rack and half-close the lid. Place the smoker on an electric burner preheated to medium or on a gas burner turned to medium-high. When the first wisps of smoke appear, close the lid. Smoke for approximately 15 minutes, until the scallops are opaque.

4. Serve immediately, with a dollop (1 tablespoon) of the ketchup on each plate. Pass the extra ketchup on the side.

Note: Smoking times are highly variable.

Zone yield per recipe: 16 protein blocks, 4 carbohydrate blocks (1 tablespoon ketchup = 0 protein blocks, ⅟₇ carbohydrate block)

Scallops with Smoked Leeks   4 SERVINGS   Bacon-wrapped scallops, classic and treacherous

party hors d'oeuvres, illustrate the affinity of these sweet mollusks for salt and smoke. In this Chinese-style

preparation, salty soy sauce and smoked leeks satisfy a craving for bacon without adding saturated fat.

NUTRITIONAL ANALYSIS PER SERVING: 283 CALORIES, 31 G PROTEIN, 25 G CARBOHYDRATE,
6 G FAT (1 G SATURATED), 56 MG CHOLESTEROL, 869 MG SODIUM, 2 G FIBER

Sauce

1   tablespoon soy sauce

1   tablespoon Shaoxing rice wine or
    dry sherry

1   teaspoon chili bean sauce (also
    known as hot bean paste or
    Sichuan bean paste)

1   teaspoon fructose

1½ pounds large sea scallops, rinsed
    and dried well on paper towels

    Salt and freshly ground black
    pepper

1   teaspoon peanut or canola oil

2   teaspoons toasted sesame oil

1   tablespoon minced garlic

1   tablespoon minced fresh ginger

2   tablespoons minced scallions (white
    parts only)

2   cups sliced Smoked Leeks (page 28)

1. To make the sauce, combine the soy sauce, rice wine, bean sauce, and fructose in a small bowl or measuring cup and whisk to dissolve the fructose. Set aside.

2. Season the scallops on both sides with salt and pepper. Combine the oils in a large nonstick skillet that will hold the scallops without crowding. Heat over medium-high heat. Add the scallops and cook for 3 minutes per side, until nearly firm and slightly browned. Remove the scallops with a slotted spoon and transfer to a bowl.

3. Place the skillet over medium heat and add the garlic, ginger, scallions, and leeks. Stir-fry for 1 minute. Return the scallops to the skillet with any collected juices and stir-fry for 1 minute. Add the sauce and stir-fry for 1 to 2 minutes, until the scallops are cooked through. Serve immediately.

Zone yield per recipe: 16 protein blocks, 6 carbohydrate blocks

Warm Salad of Grilled Scallops and Wilted Frisée with Smoky Ranch Dressing

4 SERVINGS One summer morning when fresh scallops were unavailable, I noticed some enormous Japanese sea scallops at the fish counter of my local Bread and Circus Whole Foods Market. Because they were "previously frozen," I automatically dismissed them. But after a lengthy discussion with my trusty fish consultant, Borys Gojnycz, I decided to give the monsters a try. They turned out to be manageable on the grill (a first in my experience of scallops) and also exceptionally tasty. The addition of grilled frisée and smoky ranch dressing made them truly extraordinary. I caution you against trying to substitute another green for the frisée. On the other hand, given its negligible carbohydrate content, frisée can be increased in quantity without qualms. Serve with a fruit salad for dessert.

NUTRITIONAL ANALYSIS PER SERVING: 215 CALORIES, 31 G PROTEIN, 13 G CARBOHYDRATE, 4 G FAT (1 G SATURATED), 57 MG CHOLESTEROL, 533 MG SODIUM, 2 G FIBER

Smoky Ranch Dressing

½   cup nonfat buttermilk

2   tablespoons Smoked Allium Paste (page 22)

2   tablespoons low-fat mayonnaise

¼   teaspoon salt or to taste
    Freshly ground black pepper

1   tablespoon minced flat-leaf parsley

1   tablespoon minced fresh chives

1½ pounds large sea scallops

1   teaspoon extra virgin olive oil
    Salt and freshly ground black pepper

2   heads frisée, sliced in half with stem intact

1. To make the dressing, combine the buttermilk, smoked allium paste, mayonnaise, salt, and pepper to taste in a bowl or 2-cup measure. Emulsify using a stick blender. (Alternatively, emulsify in a traditional blender and transfer to a bowl.) Stir in the parsley and chives. Adjust the seasoning and set aside for 30 minutes. (The dressing can be made up to 24 hours in advance and refrigerated. Bring to room temperature before serving.)

2. Prepare a hot fire in a grill. Combine the scallops and oil in a bowl and toss well to coat. Season well with salt and pepper. Season the frisée halves with salt and pepper.

3. Grill the scallops for 2 to 3 minutes per side until lightly browned and opaque. Grill the frisée halves, turning once or twice, for 1 to 2 minutes, until slightly browned and wilted.

4. To serve, divide the frisée and scallops among 4 plates. Drizzle 1 tablespoon of the dressing over each plate and serve immediately, passing the extra dressing on the side.

Zone yield per recipe: 16 protein blocks, 4 carbohydrate blocks (1 tablespoon dressing = 0 protein blocks, ⅕ carbohydrate block)

Warm Salad of Grilled Scallops and Wilted Frisée with Smoky Ranch Dressing

Grilled Shrimp with Red Pepper-Caper Sauce 4 SERVINGS

One summer evening in the Berkshires, my father grilled a mountain of jumbo shrimp "to clean out the freezer." I contributed two sauces: A Red Pepper-Caper Sauce and a Spicy Cashew Sauce (see variation opposite). Our taste-test/dinner produced a rare culinary generation gap: My parents lined up squarely on the Mediterranean side (peppers and capers) while my husband and I staked out the Pacific Rim (the cashew sauce). Neither team could persuade the other, but during the judging, both sauces disappeared. As a result, I decided to include them both.

NUTRITIONAL ANALYSIS PER SERVING: 215 CALORIES, 31 G PROTEIN, 13 G CARBOHYDRATE, 4 G FAT (1 G SATURATED), 215 MG CHOLESTEROL, 335 MG SODIUM, 3 G FIBER

Red Pepper-Caper Sauce

2   red bell peppers

¼   cup Smoked Garlic Paste or Roasted Garlic Paste (page 25 or 24)

4   teaspoons cider vinegar

¼   teaspoon cayenne pepper

1½ tablespoons capers

    Salt and freshly ground black pepper

1¼ pounds jumbo shrimp, peeled and deveined

    Salt and freshly ground pepper

1   teaspoon extra virgin olive oil

1. To make the sauce, roast the peppers by thoroughly charring the skins under the broiler. Transfer to a paper bag and allow to steam for 10 to 15 minutes to loosen the skins. Remove stems, skins, seeds, and membranes.

2. Combine the peppers, garlic paste, vinegar, and cayenne in a blender or food processor and puree. Transfer to a small bowl, add the capers, and season with salt and pepper. Blend well. (This sauce can be made in advance and refrigerated for up to 1 week. Bring to room temperature before serving.)

3. Prepare a hot fire in the grill. Place the shrimp in a bowl. Season generously with salt and pepper and drizzle with the oil. Toss to coat. Grill the shrimp for 2 to 3 minutes per side, until bright pink and opaque.

4. To serve, arrange the shrimp on a platter, spoon 4 tablespoons of the sauce over the shrimp, and serve immediately, passing the extra sauce at the table.

Zone yield per recipe: 16 protein blocks, 4 carbohydrate blocks (1 tablespoon sauce = 0 protein blocks, ⅕ carbohydrate block)

Grilled Shrimp with Spicy Cashew Sauce *(Variation)* 4 **SERVINGS**

NUTRITIONAL ANALYSIS PER SERVING: 279 CALORIES, 31 G PROTEIN, 10 G CARBOHYDRATE,
12 G FAT (1 G SATURATED), 215 MG CHOLESTEROL, 759 MG SODIUM, 0 G FIBER

1. To make the sauce, combine 2 tablespoons smooth roasted cashew butter, ¼ cup Smoked Allium Paste (page 22), 2 tablespoons Japanese soy sauce, 2 tablespoons rice vinegar, 1 tablespoon fresh lime juice, 2 teaspoons fructose, 1 teaspoon grated fresh ginger, and 1 teaspoon Thai chili paste or to taste. Emulsify with a stick blender or in a traditional blender. (The sauce can be made up to 2 days in advance and refrigerated.) Bring to room temperature before serving.

2. Grill the shrimp as above. Serve the shrimp with 1 tablespoon of the sauce per serving, passing the extra sauce at the table.

Zone yield per recipe: 16 protein blocks, 3 carbohydrate blocks (1 tablespoon sauce = 0 protein blocks, ¼ carbohydrate block)

Grilled Shrimp with Grapefruit Zest 4 **SERVINGS** After discovering that

grapefruit raises blood sugar more slowly than other fruits, I went through a "grapefruit phase." Experiments with cooked, raw, sectioned, and pureed grapefruit generated countless dinners. Ultimately, when I had exhausted my ideas for the pulp, I turned to the zest and immediately appreciated its power to transform protein without affecting insulin levels. This modest preparation takes little time but yields an unusual and tasty result. It works equally well as an appetizer or main course.

NUTRITIONAL ANALYSIS PER SERVING: 187 CALORIES, 29 G PROTEIN, 3 G CARBOHYDRATE,
6 G FAT (1 G SATURATED), 215 MG CHOLESTEROL, 502 MG SODIUM, 0 G FIBER

1   tablespoon extra virgin olive oil

2   tablespoons grated grapefruit zest

1   teaspoon fructose

½   teaspoon kosher salt or to taste

½   teaspoon freshly ground black pepper or to taste

1¼ pounds extra large shrimp, peeled and deveined

1. In a large bowl, combine the oil, zest, fructose, salt, and pepper. Whisk to blend. Add the shrimp and toss to coat evenly.

2. Prepare a hot fire in the grill. Grill the shrimp for 2 to 3 minutes per side, until bright pink and opaque. Serve hot, warm, or at room temperature.

Zone yield per recipe: 16 protein blocks, 1 carbohydrate block

Smoked Shrimp "Fajitas" 4 SERVINGS

Before I discovered the perils of excess insulin, I wrapped all sorts of things in tortillas. Now I use lettuce leaves which function well enough and add almost no carbohydrate to a meal. Without a doubt, their insulin-controlling value outweighs the messiness associated with their use. If you do not have a smoker, you can grill or broil the shrimp for this recipe, but you will sacrifice some depth of flavor. To compensate for this loss of intensity, use Slow-Roasted Plum Tomatoes (page 34) instead of fresh ones, but halve the amount to keep the carbohydrate counts the same.

NUTRITIONAL ANALYSIS PER SERVING: 283 CALORIES, 35 G PROTEIN, 13 G CARBOHYDRATE, 11 G FAT (4 G SATURATED), 192 MG CHOLESTEROL, 647 MG SODIUM, 3 G FIBER

Vegetables

1 tablespoon roasted pepper oil or extra virgin olive oil

1 tablespoon minced garlic

1 cup thinly sliced onion

¾ cup thinly sliced red bell pepper

¾ cup thinly sliced green or yellow bell pepper

1 cup drained, diced canned tomatoes

1 tablespoon fresh lime juice

Salt and freshly ground black pepper

Spice Rub

¾ teaspoon ancho chile powder

½ teaspoon sweet paprika

¼ teaspoon Mexican oregano

¼ teaspoon fructose

¼ teaspoon kosher salt

¼ teaspoon freshly ground white or black pepper

1 pound extra large shrimp, peeled and deveined

4 ounces grated reduced-fat cheddar cheese

1 to 2 heads Boston lettuce, leaves separated

1. To prepare the vegetables, heat the oil in a nonstick skillet over medium heat. Add the garlic, onion, peppers, and tomatoes. Sauté until the vegetables are tender and most of the liquid has evaporated. Stir in the lime juice, salt, and pepper. Set aside. (The vegetables can be made up to 1 day in advance and refrigerated. Bring to room temperature or reheat in the microwave before serving.)

2. To make the spice rub, combine the chile powder, paprika, oregano, fructose, salt, and pepper in a small bowl and stir with a fork to blend well. Apply the rub lightly to the shrimp.

3. Prepare a stovetop smoker with 1 tablespoon apple or heart of corn cob smoking chips. Arrange the shrimp on the rack and half-close the lid. Place the smoker on an electric burner preheated to medium or on a gas burner turned to medium-high. When the first wisps of smoke appear, close the lid. Smoke for 10 to 15 minutes, until the shrimp are opaque. Remove to a platter.

4. To serve, divide the shrimp, vegetables, cheese, and lettuce leaves among 4 plates. To eat: place a shrimp in the center of a leaf, top with some of the vegetables and cheese. Roll and eat.

Note: Smoking times are highly variable.

Zone yield per recipe: 16 protein blocks, 4 carbohydrate blocks

Smoked Shrimp "Fajitas"

Smoked Shrimp with Spinach, Avocado, and Grapefruit

4 SERVINGS This salad represents insulin-modulating food at its best: nutritious, refreshing, and beautiful. Grapefruit is converted to glucose and released into the bloodstream more slowly than most fruits and many vegetables. As a result, it has a particularly low glycemic index. Combined with spinach and avocado, it creates a high-fiber salad full of vitamin A and folate. Smoked shrimp, lovely against the dark green spinach leaves, contribute lean protein.

NUTRITIONAL ANALYSIS PER SERVING: 312 CALORIES, 35 G PROTEIN, 21 G CARBOHYDRATE, 11 G FAT (2 G SATURATED), 215 MG CHOLESTEROL, 369 MG SODIUM, 6 G FIBER

1¼ pounds extra large shrimp, peeled and deveined

Salt and freshly ground black pepper

2 ruby red grapefruits

2 teaspoons extra virgin olive oil

2 tablespoons red wine vinegar

1 tablespoon mild Dijon mustard

3 tablespoons water

Salt and freshly ground black pepper

12 cups fresh spinach, stems removed

¼ cup thinly sliced red onion

1 small ripe Haas avocado, diced

1. Prepare a stovetop smoker with 1 tablespoon smoking chips (alder, cherry, apple, or heart of corn cob). Season the shrimp generously with salt and pepper, place on the rack, and half-close the lid. Place the smoker on an electric burner preheated to medium or on a gas burner turned to medium-high. When the first wisps of smoke appear, close the lid. Smoke for 10 to 15 minutes, until the shrimp are opaque. Do not overcook. Remove from the smoker and set aside.

2. Meanwhile, prepare the grapefruit. First grate and set aside 1 tablespoon grapefruit zest. Then, section the grapefruits and squeeze the membranes, reserving the juice.

3. To make the dressing, fill a 2-cup measure to the half-cup level with grapefruit sections and juice. Add the oil, vinegar, mustard, and water. Puree using a stick blender. (Alternatively, puree in a traditional blender.) Stir in the zest, add salt and pepper to taste, and set aside.

4. Combine the spinach and red onion in a large bowl. Toss with half the dressing to moisten well. Divide the spinach mixture among 4 plates. Distribute the remaining grapefruit sections, avocado, and shrimp on top of each salad. Serve the extra dressing on the side.

Note: Smoking times are highly variable.

Zone yield per recipe: 16 protein blocks, 6 carbohydrate blocks

Spinach, Avocado, and Grapefruit Salad *(Variation)* 4 SERVINGS

NUTRITIONAL ANALYSIS PER SERVING: 162 CALORIES, 7 G PROTEIN, 19 G CARBOHYDRATE, 9 G FAT (1 G SATURATED), 0 MG CHOLESTEROL, 158 MG SODIUM, 6 G FIBER

1. Prepare the salad as above, omitting the shrimp. Serve as an appetizer or side dish.

Zone yield per recipe: Less than one protein block, 6 carbohydrate blocks

Cuban Shrimp 4 SERVINGS Lourdes Rossell, a family friend from Cuba, taught me to make a *sofrito* when I was barely more than a child. By the time I went to college, I could make all of her signature dishes, and they sustained me through four harsh winters at Harvard. Shrimp à la Lourdes, as my family referred to it, had a thin tomato sauce that was deliciously absorbed by the mountain of rice Lourdes served with it. This recipe concentrates the sauce elements and eliminates the rice, but Lourdes's authentic sofrito remains unchanged.

NUTRITIONAL ANALYSIS PER SERVING: 248 CALORIES, 31 G PROTEIN, 13 G CARBOHYDRATE, 6 G FAT (1 G SATURATED), 215 MG CHOLESTEROL, 639 MG SODIUM, 3 G FIBER

1   tablespoon extra virgin olive oil

½   cup finely chopped onion

½   cup finely chopped green bell pepper

1   tablespoon minced garlic

1½ teaspoons ground cumin

½   teaspoon paprika

1   (28-ounce) can whole peeled tomatoes, drained

1   teaspoon dried oregano

1¼ pounds jumbo shrimp, peeled and deveined

    Salt and freshly ground black pepper

2   tablespoons minced flat-leaf parsley

1. Heat the oil in a nonstick skillet over medium heat. Add the onion, green pepper, garlic, cumin, and paprika. Sauté until soft, 2 to 3 minutes. Stir in the tomatoes and oregano. Use a potato masher to break up the tomatoes. Cook for about 20 minutes, until the sauce thickens and most of the liquid has evaporated.

2. Add the shrimp and cook, turning in the sauce, for 5 to 6 minutes, until the shrimp are curled, bright pink, and opaque. Season generously with salt and pepper.

3. Remove from heat and garnish with the parsley. Serve immediately.

Zone yield per recipe: 16 protein blocks, 4 carbohydrate blocks

Poultry

Poultry In the world of protein, poultry lacks the diversity of fish and shellfish, but it offers considerable versatility and economy to the home cook. As a result, chicken, duck, and turkey frequently appear on my shopping list. I choose cuts depending on my cooking plans. For example, I might grill or sauté chicken or duck breasts; I might braise chicken thighs, smoke turkey tenderloins, or roast a split broiler or a boneless turkey breast. Regardless of the cut or technique, I always remove the skin before eating (and often before cooking) because 50 to 85 percent of a fowl's fat lies in and just under its skin. I also remove as much visible fat as possible.

Many people know that skinless poultry qualifies as lean protein, but few appreciate its vitamin and mineral contributions. Actually, all types of poultry contain important B vitamins as well as magnesium, phosphorus, potassium, and zinc. In addition, the dark meat of chicken supplies much needed iron in the diet, while the light meat contains significant amounts of magnesium. Surprisingly, duck provides more iron per gram of protein than beef.

With 1.7 grams of fat per ounce, skinless duck contains 4 times as much fat as light meat chicken or turkey (0.4 grams per ounce), but it compares fairly well with dark meat (1.2 grams of fat per ounce). In my opinion, its distinctive flavor and mineral richness make it well worth eating once in a while. So, if you love duck *and* your health, you need to learn how to skin one to minimize its fat content.

Begin with a split duck, which is much easier to manage than a whole one. Place the duck half skin side up on a cutting board, neck end to your right. (Reverse directions if you are left handed.) With your left hand, grab the edge of the skin (and its adherent fat) at the neck end and lift up slightly, separating it from the flesh

beneath. Place a sharp boning knife on the duck surface at the border between the flesh and the skin flap, with the sharp edge lying against the underside of the lifted skin and the dull edge pressing down onto the flesh. With your left hand, exert continuous tension on the skin flap, pulling gently up and back. Meanwhile, without actually cutting, wiggle the knife back and forth, keeping the dull end on the flesh and allowing the sharp edge to coax the skin off the meat. This dislodges the connective tissue attaching the skin and fat to the flesh without actually cutting the skin or the flesh. You should be able to remove the skin from the entire duck, except for the wings. Repeat with the second half.

Favorite Protein/Carbohydrate Pairings:

Roast Chicken with Rosemary-Garlic Paste (page 87) and Sauté of Roasted Fennel and Tomatoes with Smoked Peppers page 178)

Boneless Turkey Breast with Sun-Dried Tomato Infusion (page 98) and Broiled Zucchini with Double Basil (page 183)

Turkey Patties with Apples and Smoked Leeks (page 93) and Turnip "Fries" (page 182)

Chicken Kebabs with Spicy Lime Sauce (page 78) served with Black Bean Salad with Avocado (page 187)

Chicken Kebabs with Spicy Lime Sauce 4 SERVINGS

Because they contain so little intrinsic fat, skinless chicken breasts tend to dry out on the grill, but an acid-free marinade flavors and moistens the chicken without precooking it. As presented below, the skewers hold protein only, but you could easily add carbohydrate in the form of vegetables in 1- to 1½-inch chunks. Onions, shallots, mushrooms, cherry tomatoes, bell peppers, zucchini, and summer squash would all be suitable for this purpose. My clever friend, Diana Bateman, developed this recipe as a quick adaptation of "Guadeloupean Grilled Chicken" from the *Boston Globe's* endlessly inventive Sheryl Julian and Julie Riven. Be careful not to thread the skewers too tightly or the chicken will not cook through properly. Wear gloves to handle the Scotch bonnet! (Pictured on page 77.)

NUTRITIONAL ANALYSIS PER SERVING: 191 CALORIES, 26 G PROTEIN, 3 G CARBOHYDRATE, 8 G FAT (1 G SATURATED), 69 MG CHOLESTEROL, 160 MG SODIUM, 0 G FIBER

4   teaspoons extra virgin olive oil

1½ tablespoons minced garlic

1   Scotch bonnet chile, seeded and finely chopped

2   shallots, finely chopped

4   tablespoons minced fresh chives

4   tablespoons minced flat-leaf parsley

1   pound skinless boneless chicken breasts, visible fat removed, cut into 1- to 1½-inch chunks

½   cup chicken broth

2   teaspoons chopped fresh thyme

2   to 3 tablespoons fresh lime juice

Salt and freshly ground black pepper

1. In a large bowl, combine 2 teaspoons of the oil with 2 teaspoons of the garlic, half the chile, half the shallots, 2 tablespoons of the chives, and 2 tablespoons of the parsley. Add the chicken and refrigerate for at least 1 hour or up to 1 day.

2. To make the sauce, heat the remaining 2 teaspoons oil in a small nonstick skillet over medium heat. Add the remaining 2½ teaspoons garlic, and the remaining chile and shallot. Sauté for 1 minute. Add the broth and simmer for 1 minute. Remove from the heat and add the remaining 2 tablespoons chives, 2 tablespoons parsley, and thyme. Stir in the lime juice and season to taste with salt and pepper. Keep warm.

3. Prepare a hot fire in the grill. Thread the chicken loosely on the skewers. (You may want to double skewer them for stability.) Grill for 2 minutes per quarter turn for a total of 8 minutes, until the chicken is cooked through but not dry.

4. Serve immediately with 1 tablespoon of the sauce drizzled over each serving. Pass the extra sauce at the table.

Zone yield per recipe: 16 protein blocks, 1 carbohydrate block

Grilled Chicken Skewers with Vegetables and Almond Dipping Sauce

4 SERVINGS Although ultimately derived from the chicken satay of Malaysia, this dish involves significantly less fat and carbohydrate. Most satay sauces combine large quantities of peanuts with equally distressing amounts of oil or coconut milk. In addition, they routinely call for up to 3 tablespoons of sugar. The sauce below contains only 14 grams of fat (equal to 1 tablespoon olive oil) in the form of almond butter and a modest teaspoon of fructose. A mellow paste of roasted garlic serves as a binding agent, eliminating the need for additional fat. You will not believe the richness it conveys.

NUTRITIONAL ANALYSIS PER SERVING: 314 CALORIES, 35 G PROTEIN, 23 G CARBOHYDRATE, 11 G FAT (2 G SATURATED), 69 MG CHOLESTEROL, 661 MG SODIUM, 9 G FIBER

1 pound skinless boneless chicken breasts, visible fat removed, cut into 1- to 1½-inch chunks

1 teaspoon extra virgin olive oil

4 cups cooked broccoli florets, at room temperature or chilled

4 cups cooked cauliflower florets, at room temperature or chilled

Salt and freshly ground black pepper

Almond Dipping Sauce

¼ cup Roasted Garlic Paste (page 24)

2 tablespoons soy sauce

2 tablespoons brown rice vinegar

2 tablespoons smooth almond butter

½ to 1 teaspoon Chinese or Thai chili paste

1 teaspoon fructose

Salt and freshly ground black pepper

1. To make the dipping sauce, combine the roasted garlic paste, soy sauce, vinegar, almond butter, chili paste, and fructose in a 2-cup measure. Emulsify using a stick blender. (Alternatively, emulsify in a traditional blender and transfer to a small bowl.) Season with salt and pepper and set aside. (The sauce can be made in advance and refrigerated for up to 1 week or frozen for up to 6 months. Bring to room temperature before serving.)

2. Prepare a hot fire in the grill. Thread the chicken loosely on skewers to permit even cooking. (You may want to double skewer them for stability.) Grill for 2 minutes per quarter turn, for a total of 8 minutes, until the chicken is cooked through but not dry.

3. Serve a quarter of the chicken, a quarter of the vegetables, and 1 tablespoon of dipping sauce per person. Pass the remaining sauce at the table.

Zone yield per recipe: 16 protein blocks, 6 carbohydrate blocks (1 tablespoon sauce = 0 protein blocks, ⅓ carbohydrate block)

Composed Chicken Salad with Garlic Mayonnaise 4 SERVINGS

A composed chicken salad makes a refreshing and beautiful luncheon dish or light supper. But for the best texture, the asparagus should be peeled. To make the task bearable, use the correct tool: a horizontal vegetable peeler. Once you have been initiated into the soothing art of asparagus peeling, you will not mind. And you will never want to eat asparagus any other way.

NUTRITIONAL ANALYSIS PER SERVING: 275 CALORIES, 34 G PROTEIN, 26 G CARBOHYDRATE, 5 G FAT (1 G SATURATED), 70 MG CHOLESTEROL, 534 MG SODIUM, 7 G FIBER

4   small skinless boneless chicken breast halves (1 pound), visible fat removed

1½ pounds asparagus

2   large orange bell peppers

4   whole red leaf lettuce leaves

     Salt and freshly ground black pepper

1   tablespoon minced flat-leaf

Garlic Mayonnaise

¾   cup nonfat plain yogurt

¼   cup low fat mayonnaise

1½ tablespoons Roasted Garlic Paste (page 24)

½   teaspoon salt or to taste

     Freshly ground black pepper

1. Combine the chicken and 4 cups water in a medium saucepan. Bring to a boil, reduce the heat to low, and simmer for 5 to 8 minutes, until the chicken is just cooked through. Rinse under cold water, pat dry, and refrigerate.

2. Meanwhile, peel the asparagus. To do so, place one asparagus spear on a cutting board with the tip pointing to your left. Stabilize it with your left hand. Starting just below the tip, draw the peeler blade left to right, down the length of the stem. Roll and draw, roll and draw. (Reverse directions if you are left-handed.) Blanch the peeled asparagus in boiling water until crisp-tender. (Timing depends on thickness.) Transfer to an ice water bath. Drain and dry well on kitchen towels. Refrigerate until you are ready to serve.

3. Roast the peppers by thoroughly charring the skins under the broiler. Transfer to a paper bag and allow to steam for 10 to 15 minutes to loosen the skins. Remove stems, skins, seeds, and membranes. Julienne the flesh and set aside.

4. To make the garlic mayonnaise, combine the yogurt, mayonnaise, roasted garlic paste, salt, and pepper to taste in a small bowl or measuring cup and whisk to blend. Adjust the seasoning. (The mayonnaise can be made up to 3 days in advance and refrigerated.)

5. To serve, place a lettuce leaf on each of 4 plates. Lay the asparagus on top of the lettuce. Slice the chicken on the diagonal and overlap the slices on top of the asparagus, leaving the asparagus tips exposed. Season with salt and pepper. Decorate with the roasted pepper strips. Place a 1-tablespoon dollop of the dressing on each serving, garnish with minced parsley, and serve immediately.

Zone yield per recipe: 16 protein blocks, 8 carbohydrate blocks (1 tablespoon mayonnaise = 0 protein blocks, ⅙ carbohydrate block)

Grilled Chicken Breasts with Sun-Dried Tomato Ketchup

4 SERVINGS Sun-dried tomatoes weigh little and occupy a small volume, but they contain a fair amount of carbohydrate—about 11 grams per ounce. Fortunately, considerably less than 1 ounce suffices to make an interesting ketchup, without the long simmering usually required. Add a salad and you have a quick, easy, tasty meal. The ketchup will keep at least a week in the refrigerator or up to 6 months in the freezer.

NUTRITIONAL ANALYSIS PER SERVING: 193 CALORIES, 26 G PROTEIN, 6 G CARBOHYDRATE, 7 G FAT (1 G SATURATED), 69 MG CHOLESTEROL, 133 MG SODIUM, 1 G FIBER

Sun-Dried Tomato Ketchup

⅔ ounce sun-dried tomatoes (not packed in oil) (about 1/4 cup)

1 cup water

⅓ cup Smoked Allium Paste (page 22)

2 teaspoons chopped fresh rosemary or to taste

Salt and freshly ground black pepper

4 small boneless skinless chicken breast halves (1 pound), visible fat removed

2 teaspoons extra virgin olive oil

Salt and freshly ground black pepper

1. To make the ketchup, combine the tomatoes and water in a small saucepan. Bring to a boil, reduce the heat to low, and simmer for 20 minutes. Remove the tomatoes with a slotted spoon, reserving the cooking liquid. Strain the liquid through a cheesecloth-lined sieve into a clean saucepan. Bring to a boil and reduce to 1 tablespoon tomato syrup. Remove from the heat and cool to room temperature.

2. Meanwhile, rinse the tomatoes under cold running water, rubbing them with your fingers to remove all grit and seeds. (The seeds tend to hide under the curled edges of the tomatoes.) Pat dry on paper towels. Finely chop.

3. In a small bowl, combine the chopped tomatoes, tomato syrup, smoked allium paste, and rosemary. Blend well and season generously with salt and pepper. Set aside until you are ready to serve. (The ketchup can be made ahead and refrigerated for up to 1 week or frozen for up to 6 months. Bring to room temperature before serving.)

4. Prepare a hot fire in the grill. Flatten the chicken breasts slightly for even cooking. Brush both sides with the oil and season generously with salt and pepper. Grill for about 4 minutes per side, until cooked through but not dry.

5. To serve, slice the chicken on an angle and arrange on 4 plates. Serve with 1 tablespoon ketchup spooned on the side of each plate. Pass the extra ketchup at the table.

Zone yield per recipe: 16 protein blocks, 2 carbohydrate blocks (1 tablespoon ketchup = 0 protein blocks, ⅙ carbohydrate block)

Sautéed Chicken Breasts with Blueberry Sauce 4 SERVINGS My father

spent the happiest part of his childhood in the Catskills where my grandmother worked as a chef. He spent summer days exploring the countryside on his own, eating his fill of wild blueberries. His idyllic recollections inspired my husband to plant a stand of blueberries when my son was a toddler, in hopes that he would have memories of similarly blissful (if less risky) berry-picking. Ironically, it is my husband who returns blue-stained from the yard on summer evenings. | Since a serving of chicken requires only about 2 tablespoons of sauce, you will have more sauce than you need for 4 servings of protein. The remainder can be refrigerated for up to 1 week or frozen for up to 6 months. For variety, try it on pork or duck.

NUTRITIONAL ANALYSIS PER SERVING: 173 CALORIES, 25 G PROTEIN, 5 G CARBOHYDRATE,
5 G FAT (1 G SATURATED), 69 MG CHOLESTEROL, 61 MG SODIUM, 1 G FIBER

Blueberry Sauce

2   cups blueberries, picked over, rinsed, and drained

2   tablespoons blueberry, raspberry, or black currant vinegar

1   tablespoon fructose

1   tablespoon water

2   teaspoons chopped fresh thyme

    Salt and freshly ground black pepper

4   small boneless skinless chicken breast halves (1 pound), visible fat removed

    Salt and freshly ground black pepper

2   teaspoons extra virgin olive oil

2   tablespoons blueberry, raspberry, or black currant vinegar

1. To make the sauce, combine the berries, vinegar, fructose, and water in a medium saucepan and bring to a boil. Reduce the heat and simmer, stirring occasionally, for about 10 minutes, until the berries break down. Pass through a fine-mesh sieve into a bowl. Work the berry mass vigorously with a wooden spoon to push the pulp through the sieve. Scrape into the bowl any pulp that collects on the underside and discard the residue inside the sieve. Stir in the thyme and season with salt and pepper. Reserve ½ cup of the sauce to be served with the chicken. Set aside the remainder for another use.

2. Place the chicken between layers of plastic wrap and flatten slightly with the bottom of a heavy skillet. Remove from the plastic. Season generously on both sides with salt and pepper.

3. Using ½ teaspoon oil for each, make 4 oil "footprints" in the shape of the breast halves in a large non-stick skillet over medium-high heat. Place the chicken breasts on the oil and sauté for 4 to 5 minutes. Reduce the heat as needed after browning to prevent burning. Turn and repeat on the second side until the chicken is cooked through. Remove from heat and transfer to a platter.

4. Add the remaining 2 tablespoons vinegar to the skillet and stir, scraping up any brown bits. Add the reserved ½ cup blueberry sauce. Turn the heat to low and stir well to combine.

5. To serve, spoon 2 tablespoons of the sauce on each of 4 plates and top with a chicken breast. Serve immediately.

Zone yield per recipe: 16 protein blocks, 2 carbohydrate blocks (1 tablespoon sauce = 0 protein blocks, ¼ carbohydrate block)

Sautéed Chicken Breasts with Blueberry Sauce served with Broiled Zucchini with Double Basil (page 183)

Poached Chicken with Asparagus-Basil Mayonnaise 4 SERVINGS

Poached chicken is one of my favorite blank canvases, especially in the spring when poultry emerges from dark sauces and hearty braising liquids. I poach a whole chicken when I can and spend the week using every last bit, including the poaching liquid. But when life gets complicated, I resort to chicken breasts, which poach quickly and eliminate the need for carving. They benefit from delicate sauces, such as the sweet, mellow mayonnaise below, in which an asparagus puree evokes the spirit of spring. If you wish to serve your chicken warm, substitute 1 tablespoon extra virgin olive oil for the 2 tablespoons low-fat mayonnaise. Season the sauce generously with salt and pepper.

NUTRITIONAL ANALYSIS PER SERVING: 188 CALORIES, 27 G PROTEIN, 8 G CARBOHYDRATE, 5 G FAT (1 G SATURATED), 69 MG CHOLESTEROL, 133 MG SODIUM, 2 G FIBER

4 small boneless skinless chicken breast halves (1 pound), visible fat removed

2 sprigs flat-leaf parsley

2 sprigs fresh thyme

1 bay leaf

1 garlic clove, peeled

½ carrot

½ small onion

Salt and freshly ground black pepper

Asparagus-Basil Mayonnaise

¾ pound fresh asparagus, stems peeled

¼ cup Smoked Allium Paste (page 22)

2 tablespoons low-fat mayonnaise

¼ cup chopped fresh basil

1. Fill a large saucepan with 4 cups water. Add the chicken, water, parsley, thyme, bay leaf, garlic, carrot, and onion. Bring to a boil, reduce the heat to low, and simmer for 5 to 8 minutes, until the chicken is just cooked through. Remove the chicken, rinse under cold water, pat dry, and refrigerate until you are ready to serve. Discard the cooking liquid or save for another use.

2. To make the flavored mayonnaise, blanch the asparagus in boiling salted water until crisp-tender for 2 minutes. Transfer to an ice water bath, drain, and dry well on kitchen towels. Cut off the tips and reserve for another use. Place the stems in a food processor with the smoked allium paste and mayonnaise. Process until smooth. Transfer to a small bowl, add the basil, season to taste with salt and pepper, and blend well.

3. Serve at room temperature or chilled. Slice the chicken on the diagonal. Divide the slices among 4 plates and arrange them in an overlapping pattern. Season the chicken slices with salt and pepper and spoon 1 tablespoon of the sauce down the center of each row. Pass the extra sauce at the table.

Zone yield per recipe: 16 protein blocks, 2 carbohydrate blocks (1 tablespoon mayonnaise = 0 protein blocks, ⅟₁₀ carbohydrate block)

Poached Chicken with Assorted Vegetables and Creamy Garlic Dressing

4 SERVINGS When I made this salad for the first time, my refrigerator held 3-day-old cooked broccoli, cauliflower, and green beans which I wanted to use up. In addition, I had some roasted garlic paste on hand. Since the actual preparation of these ingredients remained only a dim memory, the resulting tasty salad seemed almost effortless. If you are starting from scratch, however, assembling the ingredients will take time and a multi-use pot with a pasta insert will help you. Bring a large amount of water to a boil and cook each vegetable in turn until crisp-tender. Immediately transfer the cooked vegetable to an ice water bath and fill the insert with the next vegetable. Dry well between kitchen towels, rolling to squeeze out excess water. The chicken and vegetables should be served at room temperature or slightly chilled.

NUTRITIONAL ANALYSIS PER SERVING: 265 CALORIES, 33 G PROTEIN, 23 G CARBOHYDRATE, 5 G FAT (1 G SATURATED), 71 MG CHOLESTEROL, 574 MG SODIUM, 8 G FIBER

2 large chicken breast halves with skin and bone (1⅓ pounds), visible fat removed

2 sprigs flat-leaf parsley

2 sprigs fresh thyme

½ small onion

1 bay leaf

1 teaspoon salt

Creamy Garlic Dressing

¾ cup nonfat buttermilk

¼ cup low-fat mayonnaise

2 tablespoons Roasted Garlic Paste (page 24)

½ teaspoon salt or to taste
   Freshly ground black pepper

Vegetables

1 cup halved cherry tomatoes

2 cups cooked green beans, chilled

2 cups cooked cauliflower florets, chilled

1 cup cooked broccoli florets, chilled
   Salt and freshly ground black pepper

8 cups torn romaine lettuce

1. Fill a large saucepan with 4 cups water. Add the chicken breasts and bring to a boil. Reduce the heat and simmer for 5 minutes, skimming off any foam. Add the parsley, thyme, onion, bay leaf, and salt. Partially cover the pot and simmer for 12 minutes. Remove from the heat and allow the chicken to cool in the broth. Drain well. (Discard cooking liquid or reserve for another use.) Remove and discard the skin and bones, as well as the onion and herbs. Shred or dice the meat and season with salt and pepper. Refrigerate until you are ready to serve.

2. To make the dressing, combine the buttermilk, mayonnaise, and roasted garlic paste in a 2-cup measure and blend using a stick blender. (Alternatively, blend in a traditional blender and transfer to a bowl.) Add salt and pepper to taste. Refrigerate until you are ready to serve. (The dressing can be made up to 3 days in advance.)

3. To serve, combine the tomatoes and cooked vegetables in a bowl. Season with salt and pepper and toss to combine. Arrange the lettuce, vegetables, and chicken on 4 plates. Spoon a tablespoon of the dressing onto each plate. Pass the extra dressing on the side.

Zone yield per recipe: 16 protein blocks, 6 carbohydrate blocks (1 tablespoon dressing = 0 protein blocks, ⅙ carbohydrate block)

Spicy Marinated Roast Chicken

4 SERVINGS To qualify as lean protein, chicken must be eaten without the skin. Since fat intensifies flavor, and most of the fat lies just under the skin, skin loss generally portends flavor loss. Consequently, I have turned toward marinades to infuse the meat with interesting tastes that are not shed with the skin.

NUTRITIONAL ANALYSIS PER SERVING: 271 CALORIES, 33 G PROTEIN, 7 G CARBOHYDRATE, 11 G FAT (3 G SATURATED), 96 MG CHOLESTEROL, 1237 MG SODIUM, 0 G FIBER

Marinade

2   tablespoons rice wine or dry sherry

1½ tablespoons soy sauce

1   tablespoon chili bean sauce
     (also known as hot bean paste or
     Sichuan bean paste)

1   tablespoon rice vinegar

1   tablespoon minced garlic

1   tablespoon minced fresh ginger

3   tablespoons minced scallions
     (white parts only)

2   teaspoons toasted sesame oil

2   teaspoons fructose

1   teaspoon salt

1   (3-pound) split broiler chicken,
     visible fat removed

1   to 1½ cups no-salt chicken broth

1. To make the marinade, combine the sherry, soy sauce, chili sauce, vinegar, garlic, ginger, scallions, oil, fructose, and salt in a small bowl or measuring cup and whisk to dissolve the fructose. Place the chicken halves in a nonreactive container and pour the marinade over it. Turn to coat well. Marinate overnight in the refrigerator, turning once or twice.

2. Preheat the oven to 400° F. Prepare a roasting pan with a rack. Remove chicken from the marinade and place skin side down on the rack, reserving the marinade. Roast the chicken for 30 minutes. Turn the chicken and add 1 cup of the broth and the reserved marinade to the roasting pan. Roast for another 30 to 45 minutes, or until the juices run clear. Transfer to a platter.

3. Scrape up the brown bits in the pan, adding more broth if needed. Transfer to a measuring cup along with any collected chicken juices and degrease. Remove the chicken skin and discard. Cut the chicken into serving pieces, and serve immediately with the pan juices.

Zone yield per recipe: 16 protein blocks, 3 carbohydrate blocks

Roast Chicken with Rosemary-Garlic Paste **4 SERVINGS** A life-long

dieting friend of mine has always divided the world of food into "WTC" and not. This used to mean "worth

the calories," but—since she entered Dr. Barry Sears's Zone—it has come to mean "worth the carbohydrate."

At 9 grams of carbohydrate per ounce, garlic is surprisingly carbohydrate-dense, but totally "WTC." I do not

hesitate to use an entire head in the following recipe. The chicken has so much flavor, it is also delicious served

cold, without the pan juices.

NUTRITIONAL ANALYSIS PER SERVING: 274 CALORIES, 34 G PROTEIN, 8 G CARBOHYDRATE,
11 G FAT (2 G SATURATED), 96 MG CHOLESTEROL, 289 MG SODIUM, 0 G FIBER

Rosemary-Garlic Paste

*1 large bulb Roasted Garlic
    (page 24), peeled*

2 teaspoons extra virgin olive oil

1 tablespoon balsamic vinegar

2 teaspoons fresh lemon juice

2 teaspoons chopped fresh rosemary

   *Salt and freshly ground black
   pepper*

*1 (3-pound) split broiler chicken,
    visible fat removed*

   *Salt and freshly ground black
   pepper*

1 teaspoon extra virgin olive oil

1 cup chicken broth

1. To make the rosemary-garlic paste, combine the roasted garlic cloves, oil, vinegar, and lemon juice in a food processor or blender and puree until smooth. Transfer to a small bowl. Stir in the rosemary and season to taste with salt and pepper. Set aside. (This flavoring paste can be made in advance and refrigerated for up to 1 week or frozen for up to 6 months.)

2. Loosen the chicken skin by slipping your hand under it, creating a space between it and the meat. Using a small spatula or your fingers, spread two-thirds of the paste under the skin. Turn the chicken halves over. Season the undersides generously with salt and pepper and spread on the remaining paste. (The chicken can be prepared up to this point, then refrigerated for up to 24 hours before roasting.)

3. Preheat the oven to 400° F. Season the chicken skin well with salt and pepper. Place the chicken skin side down on a rack in a roasting pan. Roast for 30 minutes. Turn and brush the skin with 1 teaspoon olive oil. Return to the oven and roast for 30 to 45 minutes, or until the chicken is cooked through and the juices run clear. Transfer the chicken to a platter.

4. Remove the rack from the pan and add the broth to the drippings. Stir, scraping up the brown bits. Transfer to a measuring cup along with any collected chicken juices and degrease.

5. To serve, remove the skin from the chicken and discard. Cut the chicken into serving size pieces. Serve immediately with the pan juices poured over the chicken.

Zone yield per recipe: 16 protein blocks, 4 carbohydrate blocks

Moroccan Chicken Thighs 4 SERVINGS

This fragrant chicken stew, loosely adapted from Sheryl Julian and Julie Riven of the *Boston Globe,* illustrates one of the many uses of roasted eggplant. Since the eggplant simmers in the sauce for 10 minutes, roast it until it is tender but not soft, or it will disintegrate during the final cooking. I generally leave the skin on, but you can peel it if you wish before cutting it into cubes. If you do not have roasted eggplant, zucchini cut into 1-inch chunks will cook in the allotted time. The stew is excellent (perhaps even better) reheated the next day.

NUTRITIONAL ANALYSIS PER SERVING: 388 CALORIES, 34 G PROTEIN, 23 G CARBOHYDRATE, 17 G FAT (4 G SATURATED), 99 MG CHOLESTEROL, 558 MG SODIUM, 7 G FIBER

8	bone-in chicken thighs, skin and visible fat removed
	Salt and freshly ground black pepper
1	tablespoon extra virgin olive oil
1	cup chopped onion
1	tablespoon minced fresh ginger
1	tablespoon minced garlic
2	cinnamon sticks
1	teaspoon ground cumin
1	cup diced canned tomatoes, drained
1½ cups chicken broth	
1	cup cooked and drained chickpeas
3	cups cubed Roasted Eggplant (1-inch cubes) (page 30)
2	tablespoons minced flat-leaf parsley

1. Season the chicken generously with salt and pepper. Heat the oil in a large nonstick skillet or Dutch oven over medium-high heat. Add the chicken and brown well on both sides; then remove from the skillet.

2. Reduce the heat to medium. Add the onion and sauté, stirring, until soft, about 3 minutes. Add the ginger, garlic, cinnamon sticks, and cumin. Cook, stirring, for 1 minute. Add the tomatoes, broth, and salt and pepper to taste. Return the chicken with any accumulated juices to the pan. Baste with the sauce. Cover and simmer for 15 minutes. Add the chickpeas and roasted eggplant and simmer for 10 minutes.

3. Adjust the seasoning and remove the cinnamon sticks. Garnish with the parsley. Serve immediately.

Zone yield per recipe: 16 protein blocks, 7 carbohydrate blocks

Chicken Patties with Smoked Peppers and Parsley 4 SERVINGS

In an attempt to reduce fat content, ground meats of all kinds are often extended with carbohydrates, such as bread crumbs, potatoes, couscous, bulgur, and rice. Smoked vegetables accomplish the same task more flavorfully with less insulin impact. They also lighten the mixture, as bread crumbs would, while keeping it tender and moist.

NUTRITIONAL ANALYSIS PER SERVING: 198 CALORIES, 32 G PROTEIN, 2 G CARBOHYDRATE, 6 G FAT (1 G SATURATED), 86 MG CHOLESTEROL, 659 MG SODIUM, 1 G FIBER

1¼ pounds ground white-meat chicken

1   cup diced Smoked Bell Peppers (red) (page 32)

¼   cup minced flat-leaf parsley

1   teaspoon salt or to taste

Freshly ground black pepper

2   teaspoons extra virgin olive oil

1. Combine the chicken, peppers, parsley, salt, and black pepper in a bowl and blend well without overworking. Form into 4 patties, each approximately 1 inch thick.

2. Using ½ teaspoon oil for each, make 4 patty-shaped oil "footprints" in a large nonstick skillet over medium-high heat. Place the patties in the oil and sauté for 5 minutes per side, until cooked through but not dry. Serve immediately.

Zone yield per recipe: 16 protein blocks, 1 carbohydrate block

Moroccan Chicken Thighs

Seared Duck Breasts with Red Rice Vinegar

4 SERVINGS I had been an avid vinegar collector long before I changed my diet to modulate insulin, but I began to take vinegar more seriously when I learned of its capacity to lower blood sugar. The Chinese palette includes vinegars of various hues. White rice vinegar, seasoned or unseasoned, is the most widely available, familiar, and commonly used. (Be sure to use the *unseasoned* variety to avoid unnecessary sugar.) Black rice vinegar ranks second in availability and use. It appears in savory soups and sauces with "hot and sour" character. Red rice vinegar, the most obscure, typically enhances "sweet and sour" dishes like the duck preparation below.

NUTRITIONAL ANALYSIS PER SERVING: 193 CALORIES, 31 G PROTEIN, 7 G CARBOHYDRATE, 3 G FAT (0 G SATURATED), 174 MG CHOLESTEROL, 343 MG SODIUM, 0 G FIBER

Marinade

- 2   tablespoons light soy sauce
- 2   tablespoons bean sauce
- 2   tablespoons Shaoxing rice wine
- 2   teaspoons fructose
- ½   teaspoon five-spice powder
- 1   tablespoon minced garlic
- 3   tablespoons minced scallions (white parts only)

Sauce

- 2½ tablespoons red rice vinegar
- 2   tablespoons fructose
- 4   teaspoons light soy sauce
- 1   tablespoon water

- 2   Muscovy duck breasts (1½ pounds), skin and visible fat removed

     Salt and freshly ground black pepper

- 1   teaspoon peanut or canola oil

1. To make the marinade, combine the soy sauce, bean sauce, rice wine, fructose, five-spice powder, garlic, and scallions in a small bowl or measuring cup and whisk to blend. Place the duck breasts in a nonreactive container. Add the marinade and turn to coat. Marinate overnight in the refrigerator.

2. To make the sauce, combine the vinegar, fructose, soy sauce, and water in a small bowl or measuring cup and whisk to dissolve the fructose. Set aside.

3. Preheat the oven to 450° F. Remove the duck breasts from the marinade and discard the marinade. Scrape off any residual solids and pat the duck dry between layers of paper towels. Season the duck with salt and pepper.

4. Using ½ teaspoon oil for each, make 2 breast-shaped oil "footprints" in a cast-iron skillet over medium-high heat. Place the duck in the oil and sauté for 2 minutes, until well seared. Turn the breasts, and transfer the skillet to the oven. Roast for 6 minutes for medium-rare meat, or longer if desired.

5. Remove the duck breasts to a platter. Add the sauce to the hot skillet and cook for 1 minute over medium heat, stirring and scraping up the brown bits. Pour over the duck and serve immediately.

Note: Spice Merchant Catalog (P.O. Box 524, Jackson Hole, WY 83001; 800-551-5999) offers a sampler of rice vinegars, containing white, black, and red rice varieties.

Zone yield per recipe: 16 protein blocks, 3 carbohydrate blocks

Chinese Brined and Grilled Ducks 8 SERVINGS Benjamin Nathan, one of

Boston's most promising young chefs, is a devotee of brining—a powerful marinating technique that tenderizes and flavors meat via immersion in a sweet and salty bath. When his intriguing recipe for "Orange-Soy-Chili Brine-Roasted Duck" appeared in the *Boston Globe,* I made it immediately. It yielded an irresistibly juicy and tender duck with complex Chinese flavors. Unfortunately, I could not include it in my repertoire without modifying its fat and carbohydrate contents. First, I developed a mirin substitute to decrease the glycemic burden of the brine. I also decreased the added oil and salt. Then I halved the duck and removed its skin and fat, which significantly reduced the necessary brining time as well as fat content. I noticed that my skinny duck now took up less space, leaving room for two. Finally, using the grill instead of the oven, I cut the cooking time in half. Though not as rich as the original, this recipe produces two deeply flavored aromatic grilled ducks. If this recipe does not immediately strike you as worth the effort, consider this: When I set out to obtain permission to adapt the recipe, I had tremendous difficulty locating Ben Nathan, but the vivid memory of his extraordinary duck would not let me rest. In desperation, I took my "missing persons" case to a *private detective*, and the missing chef was found to be on an extended culinary vacation in France. Here, with Ben Nathan's generous consent, is my version of "Benjamin Nathan's Orange-Soy-Chili Brine-Roasted Duck."

NUTRITIONAL ANALYSIS PER SERVING: 189 CALORIES, 32 G PROTEIN, 0 G CARBOHYDRATE,
6 G FAT (1 G SATURATED), 140 MG CHOLESTEROL, 120 MG SODIUM, 0 G FIBER

Brine

3 quarts ice water

3 cups soy sauce

1½ cups Pseudo-Mirin (page 37)

2 teaspoons peanut or canola oil

2 tablespoons minced garlic

⅓ cup minced fresh ginger

3 small dried hot chiles (such as Thai, Chinese, or chiles de arbol)

1½ cups halved and sliced oranges with peels

1½ cups halved and sliced onions

¼ cup chili garlic paste

1½ tablespoons Sichuan peppercorns

1½ tablespoons coriander seeds

2 tablespoons kosher salt

2 (4- to 5-pound) ducks, split, all skin and visible fat removed

2 teaspoons peanut or canola oil

1. Set a jumbo zippered or oven-roasting bag inside a pot or container large enough to hold the ducks and allow the edges of the bag to hang over. Begin making the brine by combining the water, soy sauce, and Pseudo-Mirin in the bag. Heat 2 teaspoons oil in a nonstick wok or large skillet over medium-high heat. Add the garlic, ginger, chiles, oranges, and onions. Stir-fry for 5 minutes, until lightly brown.

(continued)

Chinese Brined and Grilled Ducks (continued)

Add the chili paste and stir-fry for another 2 minutes. Remove from the heat and add to the liquids in the bag. Stir gently to combine.

2. Place a small nonstick skillet over medium heat and add the peppercorns and coriander seeds. Cook for 2 to 3 minutes, stirring or shaking the pan, until fragrant. Do not allow the seeds to burn. Add to the brine along with the

salt and stir to combine. Allow the brine to cool completely.

3. Submerge the ducks in the cooled brine. Seal the bag and refrigerate for 24 hours.

4. Prepare a hot fire in the grill. Remove the ducks from the brine and pat dry. Discard the brine. Brush the ducks with the remaining 2 teaspoons oil and place on the grill. Cover and grill for 20 to 30 minutes. Turn the ducks every 5 minutes or

so, moving them around from hotter to cooler spots as needed to prevent burning. Check at the leg-thigh joint for doneness. The meat should be rosy but cooked through.

5. Remove the birds to a cutting board and allow to rest for 5 minutes. Cut into serving pieces. Serve hot, warm, at room temperature, or cold.

Zone yield per recipe: 32 protein blocks, less than one carbohydrate block

Not Exactly Peking Duck **4 SERVINGS** Like tortillas, Mandarin pancakes undermine

insulin control by causing a rapid rise in blood sugar. In this recipe, they have been replaced by lettuce leaves which protect fingers and insulin status at the same time. By using skinless duck breasts, most of the fat has also been eliminated, thus decreasing the saturated fat load on the cardiovascular system. The resulting roll-up satisfies the desire for Peking duck without compromising one's health.

NUTRITIONAL ANALYSIS PER SERVING: 262 CALORIES, 34 G PROTEIN, 16 G CARBOHYDRATE, 7 G FAT (0 G SATURATED), 174 MG CHOLESTEROL, 381 MG SODIUM, 3 G FIBER

Sauce

5   tablespoons sweet bean sauce

1   tablespoon fructose

1   tablespoon rice vinegar

1   teaspoon toasted sesame oil

Spice Rub

½   teaspoon five-spice powder

½   teaspoon salt

½   teaspoon freshly ground black pepper

2   Muscovy duck breasts (1½ pounds), skin and visible fat removed

1   teaspoon peanut or canola oil

2   heads Boston lettuce, leaves separated

2   cups julienned scallions (white parts only)

1. To make the sauce, combine the bean sauce, fructose, vinegar, and oil in a small bowl or measuring cup and whisk to dissolve the fructose.

2. In another bowl, combine the five-spice powder, salt, and pepper. Rub over the duck breasts.

3. Preheat the oven to 450° F. Place a large cast-iron skillet over medium-high heat and brush with the oil. Place the duck breasts in the skillet and sear for 2 minutes. Turn the ducks and transfer the skillet to the oven. Roast for 6 minutes for

Not Exactly Peking Duck (continued)

medium-rare meat, or longer, if desired. The meat should be rosy but cooked through.

4. Remove the duck to a platter and let rest for 5 minutes. Slice on the diagonal and serve with the lettuce leaves, scallions, and sauce. To eat: dab a little sauce on a lettuce leaf, add some duck and scallion, roll up, and eat.

Zone yield per recipe: 16 protein blocks, 5 carbohydrate blocks (1 tablespoon sauce = 0 protein blocks, ½ carbohydrate block)

Turkey Patties with Apples and Smoked Leeks 4 SERVINGS The meteoric

rise in the popularity of ground turkey followed the trajectory of public concern about the adverse health effects of saturated fat. A 4-ounce serving of ground light meat turkey harbors less than 1 gram of saturated fat. In the world of animal protein, only ostrich, game, and fish exhibit better lipid profiles. In the presence of apples and smoked leeks, ground turkey makes a delicious lean burger. Ketchup may seem like an eccentric accompaniment; but I assure you, this combination works.

NUTRITIONAL ANALYSIS PER SERVING: 216 CALORIES, 27 G PROTEIN, 13 G CARBOHYDRATE, 6 G FAT (1 G SATURATED), 59 MG CHOLESTEROL, 744 MG SODIUM, 2 G FIBER

¾ cup peeled and chopped crisp, sweet apple (such as Fuji or Yellow Delicious)

½ cup sliced Smoked Leeks (page 28)

1⅓ pounds ground white-meat turkey

2 tablespoons minced flat-leaf parsley

2 teaspoons minced garlic

1 teaspoon salt or to taste
   Freshly ground black pepper

2 teaspoons extra virgin olive oil

¼ cup Charred Tomato Ketchup (page 38)

1. Combine the apple and leeks in a food processor and pulse to mince. Transfer to a bowl and add the ground turkey, parsley, garlic, salt, and pepper. Blend well without overworking. Form into 4 patties, each about 1 inch thick.

2. Using ½ teaspoon oil for each, make 4 patty-shaped oil "footprints" in a large nonstick skillet over medium heat. Place the patties in the oil and sauté for 5 minutes per side, until cooked through and slightly browned.

3. Serve immediately with 1 tablespoon of the ketchup per patty.

Zone yield per recipe: 16 protein blocks, 4 carbohydrate blocks

Spiced Turkey Kebabs

4 SERVINGS During the summer, my local market offers "London broil-style" turkey—half a skinless boneless breast in the form of a thick steak. I cube it, marinate it overnight in Indian spices, and grill it the next day. The meat can be skewered with or without the usual shish kebab companions (peppers, onions, cherry tomatoes). If, however, you seek adventure, try combining this recipe with Broiled Fruit Skewers (page 205). Many fruits respond well to broiling and substitute brilliantly for high-glycemic chutneys. | The recipe provides plenty of extra spice mixture to use with chicken, duck, lamb, and pork. Store the excess in an airtight container in a cool, dark place and use it as needed. It should keep for up to 6 months.

NUTRITIONAL ANALYSIS PER SERVING: 178 CALORIES, 26 G PROTEIN, 2 G CARBOHYDRATE, 7 G FAT (2 G SATURATED), 58 MG CHOLESTEROL, 297 MG SODIUM, 0 G FIBER

Spice Mix

1   tablespoon ground cumin

1   tablespoon ground coriander

1   tablespoon turmeric

½   to 1 teaspoon cayenne pepper

1   tablespoon salt

1   teaspoon freshly ground black pepper

1   tablespoon peanut or canola oil

1   tablespoon minced garlic

1   tablespoon minced fresh ginger

2   tablespoons minced onion

1⅓ pounds boneless skinless turkey breast, cut in 1½-inch chunks

1. To make the spice mix, combine the cumin, coriander, turmeric, cayenne, salt, and pepper in a small nonstick skillet over medium heat. Cook, stirring, for 2 to 3 minutes until fragrant. Remove from the heat and set aside to cool. Measure out 2 teaspoons (or more to taste) into a medium-sized bowl. Reserve the extra for another use.

2. Add the oil, garlic, ginger, and onion to the spice mix. Whisk to blend. Add the turkey chunks and toss well to coat. (The turkey can be set aside in the refrigerator for up to 24 hours at this point.)

3. Preheat the broiler or prepare a hot fire in the grill. Thread the turkey chunks loosely on skewers. Broil or grill 4 inches from the heat for about 4 minutes. Turn, broil, or grill for approximately 4 minutes longer, or until the turkey is cooked through but not dry. Serve immediately.

Zone yield per recipe: 16 protein blocks, 1 carbohydrate block

Spiced Turkey Kebabs served with Curried Slaw with Fruit and Pistachios (page 152)

Smoked Turkey Tenderloins with Raspberry-Chipotle Sauce

4 SERVINGS The magical combination of smoked turkey, fresh raspberries, and chipotle peppers in adobo originated with Norma Gillaspie, *chef de cuisine* and owner of The Cottonwood Cafe in Boston and Cambridge. With Norma's generous permission, I've adapted the sauce for modified carbohydrate diets. In this version, fructose and black currant vinegar replace sugar and port. Though considerably less sweet than the original, this sauce still manages to transform plain smoked turkey into exotic fare. For a spectacular variation, try the sauce on grilled pork tenderloin. Be sure to wear gloves when you remove the seeds and membranes from the chipotle.

NUTRITIONAL ANALYSIS PER SERVING: 170 CALORIES, 26 G PROTEIN, 5 G CARBOHYDRATE, 4 G FAT (1 G SATURATED), 58 MG CHOLESTEROL, 69 MG SODIUM, 2 G FIBER

Raspberry-Chipotle Sauce

1½ cups fresh raspberries

4   teaspoons fructose

1   tablespoon black currant or raspberry vinegar

1   tablespoon water

1   teaspoon minced chipotle chile in adobo sauce, seeds and membranes removed

2   teaspoons adobo sauce

1⅓ pounds turkey tenderloins

1   teaspoon peanut or canola oil

Salt and freshly ground black pepper

1. To make the sauce, combine the raspberries, fructose, vinegar, water, chipotle, and adobo sauce in a small nonreactive saucepan. Bring to a boil, reduce the heat, and simmer for about 5 minutes, stirring occasionally, until the raspberries break down and the fructose dissolves. Pass through a fine mesh sieve into a bowl. Work the berry mass vigorously with a wooden spoon to harvest all the pulp. Scrape into the bowl any pulp adhering to the underside of the sieve. Set aside. Discard the residue inside the sieve. Reserve ½ cup of the sauce to be served with the turkey. Set aside the remainder for another use. (The sauce can be made ahead and refrigerated for up to 1 week or frozen for up to 6 months. Bring to room temperature before serving.)

2. Prepare a stovetop smoker with 1 tablespoon apple or cherry smoking chips. Spray the rack with canola oil. Lightly brush the tenderloins with the oil and generously season with salt and pepper. Place the turkey on the rack and half-close the lid. Place the smoker on an electric burner preheated to medium or on a gas burner turned to medium-high. When the first wisps of smoke appear, close the lid. Smoke for 10 to 15 minutes, until the turkey is cooked through but not dry. Remove to a platter.

3. This dish is delicious served warm or at room temperature. Slice the tenderloins on an angle and drizzle 1 tablespoon of the sauce over each portion. Pass the extra sauce at the table.

Note: Smoking times are highly variable.

Zone yield per recipe: 16 protein blocks, 1 carbohydrate block (1 tablespoon sauce = 0 protein blocks, ⅙ carbohydrate block)

Smoked Turkey Tenderloins with Raspberry-Chipotle Sauce served with steamed spinach

Boneless Turkey Breast with Sun-Dried Tomato Infusion

4 TO 6 SERVINGS Turkey breast is naturally lean, so it requires no surgery to make it healthful. The boneless breast roasts quickly and tastes wonderful warm or cold. The skin, which serves as an automatic baster, is removed before serving.

NUTRITIONAL ANALYSIS PER SERVING: 197 CALORIES, 29 G PROTEIN, 7 G CARBOHYDRATE, 6 G FAT (1 G SATURATED), 62 MG CHOLESTEROL, 548 MG SODIUM, 1 G FIBER

Infusion Paste

1¼ ounces sun-dried tomatoes (not oil-packed) (about ½ cup)

2 cups water

⅓ cup Smoked Allium Paste (page 22)

1 tablespoon chopped fresh thyme leaves

¾ teaspoon salt or to taste

Freshly ground black pepper

1 boneless turkey breast with skin, about 2 pounds

Salt and freshly ground black pepper

1 teaspoon extra virgin olive oil

3 teaspoons chopped fresh thyme leaves

1 cup chicken broth

1. To make the infusion paste, combine the tomatoes and water in a medium saucepan and bring to a boil. Reduce the heat to low and simmer for 20 minutes. Remove the tomatoes with a slotted spoon and transfer to a colander. Strain the liquid through a cheesecloth-lined sieve into a small clean saucepan. Reduce the liquid to 1 to 2 table-spoons tomato syrup. Cool to room temperature.

2. Meanwhile, wash the tomatoes under cold running water rubbing with your fingers to remove all seeds and grit. Pat dry on paper towels. Transfer half the tomatoes to a food processor and pulse to chop finely. Remove to a bowl and set aside. Combine the remaining whole tomatoes, syrup, and smoked allium paste in the food processor and puree. Add to the chopped tomatoes, along with the thyme, salt and pepper to taste. Blend

well and set aside. (The infusion paste can be made in advance and refrigerated up to 1 week or frozen up to 6 months.)

3. Untie and unroll the turkey breast. Season both sides generously with salt and pepper. Lay the breast flat, skin side up. Loosen the skin between the ends of the breast by slipping your hand under it, but do not detach it altogether.

4. Reserve 2 tablespoons of the infusion paste for the gravy and set aside. Using a small spatula, spread half the remaining paste under the skin. Turn the turkey breast over and spread the rest of the paste over the inner surface. Roll and tie with butcher's twine. If any paste oozes out, simply spread it on the top or ends of the turkey breast.

Boneless Turkey Breast with Sun-Dried Tomato Infusion (continued)

5. Preheat the oven to 350° F. In a small flameproof roasting pan, make a roast-shaped "footprint" with ½ teaspoon extra virgin olive oil. Sprinkle 1½ teaspoons of the fresh thyme leaves over the bottom of the breast and place in the roasting pan. Brush the top of the roast with the remaining ½ teaspoon oil and sprinkle with the remaining 1½ teaspoons thyme.

6. Roast for 20 to 30 minutes per pound to an internal temperature of 160° to 165° F. Remove to a platter and allow to rest for 10 minutes.

7. To make a gravy to accompany the turkey, add the chicken broth to the roasting pan and place over low heat. Stir, scraping up the brown bits. Add the reserved 2 tablespoons infusion paste and blend well. Season to taste with salt and pepper. Transfer to a measuring cup along with any collected turkey juices and degrease.

8. Remove the skin from the turkey. Thickly slice the turkey and serve immediately with 1 tablespoon of the gravy drizzled on each portion. Pass the extra gravy at the table.

Zone yield per recipe: 20 protein blocks, 4 carbohydrate blocks

Cold Sliced Roasted Turkey Breast with Sun-Dried Tomato Infusion *(Variation)*

4 TO 6 SERVINGS

NUTRITIONAL ANALYSIS PER SERVING: 189 CALORIES, 28 G PROTEIN, 5 G CARBOHYDRATE, 5 G FAT (1 G SATURATED), 62 MG CHOLESTEROL, 283 MG SODIUM, 0 G FIBER

1. Follow the recipe as above, but do not make the gravy. Combine the reserved 2 tablespoons infusion paste with ¼ cup low-fat mayonnaise and ¼ cup nonfat yogurt. Slice the turkey thickly and serve it with a dollop of this creamy sauce.

Zone yield per recipe: 20 protein blocks, 3 carbohydrate blocks (1 tablespoon sauce = 0 protein blocks, ½ carbohydrate block)

Pork and Veal

I love the *pink meats*, pork and veal, for their savory flavors and the variety they bring to meals, but their nutritional profiles make them desirable as well. Both veal and pork contain significant amounts of minerals—especially phosphorus, potassium, and zinc. In addition, pork provides more iron than chicken and useful amounts of vitamins B12 and thiamin. Veal supplies more niacin than chicken (also a good source) and more folate than any meat except for lamb.

In fat content, the leanest cuts of pork and veal (tenderloin, loin, and sirloin) stand between chicken breast meat and beef tenderloin. Per cooked ounce, white meat chicken contains about 1 gram, pork tenderloin 1.3 grams, veal sirloin 1.7 grams, and beef tenderloin 2.9 grams of fat. Saturated fat accounts for about 25 percent of the total fat in each of these meats. In the seductive world of pork and veal, thorough trimming (before and after cooking) is essential to keep total and saturated fat as low as possible. A sharp knife and steely determination will free you to delight in their virtues without suffering from their disposable vices.

Lean pork and veal respond well to dry cooking methods (sautéing, grilling, broiling, and roasting). However, like other lean meats, they are vulnerable to drying out and caution must be taken to avoid overcooking them. I wish I could tell the doneness of a roast by poking it with my index finger, but *in truth* I rely on an instant-read thermometer for help. I even occasionally cut into a roast and peek.

Since fat intensifies flavor, well-trimmed veal and pork pose the same flavor challenge as poultry without the skin and I am consistent in my strategies for dealing with it. Brining and marinating make pork and veal tender and tasty, even without their envelopes of fat. Infusion pastes like the one in Roasted Pork Tenderloin with Ancho Chile Infusion (page 108) also turn up flavor while they keep roasts moist.

Although this section includes recipes of Mexican, Italian, and contemporary American slant, the majority reveal my predilection for intense Asian flavorings. Admittedly, I apply them in unorthodox ways. Fermented black beans and black mushrooms find their way into pork roasts. Veal, which has no place at all in Chinese cuisine, flourishes under the influence of marinades containing Chinese seasonings and condiments.

Favorite Protein/Carbohydrate Pairings:

Sirloin Pork Roast with Black Mushrooms and Smoked Leeks (page 103) and Glazed Sweet Bean Turnips (page 181)

Verjus-Marinated Grilled Pork Tenderloin (page 110) and Fresh Bean Salad with Parsley-Buttermilk Dressing (page 162)

Porcini-Laced Veal Roast (page 115) and Spicy Greens with Roasted Tomatoes and Peppers (page 174)

Brined Pork Roast with Shiitakes and Smoked Peppers (page 102) served with steamed chard

Brined Pork Roast with Shiitakes and Smoked Peppers 6 SERVINGS

Brining is a low-fat "wet cure" for lean meats that tend to dry out during roasting. This centuries-old method involves immersing the meat in a solution of salt, water, sweeteners, and seasonings to tenderize and permeate it with flavor. If brining sounds intimidating, just think of it as marinating. | After trimming, a 3-pound roast will yield about 2¼ pounds of lean pork—enough for 6 to 8 insulin-conscious diners. If your guests are not bound by health concerns, you will need a larger roast; the brine easily will accommodate one twice the size used here. Note also that the brining process takes 48 hours, so you must plan this roast well in advance. (Pictured on page 101.)

NUTRITIONAL ANALYSIS PER SERVING: 244 CALORIES, 28 G PROTEIN, 5 G CARBOHYDRATE, 12 G FAT (4 G SATURATED), 74 MG CHOLESTEROL, 294 MG SODIUM, 1 G FIBER

Brine

2   tablespoons kosher salt

2   tablespoons fructose

4   cups boiling water

1   tablespoon sesame oil

¼   cup minced garlic

½   cup minced scallions

¼   cup minced fresh ginger

½   teaspoon hot red pepper flakes

4   cups ice water

½   cup soy sauce

½   cup amontillado sherry

3   pound center-cut loin pork roast, visible fat removed (about 2¼ pounds trimmed)

     Salt and freshly ground black pepper

2   teaspoons sesame oil

1   cup chicken broth

2   tablespoons amontillado sherry

1   teaspoon peanut or canola oil

¼   cup thinly sliced scallions (white parts only)

3   cups thinly sliced shiitake mushroom caps (¾ pound with stems)

1   cup thinly sliced Smoked Bell Peppers (red) (page 32)

2   teaspoons soy sauce

1   teaspoon fructose

1. To make the brine, combine the salt and fructose in a large heatproof bowl and add the boiling water. Stir to dissolve. Heat 1 tablespoon sesame oil in a skillet. Add the garlic, scallion, ginger, and pepper flakes and sauté until soft, about 2 minutes. Add to the hot water along with the ice water, soy sauce, and ½ cup sherry. Allow to cool completely.

2. Fit a large oven-roasting bag inside a 3-quart pot and let the bag edges hang over the pot. Place the roast inside it. Pour the brine into the bag and close with a tie. Refrigerate for 48 hours.

3. Preheat the oven to 325° F. Remove the roast from the brine and discard the brine. Pat dry the meat and tie with butcher's twine. Season with salt and pepper. Brush with 1 teaspoon of the sesame oil and place in a flameproof roasting pan or cast-iron skillet just large enough to hold it. For slightly pink meat, roast for 20 to 30 minutes per pound to an internal temperature of 150° F on an instant-read thermometer. (The temperature will continue to rise during resting.) Remove the meat to a platter and allow to rest for 5 to 10 minutes.

4. Place the roasting pan over low heat and add the broth and 2 tablespoons sherry. Stir, scraping up the brown bits. Transfer to a measuring cup and degrease.

Brined Pork Roast with Shiitakes and Smoked Peppers (continued)

5. Heat the remaining 1 teaspoon sesame oil and 1 teaspoon peanut oil in a nonstick skillet over medium heat. Add the scallions and stir-fry for 20 seconds. Add the mushrooms and stir-fry for 2 to 3 minutes, until tender. Add the smoked pepper strips and season with salt and pepper. Add the broth-sherry mixture, soy sauce, and fructose. Stir to combine.

6. Carve the pork into slices about ¼ inch thick. Serve each portion with 1 tablespoon of the shiitake sauce drizzled on top. Pass the extra sauce at the table.

Zone yield per recipe: 24 protein blocks, 2 carbohydrate blocks

Sirloin Pork Roast with Black Mushrooms and Smoked Leeks **4 SERVINGS** A sirloin pork roast is a rare and beautiful thing—well worth the pursuit—but it requires careful trimming. The infusion paste replaces the fat and keeps the meat moist during roasting. You will notice that a solitary smoked leek figures in the paste. If you eliminate it, you will lose half the magic of this preparation. A fresh one will not do; an absent one is a great opportunity missed.

NUTRITIONAL ANALYSIS PER SERVING: 267 CALORIES, 29 G PROTEIN, 12 G CARBOHYDRATE, 11 G FAT (4 G SATURATED), 78 MG CHOLESTEROL, 665 MG SODIUM, 1 G FIBER

Infusion Paste

½ ounce dried Chinese black or shiitake mushrooms (about ¾ cup or 5 large)

1¼ cups water

1 Smoked Leek (page 28), coarsely chopped (about ⅓ cup)

⅓ cup Smoked Allium Paste (page 22)

3 tablespoons oyster sauce

Salt and freshly ground black pepper

2 pound sirloin pork roast, visible fat removed (1½ pounds trimmed)

Salt and freshly ground black pepper

1 cup chicken broth

1 teaspoon fructose

1. To make the infusion paste, combine the mushrooms and water in a small saucepan. Bring to a boil, reduce the heat to low, and simmer for 20 minutes. Remove the mushrooms with a slotted spoon. Strain the liquid through a cheesecloth-lined sieve into a clean saucepan. Place over medium-high heat and reduce to 2 tablespoons mushroom syrup. Set aside.

2. Meanwhile, rinse the mushrooms under cold running water, rubbing with your fingers to remove any grit. Dry on paper towels and gently squeeze out the excess water.

Remove and discard the stems and quarter the caps. Transfer the caps to a food processor along with the leek and pulse until finely chopped, but not pureed. (You should have about ⅔ cup.)

3. In a small bowl, combine the mushroom-leek mixture, smoked allium paste, oyster sauce, and 1 tablespoon of the reserved mushroom syrup. Blend well and season with salt and pepper. (The paste can be made in advance and refrigerated for up to 1 week or frozen for up to 6 months.)

(continued)

Sirloin Pork Roast with Black Mushrooms and Smoked Leeks (continued)

4. Preheat the oven to 275° F. To butterfly the roast, bisect the roast lengthwise to within ½ inch of the bottom surface. *Do not cut all the way through it.* Open up the 2 lobes like a book. Make a similar lengthwise slit through each lobe but stop again ½ inch above the bottom surface. You now have 4 lobes and the roast should lie relatively flat.

5. Lay the butterflied roast flat on a work surface and season both sides well with salt and pepper. Place cut side up. Reserve 2 tablespoons of the infusion paste for the gravy and set aside. Using a spatula, spread half the remaining paste over the exposed surface including the crevices. Roll up jelly-roll style, but not too tightly or the paste will ooze out. Secure with butcher's twine and place in a flameproof roasting pan or cast-iron skillet. Spread the remaining paste over the top and sides of the roast.

6. For slightly pink meat, roast for approximately 1¾ to 2 hours, to an internal temperature of 150° F on an instant-read thermometer. Remove the meat to a platter and allow to rest for 5 to 10 minutes. (The temperature of the meat will continue to rise during resting.)

7. Place the roasting pan over low heat and add the chicken broth, fructose, the remaining 1 tablespoon mushroom syrup, and reserved infusion paste. Stir, scraping up the brown bits. Transfer to a measuring cup, add any collected meat juices, and degrease. Adjust the seasoning.

8. To serve, carve the pork into slices ¼ inch thick. Drizzle 1 tablespoon of the gravy over each portion and pass the remaining gravy at the table.

Zone yield per recipe: 16 protein blocks, 4 carbohydrate blocks

Loin Pork Roast with Black Bean Infusion 6 TO 8 SERVINGS

Be resolute when you trim fat from pork. In the case at hand, you must psychologically prepare yourself to sever the small strip of tenderloin that usually accompanies a loin roast. Unfortunately, its attachment to the roast consists of pure, solid-at-room-temperature, saturated fat. So, if you yearn for pork tenderloin, make one; but when you make a pork roast, do not get sidetracked by concerns about "waste." If you spare that seductive morsel, its thick coat of fat may end up in your arteries and on the lipid profile at your next medical check-up. To avoid waste, I salvage any lean meat from the severed tenderloin and freeze it until I have enough for another purpose. Eventually I get around to using it in a stir-fry or stuffing. | A 3¾ pound roast at the meat counter will weigh just over 3 pounds trimmed—enough for 8 insulin-conscious eaters or fewer unconscious ones. Do not fear that it will be dry without its fat: The delicious infusion paste will keep it moist.

NUTRITIONAL ANALYSIS PER SERVING: 299 CALORIES, 32 G PROTEIN, 8 G CARBOHYDRATE, 14 G FAT (4 G SATURATED), 85 MG CHOLESTEROL, 179 MG SODIUM, 1 G FIBER

Loin Pork Roast with Black Bean Infusion (continued)

Infusion Paste

2   teaspoons peanut or canola oil

3   tablespoons minced scallions
    (white parts only)

2   tablespoons minced fresh ginger

2   tablespoons fermented black beans,
    rinsed, patted dry, and coarsely
    chopped

¼   teaspoon hot red pepper flakes

¾   cup Smoked Allium Paste (page 22)

1   teaspoon fructose
    Salt and freshly ground
    black pepper

3¾ pound boneless loin pork roast,
    visible fat removed (about
    3 pounds trimmed)
    Salt and freshly ground black
    pepper

1   teaspoon peanut or canola oil

1   cup chicken broth

1   teaspoon fructose

1. To make the infusion paste, heat the oil in a small nonstick skillet over medium heat. Add the scallions, ginger, black beans, and pepper flakes and sauté until soft, about 2 minutes. Transfer to a bowl and cool to room temperature. Add the smoked allium paste and fructose and blend well. Season to taste with salt and pepper. Set aside. (The infusion paste can be made up to 2 days in advance and refrigerated.)

2. Preheat the oven to 325° F. Untie the roast and trim all visible fat. To butterfly the roast, bisect the roast lengthwise to within ½ inch of the bottom surface. *Do not cut all the way through it.* Open up the 2 lobes like a book. Make a similar length-wise slit through each lobe but stop again ½ inch above the bottom surface. You now have 4 lobes and the roast should lie relatively flat.

3. Lay the butterflied meat flat on a work surface. Season both sides of the roast generously with salt and pepper. Place cut side up. Reserve 3 tablespoons infusion paste for flavoring the gravy. With a spatula, spread half the remaining paste over the exposed surface, including inside the crevices. Roll up the roast jelly roll style, but not too tightly or the paste will ooze out. Secure with butcher's twine.

4. Make a roast-shaped "footprint" with the oil in a large cast-iron skillet over medium-high heat. Brown the roast on all sides. Remove from the heat. Spread the remaining half of the infusion paste over the top and sides of the roast and transfer to the oven.

5. For slightly pink meat, roast for 15 to 25 minutes per pound to an internal temperature of 150° F on an instant-read thermometer. Transfer the meat to a platter and let it rest for 5 to 10 minutes. (The temperature will continue to rise during resting.)

6. In the skillet over low heat, combine the chicken broth, fructose, and 2 tablespoons of the reserved infusion paste. Simmer, stirring and scraping up the brown bits. Taste and add the remaining 1 tablespoon infusion paste, if desired. Transfer to a measuring cup, add any collected meat juices, and degrease.

7. Slice the pork and drizzle 1 table-spoon of the gravy over each portion. Pass any extra gravy at the table.

Zone yield per recipe: 32 protein blocks, 5 carbohydrate blocks

Pork Tenderloin with Plum Sauce 4 SERVINGS Most commercial plum sauces

contain high-glycemic sweetening agents, such as sugar and high-fructose corn syrup. In addition, their dull flavor rarely makes them worth their 5 or more grams of carbohydrate per tablespoon. This homemade plum sauce contains about 2 grams of low-glycemic carbohydrate per tablespoon and has the bright, tangy flavor of fresh oranges and plums. For variety, try it with sautéed chicken or duck breasts.

NUTRITIONAL ANALYSIS PER SERVING: 212 CALORIES, 30 G PROTEIN, 5 G CARBOHYDRATE,
7 G FAT (2 G SATURATED), 82 MG CHOLESTEROL, 58 MG SODIUM, 0 G FIBER

Plum Sauce

6   tablespoons fresh orange juice

1   cup pitted and halved sweet black plums

1   tablespoon fructose

1   teaspoon cider vinegar

2   teaspoons extra virgin olive oil

1¼ pounds trimmed pork tenderloin
     Salt and freshly ground black pepper

2   tablespoons cider vinegar

1. To make the sauce, place the plums, cut side down, in a nonreactive skillet or saucepan just large enough to hold them in a single layer. Add the orange juice, fructose, and vinegar. Bring to a boil, reduce the heat to low, and simmer for 5 minutes.

Turn the plums over and simmer for 10 minutes, or until the plums are very tender and the liquid is syrupy. Transfer to a food processor and puree. Set aside ½ cup and reserve the remainder for another use. (The sauce can be stored in the refrigerator for up to 1 week or frozen for up to 6 months.)

2. Preheat the oven to 375° F. Brush a flameproof roasting pan with 1 teaspoon of the oil. Brush the tenderloin with the remaining 1 teaspoon oil and season well with salt and pepper. Place the meat in the pan, folding the thin end under itself for even cooking. For slightly pink meat, roast for 20 to 30 minutes, to an internal temperature of 150° F on an instant-read thermometer inserted into the thickest portion of the meat. Transfer the meat to

a platter and let it rest for 5 to 10 minutes. (The temperature will continue to rise during resting.)

3. Add 2 tablespoons cider vinegar to the roasting pan, stirring and scraping up the brown bits. Add the reserved ½ cup plum sauce and place over low heat until warm. Season with salt and pepper.

4. Thickly slice the pork on an angle and drizzle 1 tablespoon of the sauce over each portion. Pass the extra sauce at the table.

Zone yield per recipe: 16 protein blocks, 2 carbohydrate blocks (1 tablespoon sauce = 0 protein blocks, ¼ carbohydrate block)

Roasted Pork Tenderloin with Ancho Chile Infusion 6 SERVINGS

At half the price, pork tenderloin is just as tender and flavorful as filet mignon. It also contains less than half the fat, which makes it more healthful than beef but more vulnerable to drying out. With the help of a moist infusion paste, it will stay juicy during roasting. In the savory version below, black pepper, not the ancho, contributes the heat. If you prefer mild flavors, decrease it by half.

NUTRITIONAL ANALYSIS PER SERVING: 185 CALORIES, 25 G PROTEIN, 7 G CARBOHYDRATE, 6 G FAT (2 G SATURATED), 65 MG CHOLESTEROL, 292 MG SODIUM, 1 G FIBER

Ancho Chile Infusion Paste

1	large dried ancho chile
⅓	cup Smoked Allium Paste (page 22)
1	teaspoon fructose
½	teaspoon ground cumin
½	teaspoon freshly ground black pepper
¼	teaspoon salt or to taste
⅛	teaspoon ground cloves
⅛	teaspoon cayenne pepper
2	(¾-pound) pork tenderloins, visible fat removed
	Salt and freshly ground black pepper
1	cup chicken broth
1	teaspoon fructose
	Salt and freshly ground black pepper

1. To make the infusion paste, combine the chile with water to cover in a small saucepan. Bring to a boil, reduce the heat, and simmer until soft, about 10 minutes. Remove the chile from the pot. When it is cool enough to handle, remove the stem and seeds. Coarsely chop the remaining chile flesh and transfer to a food processor. Add the smoked allium paste, fructose, cumin, black pepper, salt, cloves, and cayenne and process to a smooth puree. Transfer to a small bowl and adjust the seasoning. Set aside. (The infusion paste can be made up to 3 days in advance and refrigerated.)

2. To butterfly the roast, make a lengthwise slit down the center of each tenderloin to within ½ inch of the bottom surface. *Do not cut all the way through it.* Now make similar lengthwise slits down the center of each half, so that each tenderloin now has 4 little "lobes."

3. Lay the meat flat on a work surface. Season both sides of the tenderloins with salt and pepper. Reserve about one-third of the infusion paste for flavoring the gravy. Divide the remainder between the 2 tenderloins, spreading it evenly across the inner surfaces and within the crevices. Roll each back into its original shapes and secure with butcher's twine.

4. Preheat the oven to 350° F. Place the tenderloins in a small flame-proof roasting pan or cast-iron skillet just large enough to hold them. For slightly pink meat, roast for approximately 20 minutes, to an internal temperature of 150° F on an instant-read thermometer. Transfer the meat to a platter and allow to rest for 5 to 10 minutes. (The temperature of the meat will continue to rise.)

5. Place the roasting pan over medium heat and add the chicken broth. Stir, scraping up the brown bits. Add the reserved infusion paste and 1 teaspoon fructose and blend well.

6. Slice the pork thickly on an angle and serve immediately with 1 tablespoon of the gravy drizzled on each portion. Pass the extra gravy at the table.

Zone yield per recipe: 21 protein blocks, 4 carbohydrate blocks

Smothered Pork Tenderloin with Vidalia Onions and Grapes

4 SERVINGS Carefully trimmed cooked pork tenderloin contains only 1.3 grams of fat per ounce. So as you trim, be thorough in your work and do not be distressed by the small amount of meat lost along with the fat. This waste is small compared to the human loss associated with excess saturated fat consumption. Also, be sure you do not overcook your lean little tenderloin. If you're careful, it will live up to its name, but it can turn tough and dry in a hurry.

NUTRITIONAL ANALYSIS PER SERVING: 213 CALORIES, 30 G PROTEIN, 9 G CARBOHYDRATE, 6 G FAT (2 G SATURATED), 82 MG CHOLESTEROL, 60 MG SODIUM, I G FIBER

1¼ pounds pork tenderloin, visible fat removed

Salt and freshly ground black pepper

1   teaspoon extra virgin olive oil

½   cup sliced Vidalia onion

1½ cups grapes (preferably Concord)

1   tablespoon balsamic vinegar

1. Preheat the oven to 450° F. Season the pork generously with salt and pepper. Heat the oil in a cast-iron skillet over medium-high heat and add the pork. (If necessary, cut the pork into 2 pieces to fit the skillet.) Brown the pork on all sides and transfer to the oven.

2. For slightly pink meat, roast for approximately 10 minutes, to an internal temperature of 150° F on an instant-read thermometer inserted into the thickest portion of the meat. Transfer the meat to a platter and allow to rest for 5 to 10 minutes. (The internal temperature of the meat will continue to rise.)

3. Meanwhile, place the skillet over medium heat and add the onion. Cook, stirring frequently, for about 3 minutes, until it begins to soften and brown. Add the grapes and continue cooking for 2 to 3 minutes, until the first few grapes split. Stir in the vinegar and any accumulated meat juices. Remove from the heat and adjust the seasoning.

4. Thickly slice the pork on the diagonal and smother with the grape-and-onion mixture. Serve immediately.

Zone yield per recipe: 16 protein blocks, 4 carbohydrate blocks

Verjus-Marinated Grilled Pork Tenderloin

4 SERVINGS Thanks to Jim Neal, a young California chef, Fusion Foods Napa Valley Verjus has become available to home cooks (see Note below). Used by the French for centuries, verjus is the unfermented, pressed juice of unripe wine grapes. Its red and white varieties evoke Beaujolais and Gewürztraminer respectively. Fruity, mildly tart verjus has many applications as a wine-friendly alternative to vinegar. Use it for dressing salads, deglazing pans, poaching fish, and marinating meats. It contains only 2 grams of carbohydrate per tablespoon, which is 25 to 50 percent less than most balsamic vinegars. | Jim generously allowed me to adapt his Napa Valley spareribs recipe to a leaner protein source. Compared to other cuts of pork, a well-trimmed tenderloin offers plenty of rich, sweet taste with much less fat. Verjus provides the perfect counterpoint.

NUTRITIONAL ANALYSIS PER SERVING: 237 CALORIES, 30 G PROTEIN, 13 G CARBOHYDRATE, 7 G FAT (2 G SATURATED), 82 MG CHOLESTEROL, 574 MG SODIUM, 0 G FIBER

Verjus Marinade

1   cup red verjus

2   tablespoons soy sauce

1½ teaspoons extra virgin olive oil

1   tablespoon fructose or molasses

1   garlic clove, crushed

⅛   teaspoon dry mustard

⅛   teaspoon ground cumin

⅛   teaspoon ground cloves

⅛   teaspoon ground nutmeg

⅛   teaspoon cayenne pepper

1¼ pounds pork tenderloin, visible fat removed

1. To make the marinade, combine the verjus, soy sauce, oil, fructose, garlic, mustard, cumin, cloves, nutmeg, and cayenne in a bowl or measuring cup and whisk to blend. Place the pork in a nonreactive container. Add the marinade and turn to coat. Refrigerate overnight, turning the meat occasionally.

2. Prepare a hot fire in the grill. Remove the pork from the marinade and transfer the marinade to a small saucepan.

3. Grill the pork for about 15 minutes, rolling it around, until cooked through but not dry. The internal temperature should register 150° F on an instant-read thermometer inserted into the thickest portion of the meat. Allow the pork to rest for 5 minutes. (The temperature will continue to rise.)

4. Meanwhile, bring the marinade to a boil, reduce the heat, and simmer until reduced in volume and syrupy.

5. Thickly slice the pork on an angle and serve with 1 tablespoon of the sauce drizzled over the meat. Pass the extra sauce at the table.

Note: Napa Valley brand verjus is available from Fusion Foods, PO Box 542, Rutherford, CA 94573; 707-963-0206.

Zone yield per recipe: 16 protein blocks, 4 carbohydrate blocks (1 tablespoon sauce = 0 protein blocks, ⅓ carbohydrate block)

Verjus-Marinated Grilled Pork Tenderloin served with Broiled Fruit Skewers (page 205)

Grilled Pork Cutlets with Orange

4 SERVINGS Pork cutlets come from the sirloin end of the pork roast and reflect its flavorful, tender character. They are wonderfully convenient—requiring less trimming and less cooking time than a tenderloin. Cutlets contain more intrinsic fat (1.9 grams per raw ounce compared with 0.7 grams), so they should be an occasional treat rather than regular fare. The sauce contains an elegant, but optional, 1½ teaspoons Grand Marnier (5 grams of carbohydrate) which will not be sorely missed if eliminated.

NUTRITIONAL ANALYSIS PER SERVING: 180 CALORIES, 24 G PROTEIN, 6 G CARBOHYDRATE, 6 G FAT (2 G SATURATED), 65 MG CHOLESTEROL, 690 MG SODIUM, 0 G FIBER

Marinade

2 tablespoons light soy sauce

1 tablespoon grated fresh ginger with juice

2 teaspoons minced orange zest

1½ teaspoons fructose

1 teaspoon toasted sesame oil

1 pound pork cutlets, about ⅓ inch thick, visible fat removed

½ cup fresh orange juice

1½ teaspoons light soy sauce

1½ teaspoons Grand Marnier (optional)

½ teaspoon toasted sesame oil

Salt and freshly ground black pepper

1. To make the marinade, combine the soy sauce, ginger, orange zest, fructose, and ½ teaspoon of the sesame oil in a small bowl or measuring cup. Whisk to dissolve the fructose. Place the pork in a nonreactive container, add the marinade, and turn to coat well. Marinate overnight in the refrigerator, turning several times.

2. Prepare a hot fire in the grill. Remove the pork from the marinade and set aside. Transfer the marinade to a small nonreactive saucepan. Add the orange juice, soy sauce, and Grand Marnier, if using. Turn the heat to medium-high and boil to reduce the volume by half. Remove from the heat and add the remaining ½ teaspoon sesame oil.

3. Season the cutlets with salt and pepper. Grill for 2 to 3 minutes per side, until cooked through but not dry. Remove to a serving platter.

4. Serve immediately with 1 tablespoon of the sauce drizzled on each portion, and the extra sauce passed at the table.

Zone yield per recipe: 16 protein blocks, 3 carbohydrate blocks

Sirloin Tip Veal Roast with Orange-Herb Infusion **6 TO 8 SERVINGS**

A sirloin tip veal roast is a lovely cut of meat, leaner and more tender than the loin. Under the moist protection of an infusion paste, it will not dry out during roasting. The elegant simplicity of this preparation makes it perfect for a dinner party.

NUTRITIONAL ANALYSIS PER SERVING: 245 CALORIES, 33 G PROTEIN, 5 G CARBOHYDRATE, 9 G FAT (3 G SATURATED), 127 MG CHOLESTEROL, 382 MG SODIUM, 0 G FIBER

Orange-Herb Infusion Paste

⅓ cup Smoked Allium Paste (page 22)

2 tablespoons minced flat-leaf parsley

2 teaspoons chopped fresh rosemary

2 teaspoons chopped fresh thyme leaves

1 teaspoon grated orange zest

1 teaspoon fructose (optional)

½ teaspoon salt

   Freshly ground black pepper

¾ cup fresh orange juice

1 sirloin tip veal roast, visible fat removed (about 2½ pounds trimmed)

   Salt and freshly ground black pepper

1 teaspoon extra virgin olive oil

1 cup chicken broth

1. To make the infusion paste, combine the smoked allium paste, parsley, rosemary, thyme, orange zest, fructose, if using, and salt in a small bowl or measuring cup. Add pepper to taste. Blend well and set aside. (The infusion paste can be made up to 24 hours in advance and refrigerated.)

2. In a small nonreactive saucepan over medium-high heat, bring the orange juice to a boil and reduce to 3 tablespoons. Cool to room temperature. Add 1 tablespoon of the concentrated juice to the infusion paste and blend well. Reserve the remaining 2 tablespoons concentrated juice for the gravy.

3. Untie the roast and season both sides generously with salt and pepper. Lay the roast flat on a work surface, with the interior surface up. Spread half the infusion paste over the exposed surface and reserve the remaining paste. Roll up the roast and tie with butcher's twine. Any paste that oozes out can be added to the reserved infusion paste.

4. Preheat the oven to 350° F. Over medium-high heat, make a roast-shaped "footprint" with 1 teaspoon oil in a cast-iron skillet or small flameproof roasting pan just large enough to hold the roast. Brown the meat on all sides. Remove the skillet from heat. Spread the remaining paste over the top and sides of the roast and transfer to the oven.

5. Roast for 15 to 25 minutes per pound, to an internal temperature of 135° to 140° F for rare to medium-rare, or to 150° to 155° F for medium. Transfer the meat to a platter and allow it to rest for 5 to 10 minutes.

6. Add the chicken broth and the reserved concentrated orange juice to the skillet over medium heat. Stir, scraping up the brown bits and reduce until slightly syrupy. Add any collected meat juices and degrease.

7. Thickly slice the roast and serve with 1 tablespoon of the gravy spooned over each portion. Pass the additional gravy at the table.

Zone yield per recipe: 32 protein blocks, 4 carbohydrate blocks

Porcini-Laced Veal Roast   8 TO 10 SERVINGS   The night before my sister's wedding,

I wandered into my parents' kitchen at 4 in the morning, where I found my father at the stove, Vulcan-like, tending six enormous veal roasts. He had already hand-washed the quart of porcini he had carried back from Italy expressly for this purpose. When I later made the roast in his honor, he suggested adding a little truffle oil to the dish. If you have this luxury item on hand, taste the sauce first without it and then with—and learn the difference between a cook and a chef.   If you are lucky enough to have an old-fashioned butcher like my *artiste*, Ken O'Reilly, request a roast cut from the hip or, in current parlance, the top butt. Otherwise, use a loin roast.

NUTRITIONAL ANALYSIS PER SERVING: 273 CALORIES, 38 G PROTEIN, 3 G CARBOHYDRATE, 11 G FAT (4 G SATURATED), 150 MG CHOLESTEROL, 147 MG SODIUM, 0 G FIBER

Porcini Paste

2   (⅓-ounce) packages dried porcini (about ⅔ cup)

1   cup water

¼   cup Smoked Allium Paste (page 22)

½   to 1 teaspoon white truffle oil (optional)

Salt and freshly ground black pepper

4   pound boneless veal roast, visible fat removed (about 3¾ pounds trimmed)

Salt and freshly ground black pepper

1   tablespoon minced fresh sage

1   teaspoon extra virgin olive oil

1   cup brown chicken stock or chicken broth

½   to 1 teaspoon white truffle oil (optional)

Porcini-Laced Veal Roast served with steamed green beans

1. To make the porcini paste, combine the mushrooms and water in a small saucepan and bring to a boil. Reduce the heat to low and simmer for 20 minutes. Remove the mushrooms with a slotted spoon and reserve the cooking liquid. Rinse the mushrooms under cold running water, rubbing with your fingers to remove grit. Pat dry on paper towels. Mince by hand or in a food processor.

2. Strain the cooking liquid through a cheesecloth-lined sieve into a clean saucepan. Boil to reduce to 1 tablespoon porcini syrup. Cool to room temperature. In a small bowl, combine the minced mushrooms, porcini syrup, smoked allium paste, truffle oil, if using, and salt and pepper to taste. Blend well. (This paste can be made in advance and refrigerated for up to 1 week or frozen for up to 6 months.)

3. Preheat the oven to 325° F. To butterfly the roast, untie the roast and bisect the roast lengthwise to within ½ inch of the bottom surface. *Do not cut all the way through it.* Open up the 2 lobes like a book. Make a similar lengthwise slit through each lobe but stop again ½ inch above the bottom surface. You now have 4 lobes and the roast should lie relatively flat.

4. Season the meat on both sides with salt and pepper. Lay it flat on a work surface, interior side up. Reserve 1 tablespoon of the porcini paste for flavoring the gravy. Spread the remaining porcini paste evenly over the exposed surface. Starting at one end, roll up the roast jelly roll fashion. Tie with butcher's twine. Rub the minced sage over the exterior.

(continued)

Porcini-Laced Veal Roast (continued)

5. Make a roast-shaped "footprint" with 1 teaspoon oil in a cast iron skillet or flameproof roasting pan over medium-high heat. Brown the roast well on all sides and transfer to the oven.

6. Roast for 15 to 25 minutes per pound, to an internal temperature of 135° to 140° F for rare to medium-rare, 150° to 155° F for medium. Transfer the meat to a platter and let it rest for 5 to 10 minutes.

7. Add the stock and the reserved 1 tablespoon paste to the skillet and stir, scraping up the brown bits. Transfer to a measuring cup along with any collected meat juices and degrease. Add the truffle oil, if using. Season with salt and pepper.

8. Thickly slice the roast and serve immediately with 1 tablespoon of the gravy spooned on each portion. Pass the remaining gravy at the table.

Zone yield per recipe: 48 protein blocks, 3 carbohydrate blocks

Roasted Veal Chops with Sweet Onions and Smoked Portobello Mushrooms **4 SERVINGS** This recipe demonstrates the power of smoked portobello mushrooms. Raw ones need significantly more oil for effective sautéing and contribute much less flavor. So, fill your smoker with portobellos and fire it up.

NUTRITIONAL ANALYSIS PER SERVING: 213 CALORIES, 25 G PROTEIN, 11 G CARBOHYDRATE, 8 G FAT (2 G SATURATED), 96 MG CHOLESTEROL, 88 MG SODIUM, 3 G FIBER

---

4 *(8- to 10-ounce) bone-in veal chops, about 1 inch thick, visible fat removed*

   Salt and freshly ground black pepper

1 *teaspoon extra virgin olive oil*

2 *cups sliced red, Spanish, or Vidalia onions*

2 *cups sliced Smoked Portobello Mushrooms (page 29)*

1. Preheat the oven to 450° F. Season the chops on both sides with salt and pepper. Heat 1 teaspoon olive oil in a cast-iron skillet over high heat. Sear the chops on one side for 2 minutes, then turn the chops and transfer the skillet to the oven. Roast for 6 to 8 minutes for rare to medium-rare. Remove the meat to a platter.

2. Add the onions to the skillet and sauté 2 for 3 minutes over medium-high heat until they soften and brown. At the last minute, stir in the mushrooms, along with any accumulated meat juices. Season well with salt and pepper.

3. Spoon the onions and mushrooms over the meat. Serve immediately.

Zone yield per recipe: 16 protein blocks, 4 carbohydrate blocks

Broiled Veal Chops with Asian Flavors **4 SERVINGS** Loin and rib veal chops

may be pricey, but they are also delicious and easy to prepare. Be aware, however, that chop size varies tremendously and that rib chops generally contain more meat than loin chops of equivalent weight. Naturally, this affects protein content. To be precise about serving size, weigh the meat without the bone after cooking: 1 serving equals 4 ounces, for 29 grams of protein, or 4 Zone protein blocks.

NUTRITIONAL ANALYSIS PER SERVING: 210 CALORIES, 23 G PROTEIN, 6 G CARBOHYDRATE, 9 G FAT (3 G SATURATED), 90 MG CHOLESTEROL, 749 MG SODIUM, 0 G FIBER

Marinade

1½ tablespoons soy sauce

1½ tablespoons sweet bean sauce

2   tablespoons Shaoxing rice wine or dry sherry

2   teaspoons fructose

2   teaspoons toasted sesame oil

4   (8- to 10-ounce) bone-in veal chops, 1 inch thick, visible fat removed

2   tablespoons water

1   tablespoon soy sauce

1   tablespoon Shaoxing rice wine

Salt and freshly ground black pepper

1. To make the marinade, combine the soy sauce, bean sauce, wine, fructose, and sesame oil in a small bowl or measuring cup and whisk to dissolve the fructose. Place the chops in a nonreactive container and add the marinade. Turn to coat the chops. Marinate overnight, turning the chops occasionally.

2. Preheat the broiler with the broiler rack 6 to 8 inches from the flame. Pour the marinade into a small saucepan and bring to a boil. Reduce the heat and simmer for 2 minutes. Remove from the heat. Broil the chops in a flameproof pan for 4 to 6 minutes per side for medium-rare meat, or longer to desired doneness. Transfer the chops to a platter.

3. Add the water, 1 tablespoon soy sauce, 1 tablespoon rice wine, and the marinade to the drippings in the pan. Stir, scraping up the brown bits. Transfer to a measuring cup and degrease.

4. Serve the chops immediately, drizzling 1 tablespoon of the sauce over each portion and passing the extra at the table.

Zone yield per recipe: 16 protein blocks, 2 carbohydrate blocks (1 tablespoon sauce = 0 protein blocks, ⅙ carbohydrate block)

Grilled Veal Flank

4 SERVINGS Veal flank is the smaller, pinker, leaner version of beef flank steak. It responds well to marinades with a hint of sweetness, cooks quickly, and requires close supervision on the grill. If veal flank is unavailable, substitute loin or rib veal chops and grill 3-5 minutes per side for medium rare.

NUTRITIONAL ANALYSIS PER SERVING: 168 CALORIES, 27 G PROTEIN, 0 G CARBOHYDRATE, 6 G FAT (2 G SATURATED), 112 MG CHOLESTEROL, 93 MG SODIUM, 0 G FIBER

Marinade

3   tablespoons Japanese soy sauce

1   tablespoon Dijon mustard

1   tablespoon fructose

1   teaspoon toasted sesame oil

1½ pound veal flank

   Salt and freshly ground
   black pepper

1. To make the marinade, combine the soy sauce, mustard, fructose, and oil in a small bowl or measuring cup and whisk to blend. Place the veal in a nonreactive container and add the marinade. Turn the meat several times to coat with the marinade. Marinate overnight in the refrigerator.

2. Prepare a hot fire in the grill. Remove the veal from the marinade and pat dry with paper towels. Season both sides with salt and pepper. Grill for about 3 minutes per side. Transfer the meat to a cutting board and allow to rest for 5 minutes.

3. To serve, slice the meat on an angle and serve with any accumulated juices.

Zone yield per recipe: 16 protein blocks, less than one carbohydrate block

Spicy Grilled Chinese Veal Chops **4 SERVINGS** Through a business venture begun

by my father more than 30 years ago, my family has become deeply attached to China and the Chinese people.

My parents, brother, and sister have spent considerable time there wheeling, dealing, and eating (not necessarily

in that order). As far as we know, the Chinese do not eat veal, but if they did, they might prepare it this way.

The marinade evolved from the extraordinarily flavorful "Barbecued Chinese Spareribs" in Ken Hom's *Quick*

and Easy Chinese Cooking.

NUTRITIONAL ANALYSIS PER SERVING: 228 CALORIES, 24 G PROTEIN, 11 G CARBOHYDRATE,
9 G FAT (2 G SATURATED), 96 MG CHOLESTEROL, 795 MG SODIUM, 1 G FIBER

Marinade

2   tablespoons sweet bean sauce

2   tablespoons light soy sauce

2   tablespoons tomato paste
    (preferably double concentrated)

2   tablespoons Shaoxing rice wine
    or dry sherry

2   tablespoons minced garlic

2   tablespoons minced fresh ginger

1   tablespoon fructose

2   teaspoons chili bean sauce
    (also known as hot bean paste
    or Sichuan bean paste)

1   teaspoon toasted sesame oil

4   *(8- to 10-ounce) bone-in veal*
    chops, 1-inch thick, visible fat
    removed

1. To make the marinade, combine the bean sauce, soy sauce, tomato paste, wine, garlic, ginger, fructose, chili bean sauce, and sesame oil in a small bowl or measuring cup and whisk to dissolve the fructose. Place the chops in a nonreactive container and add the marinade. Turn to coat the chops. Marinate overnight, turning the chops occasionally.

2. Prepare a hot fire in the grill. Pour the marinade into a small saucepan and bring to a boil. Reduce the heat to low and simmer for 3 minutes. Set aside. Grill the chops for 3 to 5 minutes per side for medium-rare.

3. Serve immediately, spooning 1 tablespoon of the sauce over each chop and passing the remaining sauce at the table.

Zone yield per recipe: 16 protein blocks, 4 carbohydrate blocks (1 tablespoon sauce = 0 protein blocks, 1/3 carbohydrate block)

Spicy Grilled Chinese Veal Chops served with
Hot Sesame Green Beans (page 171)

Beef, Lamb, and Ostrich

Red meat has been the bad boy of American gastronomy since the famous Framingham Heart Study (begun in Massachusetts in 1948) established a positive correlation between blood cholesterol levels and heart attacks. Although the precise roles of *dietary* cholesterol and saturated fat (a building block of cholesterol) have been questioned, health-conscious Americans—including myself—responded by limiting their intake of red meat. Over the last few years, I have also learned that saturated fat raises insulin levels through a negative effect on muscle cell membranes. As a result, I am especially careful about the saturated fat content in the food I eat.

Can anything be said in favor of red meat? Absolutely! First, it tastes great and adds a delicious set of protein possibilities to the challenge of balancing carbohydrate. In that sense, it helps me avoid my greatest enemy: food boredom. Nutritionally it's a potent source of B vitamins and minerals. Since I love red meat, and value its nutrient contribution, I have found ways to minimize saturated fat content so that I can include it in my diet once in a while.

First, I start with the leanest cuts: loin, tenderloin, and sirloin. Then, because I have zero tolerance for visible (i.e., saturated) fat, I trim meat meticulously—in most cases, before cooking. (If I grill a whole sirloin steak, I generally trim it after cooking to keep the perimeter from drying out.) I frequently cook meat by grilling or broiling, methods that decrease total fat, taking saturated fat along with it. Degreasing sauces also helps. Finally, I take advantage of a revolutionary development in the world of red meat: the rise of ostrich.

Ostrich is a tasty, tender, extremely lean red meat with a flavor that evokes both beef and lamb. It contains less than 1 gram of fat per ounce (cooked weight), making it equivalent in fat content to venison or about 70 percent leaner than beef tenderloin. Ostrich boasts a lower cholesterol content than chicken, turkey, venison, or buffalo. In additional, it packs more iron per ounce than beef. Recently, fresh ground ostrich and fillets have become available in specialty food markets. They cost about as much per pound as beef tenderloin, but there is absolutely no waste. I highly recommend them for red meat lovers who wish to limit their saturated fat intake.

Favorite Protein/Carbohydrate Pairings:

Grilled Sirloin with Spiced Ancho Sauce (page 126) and Black-eyed Pea Salad with Radishes and Cucumbers (page 190)

Roast Leg of Lamb with Pesto Infusion (page 136) and Roasted Garlic Asparagus (page 167)

Grilled Ostrich Fillets with Rosemary (page 138) and Lentil Salad with Hijike and Roasted Red Peppers (page 200)

Filet Mignons with Porcini "Butter" (page 122) served with sautéed broccoli rabe and garlic

Filet Mignons with Porcini "Butter" 4 SERVINGS In recent years, flavored

butters have slipped into vogue as garnishes for all types of protein. They enrich and embellish meat, making it more festive and interesting. Unfortunately, they also saturate it with undesirable fat. With only 2 grams of carbohydrate per tablespoon, the pseudo-butter in this recipe adds negligible fat to the beef while investing it with intense flavor and elegance. (Pictured on page 121.)

NUTRITIONAL ANALYSIS PER SERVING: 211 CALORIES, 25 G PROTEIN, 5 G CARBOHYDRATE, 10 G FAT (3 G SATURATED), 71 MG CHOLESTEROL, 55 MG SODIUM, 1 G FIBER

Porcini "Butter"

1   *(⅓-ounce) package dried porcini
     mushrooms (about ⅓ cup)*

1   *cup water*

¼   *cup Smoked Allium Paste (page 22)*
     Salt and fresh ground black pepper

1   *pound filet mignons, 1½ to 2 inches
     thick, visible fat removed*
     *Salt and freshly ground
     black pepper*

2   *tablespoons chopped fresh chives*

1. To make the porcini butter, combine the porcini and water in a small saucepan and bring to a boil. Reduce the heat to very low and simmer for 20 minutes. Reserving the liquid, remove the mushrooms with a slotted spoon. Set the mushrooms aside. Strain the liquid through a cheesecloth-lined sieve into a clean saucepan. Over high heat, boil the liquid to reduce to 2 tablespoons mushroom syrup.

2. Meanwhile, wash the mushrooms under running water, rubbing with your fingers to remove any grit. Pat dry between layers of paper towels. Gently squeeze to remove excess water. Mince in a food processor. Transfer to a small bowl and add the mushroom syrup and smoked allium paste. Season with salt and pepper and blend well. (The "butter" can be made up to 24 hours in advance and refrigerated. Bring to room temperature or warm in a microwave before serving.)

3. Set the rack in the upper third of the oven and preheat to 500° F. Place a roasting pan or cast-iron skillet in the oven for 5 minutes. Season the beef generously with salt and pepper. Place the meat in the hot pan and roast for 12 to 15 minutes, or until an instant-read thermometer inserted into the

thickest part of the meat reads 120° F for rare, 125° to 130° F for medium-rare, 135° to 140° F for medium. Transfer the meat to a cutting board and allow to rest for 5 minutes. (The temperature of the meat will continue to rise.)

4. Thickly slice on the diagonal and distribute among 4 plates. Spoon a tablespoon of the porcini "butter" across the slices and garnish with the chives. Serve immediately, passing the extra porcini "butter" at the table.

Zone yield per recipe: 16 protein blocks, 1 carbohydrate block (1 tablespoon "butter" = 0 protein blocks, ¼ carbohydrate block)

Filet Mignons with Shallots and Garlic 4 **SERVINGS** Meticulously trimmed

beef tenderloin contains just under 3 grams of fat per ounce, about a third of which is saturated. While a chicken

breast contains significantly less fat, beef supplies 4 times as much iron, so enjoying beef on occasion is completely

justified.   My husband, however, needs no such justification. He grew up in Texas where beef was practically

the state food. He loves it and considers himself quite the expert. First, it must be perfectly cooked. (The method

below is almost foolproof.) Second, it must have the perfect accompaniment, and mushrooms lead his list.

I serve these steaks with Mushroom Hash (page 176) or Smoked Portobello Mushrooms (page 29).

NUTRITIONAL ANALYSIS PER SERVING: 194 CALORIES, 24 G PROTEIN, 1 G CARBOHYDRATE, 10 G FAT (3 G SATURATED), 71 MG CHOLESTEROL, 54 MG SODIUM, 0 G FIBER

1   *pound filet mignons, 1½ to 2 inches thick, visible fat removed*

Salt and freshly ground black pepper

1   *teaspoon extra virgin olive oil or porcini mushroom oil*

Sauce

1   *tablespoon minced shallots*

1   *teaspoon minced garlic*

1   *tablespoon balsamic or sherry vinegar*

¼   *cup water or fat-free beef broth*

Salt and freshly ground black pepper

1. Set the rack in the upper third of the oven and preheat to 500° F. Place a cast-iron skillet in the oven for 5 minutes. Season the beef generously with salt and pepper, brush on both sides with the oil, and place in the hot pan. Roast for 12 to 15 minutes, or until an instant-read thermometer inserted into the thickest part of the meat reads 120° F for rare, 125° to 130° F for medium-rare, or 135° to 140° F for medium. Transfer the meat to a cutting board and allow to rest for 5 minutes. (The temperature of the meat will continue to rise.)

2. Place the skillet over low heat. Add the shallots, garlic, vinegar, water, salt and pepper to taste, and any collected meat juices. Simmer, scraping up the brown bits, for about 2 minutes, until the garlic and shallots are tender. Remove from the heat.

3. Thickly slice the beef on the diagonal, distribute among 4 plates, and drizzle 1 tablespoon of the sauce on each portion. Serve immediately, passing the extra sauce at the table.

Zone yield per recipe: 16 protein blocks, less than one carbohydrate block

Five-Spice Flank Steak 4 SERVINGS A Chinese condiment used in sauces and marinades, sweet bean sauce is the standard accompaniment to Peking duck in northern China. In the United States, Chinese restaurants frequently present the dish with hoisin sauce. This substitution imports more than a subtle difference in flavor: It increases carbohydrate density. Hoisin sauce contains approximately 10 grams of carbohydrate per tablespoon compared with 4 grams in sweet bean sauce. In the potent five-spice marinade below, it means the difference between 30 grams of carbohydrate and 12 grams. Saving those 18 grams of carbohydrate makes sweet bean sauce just a little bit sweeter.

NUTRITIONAL ANALYSIS PER SERVING: 273 CALORIES, 29 G PROTEIN, 11 G CARBOHYDRATE, 11 G FAT (4 G SATURATED), 47 MG CHOLESTEROL, 984 MG SODIUM, 1 G FIBER

Five-Spice Seasoning Paste

3   tablespoons sweet bean sauce

3   tablespoons minced scallions (white parts only)

1   tablespoon minced garlic

1   tablespoon minced fresh ginger

2½ tablespoons soy sauce

1   tablespoon Shaoxing rice wine or dry sherry

1   tablespoon bean sauce

1   tablespoon fructose

1   teaspoon five-spice powder

1   teaspoon peanut or canola oil

1   pound flank steak, visible fat removed

1. To make the seasoning paste, combine the sweet bean sauce, scallions, garlic, ginger, soy sauce, rice wine, bean sauce, fructose, five-spice powder, and oil in a small bowl or measuring cup and whisk to dissolve the fructose. Place the steak in a nonreactive container and spread the seasoning paste over both sides. Cover and refrigerate overnight.

2. Prepare a hot fire in the grill. Grill the steak for 4 to 7 minutes per side for rare (120° F) to medium rare (125° to 130° F). Remove to a cutting board and allow to rest for 5 minutes.

3. Slice on an angle and serve immediately.

Zone yield per recipe: 16 protein blocks, 5 carbohydrate blocks

Flank Steak with Sichuan Peppercorns **4 SERVINGS** Reddish-brown Sichuan

peppercorns are not really peppercorns at all, but rather dried berries. They appear in five-spice powder as well as in Chinese marinades, sauces, and seasoned dipping salt. Their distinctive, sharp flavor often defines a dish and no adequate substitutes exist. Toasting optimizes their flavor.

NUTRITIONAL ANALYSIS PER SERVING: 258 CALORIES, 28 G PROTEIN, 8 G CARBOHYDRATE, 12 G FAT (4 G SATURATED), 47 MG CHOLESTEROL, 177 MG SODIUM, 1 G FIBER

Sichuan Peppercorn Seasoning Paste

- ¼ cup minced scallions (white parts only)
- 2 tablespoons sweet bean sauce
- 1 tablespoon minced garlic
- 1 tablespoon minced fresh ginger
- 1 tablespoon fructose
- 2 teaspoons chili bean sauce (also known as hot bean paste or Sichuan bean paste)
- 2 teaspoons toasted sesame oil
- 1 teaspoon Sichuan peppercorns, toasted and ground
- 1 pound flank steak, visible fat removed

1. To make the seasoning paste, combine the scallions, sweet bean sauce, garlic, ginger, fructose, chili bean sauce, sesame oil, and ground peppercorns in a small bowl or measuring cup. Whisk to dissolve the fructose. Place the steak in a nonreactive container and apply the paste to both sides. Cover and refrigerate overnight.

2. Prepare a hot fire in the grill. Grill the steak for 4 to 7 minutes per side for rare (120° F) to medium-rare (125° to 130° F). Remove to a cutting board and allow the meat to rest for 5 minutes.

3. Slice on an angle and serve immediately.

Note: To toast Sichuan peppercorns, place a skillet over medium heat and add the peppercorns. Roll them around either by shaking the skillet or stir-frying for 3 to 5 minutes, until they begin to brown slightly. Remove from heat and allow to cool. Grind in a pepper mill or spice grinder.

Zone yield per recipe: 16 protein blocks, 3 carbohydrate blocks

Grilled Sirloin with Spiced Ancho Sauce 4 SERVINGS The ancho chile, a dried

poblano, is the most commonly used chile in Mexico and the predominant constituent of chili powder (comprising up to 80 percent). Its large, burgundy-black pod provides rich flavor, little heat, and more pulp than most other chiles. Combined with smoked allium paste and a few spices, the ancho needs only a charcoal-grilled steak to create a spectacular protein centerpiece. One tablespoon of the sauce contains 3 grams of carbohydrate.

NUTRITIONAL ANALYSIS PER SERVING: 237 CALORIES, 29 G PROTEIN, 10 G CARBOHYDRATE, 9 G FAT (3 G SATURATED), 81 MG CHOLESTEROL, 260 MG SODIUM, 1 G FIBER

Spiced Ancho Sauce

1   dried ancho chile

⅓   cup Smoked Allium Paste (page 22)

1   teaspoon Worcestershire sauce

1   teaspoon tomato paste

1   teaspoon fructose

½   teaspoon ground cumin

½   teaspoon freshly ground black pepper

¼   teaspoon salt or to taste

⅛   teaspoon ground allspice

⅛   teaspoon cayenne pepper

Water (optional)

1   boneless sirloin steak, 1 inch thick (about 1¼ pounds)

Salt and freshly ground black pepper

1. To make the sauce, place the ancho chile in a small saucepan with water to cover. Bring to a boil, reduce the heat, and simmer until soft, about 10 minutes. Remove from the pot and let cool. When the chile is cool enough to handle, remove the stem and seeds. Coarsely chop the flesh and transfer to a food processor. Add the smoked allium paste, Worcestershire, tomato paste, fructose, cumin, pepper, salt, allspice, and cayenne. Process to a smooth puree. Thin with a little water, if necessary. Place in a small bowl and set aside. (The sauce can be made in advance and refrigerated for up to 1 week or frozen for up to 6 months. Bring to room temperature before serving.)

2. Prepare a hot fire in the grill. Season the steak generously with salt and pepper. Grill for 3 to 5 minutes per side for rare (120° F) to medium-rare (125° to 130° F). Remove to a cutting board and allow the meat to rest for 5 minutes.

3. Trim away all visible fat, slice, and serve with 1 tablespoon of the sauce alongside. Pass the extra sauce at the table.

Zone yield per recipe: 16 protein blocks, 4 carbohydrate blocks (1 tablespoon sauce = 0 protein blocks, ⅓ carbohydrate block)

Sirloin Burger on a Smoked Portobello "Bun" 4 SERVINGS

When I presented this for dinner one night, it immediately transported my husband back to high school, evoking midnight rides to Dallas burger joints. The grown-up, low-glycemic platter below no more resembles those of memory's greasy spoon than he does his high school self. They have both evolved in more interesting and less risky directions. | Serve with a fresh fruit salad for dessert or increase the carbohydrate components below (mushrooms, tomato, onion, lettuce, and ketchup).

NUTRITIONAL ANALYSIS PER SERVING: 323 CALORIES, 35 G PROTEIN, 14 G CARBOHYDRATE, 15 G FAT (8 G SATURATED), 99 MG CHOLESTEROL, 500 MG SODIUM, 4 G FIBER

Blue-Cheese Dressing

¼ cup nonfat buttermilk

1 ounce blue cheese, crumbled

1 tablespoon low-fat mayonnaise

1 tablespoon white balsamic or white wine vinegar

2 tablespoons minced flat-leaf parsley

¼ teaspoon salt or to taste

1⅓ pounds extra-lean ground sirloin

Salt and freshly ground black pepper

8 cups chopped romaine lettuce

4 medium Smoked Portobello Mushrooms (page 29)

4 slices ripe tomato

4 slices red onion (optional)

4 tablespoons Smoked Tomato Ketchup (page 39)

1. To make the dressing, combine the buttermilk, blue cheese, mayonnaise, and vinegar in a small bowl or 2-cup measure and emulsify using a stick blender. (Alternatively, combine the ingredients in a traditional blender and emulsify.) Stir in the parsley and salt. Set aside.

2. Prepare a hot fire in the grill. Place the beef in a bowl and season generously with salt and pepper. Form into 4 patties approximately 1 inch thick. Grill for 4 minutes per side for medium-rare.

3. Meanwhile, place the romaine in a bowl and toss with the dressing. When the burgers are almost done, warm the mushrooms in the microwave and place gill side up on 4 plates. Place 1 burger on each mushroom and top with a slice each of tomato and onion. Spoon a dollop of the ketchup on top. Place a serving of the romaine salad to the side. Serve immediately.

Zone yield per recipe: 17 protein blocks, 4 carbohydrate block

Hamburgers with Oyster Sauce

4 SERVINGS A classic Chinese condiment, oyster sauce is a silky brown sauce made from extracts of oysters cooked in soy sauce and seasonings. In the proper company, its rich consistency compensates for absent fat. Ironically, the best brands come from Thailand. They provide more intense flavor and lower carbohydrate counts per tablespoon than most Chinese varieties. Chuew Huad oyster sauce, for example, contains only 1 gram of carbohydrate per tablespoon. It is available in Asian markets.

NUTRITIONAL ANALYSIS PER SERVING: 270 CALORIES, 30 G PROTEIN, 8 G CARBOHYDRATE, 13 G FAT (6 G SATURATED), 96 MG CHOLESTEROL, 631 MG SODIUM, 1 G FIBER

⅓ cup sliced Smoked Leeks (page 28)

⅓ cup sliced Slow-Roasted Plum Tomatoes (page 34)

1⅓ pounds extra-lean ground beef

2 tablespoons oyster sauce

1 tablespoon soy sauce

1 teaspoon fructose

Salt and freshly ground black pepper

1 teaspoon peanut or canola oil

1. Combine the leeks and tomatoes in a food processor and pulse until minced, scraping down the sides as needed. Transfer to a bowl. Add the beef, oyster sauce, soy sauce, fructose, and salt and pepper to taste. Blend well without overworking. Form into 4 patties, approximately 1 inch thick.

2. Preheat the broiler. Brush the broiler pan with oil, and broil the burgers for 4 to 5 minutes per side to medium-rare. (Alternatively, you can heat the oil in a nonstick skillet and sauté the burgers over medium-high heat for 4 to 5 minutes per side.) Serve immediately.

Zone yield per recipe: 16 protein blocks, 3 carbohydrate blocks

Spicy Beef Patties with Sweet Bean Ketchup

4 SERVINGS When a burger loses its high-glycemic mate (i.e., the bun), creativity must intervene to prevent grief. If the burger remains solo, it will forever mourn the loss of its companion. To help the burger adjust to single life, treat it to new experiences. Here, lively condiments and seasonings take ground beef to China.

NUTRITIONAL ANALYSIS PER SERVING: 302 CALORIES, 31 G PROTEIN, 9 G CARBOHYDRATE, 16 G FAT (6 G SATURATED), 93 MG CHOLESTEROL, 1047 MG SODIUM, 1 G FIBER

Seasoning Paste

- 2 tablespoons light soy sauce
- 1 tablespoon bean sauce
- 2 teaspoons chili bean sauce (also known as hot bean paste or Sichuan bean paste) or to taste
- 2 teaspoons toasted sesame oil
- 1½ tablespoons minced garlic
- 1½ tablespoons minced scallions (white parts only)

- 1⅓ pounds extra-lean ground beef

  Salt and freshly ground black pepper

- 3 tablespoons Charred Tomato Ketchup (page 38)
- 1½ tablespoons sweet bean sauce

1. To make the seasoning paste, combine the soy sauce, bean sauce, oil, garlic, and scallions in a small bowl or measuring cup.

2. In a medium-sized bowl, combine the beef, seasoning paste, and salt and pepper to taste. Blend well without overworking and form into 4 patties, about 1 inch thick.

3. Combine the ketchup and sweet bean sauce in a small bowl or measuring cup and whisk to blend. Set aside.

4. Prepare a hot fire in the grill. Grill the patties for approximately 6 minutes per side for medium-rare.

5. Serve immediately, spooning a rounded tablespoon of the sweet bean ketchup on top of each burger.

Zone yield per recipe: 16 protein blocks, 3 carbohydrate blocks (1 tablespoon ketchup = 0 protein blocks, ⅓ carbohydrate block)

Top Loin Roast with Morels, Chanterelles, and Madeira

8 SERVINGS When I bought my first top loin roast, my butcher told me it was his most popular cut for roasting. This is probably due to its exceptional porterhouse steak flavor. Under an extravagant paste of morels and chanterelles, it will roast to irresistible tenderness even without its fat. Do not be alarmed by the presence of chopped carrots in the recipe. They flavor the drippings, but are removed before serving. | Although this roast is irregularly shaped compared to a loin of pork, the technique for butterflying remains the same. You want to end up with 4 lobes of meat, attached to each other if possible. If you accidentally sever any of the pieces, simply approximate the original form when you roll the roast back up. Butcher's twine will hold everything in place. Your goal is lean beef with rich veins of infusion paste.

NUTRITIONAL ANALYSIS PER SERVING: 315 CALORIES, 38 G PROTEIN, 7 G CARBOHYDRATE, 14 G FAT (5 G SATURATED), 97 MG CHOLESTEROL, 410 MG SODIUM, 1 G FIBER

Infusion Paste

⅓ ounce dry chanterelles (about ½ cup)

⅓ ounce dry morels (about ⅓ cup)

2 cups water

1 tablespoon Madeira

⅓ cup Smoked Allium Paste (page 22)

1 tablespoon minced fresh chives

¾ teaspoon salt or to taste

Freshly ground black pepper

3½ pound beef top loin roast, completely trimmed of fat (about 3 pounds trimmed)

Salt and freshly ground black pepper

1 teaspoon extra virgin olive oil

½ cup finely chopped onion

½ cup finely chopped carrots

2 tablespoons Madeira

1 cup beef broth

1. To make the infusion paste, combine the mushrooms and water in a medium saucepan. Bring to a boil, reduce the heat to low, and simmer for 20 minutes. Reserving the liquid, remove mushrooms with a slotted spoon. Set the mushrooms aside. Strain the liquid through a cheesecloth-lined sieve into a small clean saucepan and add 1 tablespoon Madeira. Over high heat, reduce the liquid to 1 tablespoon mushroom syrup. Cool to room temperature.

2. Clean the mushrooms under cold running water, rubbing with your fingers to remove any grit. Dry on paper towels and gently squeeze out any excess water. Transfer to a food processor and pulse to chop finely. Reserve half the mushrooms for the gravy and set aside.

3. Combine the remaining mushrooms with the mushroom syrup, smoked allium paste, chives, and salt in a small bowl. Add black pepper to taste, blend well, and set aside.

4. To butterfly the roast, bisect the roast lengthwise to within ½ inch of the bottom surface. Do not cut all the way through it. Open up the 2 lobes like a book. Make a similar

lengthwise slit through each lobe, but stop again ½ inch above the bottom surface. You now have 4 lobes, and the roast should lie relatively flat. Season all the surfaces well with salt and pepper. Place it cut side up. Using a spatula, spread half the infusion paste over the exposed surface area. Fit the roast back together by gently rolling, reassembling it as you go. Secure with butcher's twine, but not so tightly as to squeeze out all the paste.

5. Preheat the oven to 350° F. Make a roast-shaped footprint with the oil in a cast-iron skillet. Brown the roast on all sides over medium-high heat. Adjust the flame as needed to avoid burning. Remove from the heat. Spread the remaining infusion paste over the top and sides of the roast and transfer to the oven.

6. For rare to medium rare meat, roast for about 50 minutes, to an internal temperature of 120° to 125° F on an instant-read thermometer. Transfer the meat to a platter and allow to rest for 10 minutes. (The temperature of the meat will continue to rise.)

7. Add the carrots and onions to the skillet over low heat. Sauté for 2 minutes, stirring. Add 2 tablespoons Madeira and the broth to the skillet. Stir, scraping up the brown bits. Strain into a measuring cup, along with any collected meat juices, and degrease. Add the reserved mushrooms. Season well with salt and pepper. Reheat if necessary.

8. Thickly slice the roast and serve with 1 tablespoon of the gravy drizzled over each portion. Pass the remaining gravy at the table.

Zone yield per recipe: 42 protein blocks, 5 carbohydrate blocks

Top Loin Roast with Morels, Chanterelles, and Madeira served with Roasted Garlic Asparagus (page 167)

Broiled Lamb Skewers with Spicy Eggplant Hash 4 SERVINGS

Because my husband has an aversion to eggplant, I must play Ulysses, the great tactician, and cleverly disguise it. My basic strategy: conceal texture and lure with taste. The first time I served this eggplant hash, he cooed and requested more—even after the awful truth emerged. Despite its Chinese character, we now refer to it as "Trojan eggplant."

NUTRITIONAL ANALYSIS PER SERVING: 237 CALORIES, 25 G PROTEIN, 13 G CARBOHYDRATE, 9 G FAT (3 G SATURATED), 73 MG CHOLESTEROL, 863 MG SODIUM, 3 G FIBER

4   tablespoons soy sauce

2   tablespoons bean sauce

2   teaspoons chili bean sauce (also known as hot bean paste or Sichuan bean paste)

4   teaspoons fructose

1½ pounds completely trimmed lamb, preferably from the leg, cut into 1¾-inch chunks

2½ to 3 cups cubed Roasted Eggplant (page 30)

2   teaspoons peanut or canola oil

1   tablespoon minced garlic

1   tablespoon minced fresh ginger

2   tablespoons minced scallions (white part only)

1. In a large bowl, combine 2 tablespoons of the soy sauce, 1 tablespoon of the bean sauce, 1 teaspoon of the chili bean sauce, and 2 teaspoons of the fructose. Whisk until the fructose dissolves. Add the lamb chunks and toss well to coat. Cover with plastic wrap and marinate overnight.

2. In a food processor, pulse to mince the eggplant. Set aside.

3. Combine the remaining 2 tablespoons soy sauce, 1 tablespoon bean sauce, 1 teaspoon chili bean sauce, and 2 teaspoons fructose in a small bowl or measuring cup and whisk to dissolve the fructose. Set aside.

4. Preheat the broiler. Thread the lamb onto skewers. Broil 3 to 4 inches from the flame for a total of 10 minutes, turning to brown on all sides. The meat should be medium-rare. Remove to a platter.

5. Meanwhile, heat the oil in a nonstick wok or skillet over medium-high heat. Add the garlic, ginger, and scallions and stir-fry for 30 seconds. Add the minced eggplant and stir-fry for 1 minute. Add the soy-bean sauce mixture and stir-fry for another minute. Remove from the heat.

6. To serve, distribute the eggplant hash among 4 plates. Top with chunks of lamb removed from the skewers. Serve immediately.

Zone yield per recipe: 16 protein blocks, 7 carbohydrate blocks

Broiled Lamb Chops with Herbed Garlic Puree 4 SERVINGS

A 4-ounce lamb chop contains approximately 14 grams of fat, 40 percent of which is saturated. Careful trimming can reduce this to around 4 grams of total fat per chop, including 1.5 grams of saturated fat. In this recipe, a rich-tasting paste of smoked garlic and fresh herbs replaces the fat and prevents the edges of the meat from drying out. If you do not have a smoker, you can substitute roasted garlic for smoked.

NUTRITIONAL ANALYSIS PER SERVING: 212 CALORIES, 24 G PROTEIN, 6 G CARBOHYDRATE, 10 G FAT (3 G SATURATED), 74 MG CHOLESTEROL, 84 MG SODIUM, 0 G FIBER

Herbed Garlic Puree

¼   cup Smoked Garlic Paste (page 25)

2   tablespoons chicken broth

1   teaspoon extra virgin olive oil

1   teaspoon balsamic vinegar

2   teaspoons chopped flat-leaf parsley

2   teaspoons chopped fresh thyme

1   teaspoon chopped fresh rosemary

Salt and freshly ground black pepper

8   (4-ounce) bone-in loin or rib lamb chops, visible fat removed

Salt and freshly ground black pepper

1. To make the puree, combine the smoked garlic paste, broth, oil, and vinegar in a food processor or blender. Process until smooth. Stir in the parsley, thyme, and rosemary. Season with salt and pepper. (The puree can be made in advance and refrigerated for up to 1 week or frozen for up to 6 months.) Reserve half the puree and set aside.

2. Generously season the chops on both sides with salt and pepper. Using a small spatula, spread the remaining garlic puree around the trimmed edges of the chops.

3. Preheat the broiler. Broil the chops 4 inches from the flame for 4 to 5 minutes per side to medium-rare (130° F).

4. Serve immediately, with the 1 tablespoon of the remaining puree spooned onto the side of each plate.

Zone yield per recipe: 16 protein blocks, 2 carbohydrate blocks (1 tablespoon puree = 0 protein blocks, ⅓ carbohydrate block)

Grilled Lamb Chops with Smoky Pipérade 4 SERVINGS The pipérade in

this recipe still bears sufficient traces of its Basque heritage to be recognizable, despite its smoky perfume. Although it accompanies lamb here, it pairs just as readily with chicken and fish. It has miraculous staying power in the refrigerator and can be made up to a week in advance.

NUTRITIONAL ANALYSIS PER SERVING: 299 CALORIES, 28 G PROTEIN, 22 G CARBOHYDRATE, 12 G FAT (4 G SATURATED), 74 MG CHOLESTEROL, 69 MG SODIUM, 8 G FIBER

1   tablespoon extra virgin olive oil

1½ cups thinly sliced onions

1   tablespoon minced garlic

2   cups julienned Smoked Bell Peppers (page 32) (red, orange, and yellow peppers), with any accumulated juice

    Salt and freshly ground black pepper

8   (4-ounce) bone-in loin or rib lamb chops, 1½ inches thick, visible fat removed

2   tablespoons minced flat-leaf parsley

1. Heat the oil in a nonstick skillet over medium heat. Add the onions and sauté until soft and golden, 2 to 3 minutes. Add the garlic and sauté for another minute. Add the peppers with any accumulated pepper juice and stir to combine. Season generously with salt and pepper and remove from the heat.

2. Prepare a hot fire in the grill. Season the lamb chops on both sides with salt and pepper. Grill for about 4 minutes per side for medium-rare meat (130° F), or longer to desired doneness.

3. Divide the chops among 4 plates. Spoon one-quarter of the pipérade over each serving and garnish with the parsley. Serve immediately.

Zone yield per recipe: 16 protein blocks, 4 carbohydrate blocks

Grilled Lamb Chops with Smoky Pipérade served with Cannellini Beans with Rosemary (page 191)

Roast Leg of Lamb with Pesto Infusion 4 TO 6 SERVINGS I considered calling

the basil paste in this recipe "un-pesto" to distinguish it from traditional preparations. First, it involves very little oil. Second, it does not contain raw garlic—relying instead on Roasted Garlic Paste for garlic presence. In addition, Parmesan cheese plays only a minor role, and pistachios replace the more conventional pine nuts. Still, it deliciously conveys the message of pesto to this receptive cut of lamb. The meat must be trimmed with a surgeon's care to decrease fat content without cutting the roast into pieces. If a piece comes loose in the trimming process, just tuck it back in as you roll. | If the bowl of your food processor is large, it may be difficult to process the basil and nuts in the small amounts used here. You may find it necessary to double the quantities and reserve half the pesto for another dish, such as Baked Pesto Portobellos (page 177). Note that the carrots used to flavor the drippings are removed before serving.

NUTRITIONAL ANALYSIS PER SERVING: 285 CALORIES, 34 G PROTEIN, 8 G CARBOHYDRATE, 13 G FAT (4 G SATURATED), 99 MG CHOLESTEROL, 116 MG SODIUM, 1 G FIBER

Pesto Infusion Paste

½ cup densely packed fresh basil leaves

2 tablespoons dry-roasted shelled pistachios

1 tablespoon grated Parmesan cheese

¼ cup Roasted Garlic Paste (page 24)

Salt and freshly ground black pepper

½ leg of lamb, boned and butterflied, about 2½ pounds trimmed

1 teaspoon extra virgin olive oil

½ cup chopped onions

½ cup chopped carrots

1 cup brown chicken stock or chicken broth

Salt and freshly ground black pepper

1. To make the infusion paste, combine the basil, pistachios, and Parmesan in a food processor and pulse until finely chopped but not pureed. Transfer to a small bowl and combine with the roasted garlic paste. Blend well and season with salt and pepper. (The paste can be made in advance and refrigerated for up to 1 week or frozen for up to 6 months.)

2. Preheat the oven to 325° F. Place the lamb flat on a cutting board and remove as much fat as possible from both sides. Season generously with salt and pepper. Place the meat skin side down. Using a rubber spatula, spread the pesto over the exposed surface. Roll the meat jelly-roll style and tie securely with butcher's twine.

3. Make a "footprint" with the oil in the shape of the roast in a cast-iron skillet over medium-high heat. Brown the lamb on all sides, reducing the heat, if necessary, to prevent burning. Scatter the carrots and onions around the meat and transfer the pan to the oven.

4. Roast for 15 to 20 minutes per pound (trimmed weight) for medium-rare (130° F) to medium (140° F). Remove the meat from the oven and transfer to a platter. Allow to rest for 10 minutes before carving.

Roast Leg of Lamb with Pesto Infusion (continued)

5. If gravy is desired, place the skillet over low heat. Add the stock and stir, scraping up the brown bits. Strain into a measuring cup and discard the solids. Add any collected meat juices and degrease. Adjust the seasoning.

6. Thickly slice the lamb and serve immediately, drizzling 1 tablespoon of the gravy over each portion and passing the remainder at the table. Or, allow to cool. Then slice and serve at room temperature without gravy.

Zone yield per recipe: 24 protein blocks, 4 carbohydrate blocks

Lamb Chops Marinated in Spiced Yogurt 4 SERVINGS

Because I love Indian food, I have for some time coveted a little portable home tandoor oven. Unfortunately, even the smallest ones are exorbitantly priced. If I still made (and ate) traditional Indian flatbreads like naan and poori, it might be one thing; but I could never justify it simply to flavor meat. Out of respect for the tandoor and the rich tradition of its use, I do not call this preparation tandoori. It is merely a humble and affordable approximation. | For best results, use a charcoal grill. You can substitute skewered, cubed boneless leg of lamb for the chops, but grilling time will require adjustment.

NUTRITIONAL ANALYSIS PER SERVING: 170 CALORIES, 22 G PROTEIN, 0 G CARBOHYDRATE, 8 G FAT (3 G SATURATED), 74 MG CHOLESTEROL, 56 MG SODIUM, 0 G FIBER

Spice Mixture

2   teaspoons kosher salt

2   teaspoons ground cumin

2   teaspoons ground coriander

1   teaspoon turmeric

½   teaspoon cayenne pepper

¼   teaspoon ground cloves

¼   teaspoon ground cinnamon

¼   teaspoon ground cardamom

¼   teaspoon ground fenugreek

2   cups nonfat plain yogurt

2   tablespoons minced garlic

2   tablespoons minced fresh ginger

1   tablespoon extra virgin olive oil

8   (4-ounce) bone-in loin lamb chops, 1½ inches thick, visible fat removed

1. To make the spice mixture, combine the salt and all the spices in a cast-iron skillet over medium heat. Toast, stirring, for about 2 minutes, until fragrant. Remove from the heat and cool to room temperature.

2. Combine the yogurt, garlic, ginger, oil, and spice mixture in a large measuring cup and blend well. Pour half the yogurt mixture into a nonreactive container just large enough to hold the meat. Add the lamb chops and pour the remaining marinade over them. Turn to coat well on all sides. Cover and refrigerate overnight.

3. Prepare a hot fire in the grill. Scrape off most of the marinade and discard, leaving only a thin coating on the chops. Grill for about 4 minutes per side for medium-rare meat (130° F), or longer to desired doneness. Serve immediately.

Zone yield per recipe: 16 protein blocks, less than one carbohydrate block

Grilled Ostrich Fillets with Rosemary

4 SERVINGS Ostrich qualifies as a heart-healthy red meat. Recently I bought several fresh ostrich fillets and experimented with them across a range of techniques. It turns out that ostrich adapts well to grilled lamb recipes. But, unlike lamb, ostrich contains almost no fat and dries out dramatically if overcooked. It should be eaten rosy rare to medium-rare with internal temperatures of 125° to 130° F.

NUTRITIONAL ANALYSIS PER SERVING: 139 CALORIES, 31 G PROTEIN, 0 G CARBOHYDRATE, 1 G FAT (0 G SATURATED), 90 MG CHOLESTEROL, 93 MG SODIUM, 0 G FIBER

Marinade

2	tablespoons soy sauce
2	tablespoons sweet bean sauce
1	tablespoon mild Dijon mustard
1	tablespoon fructose
2	teaspoons toasted sesame oil
2	teaspoons chopped fresh rosemary
2	tablespoons minced flat-leaf parsley

1¼ pounds ostrich fillets, ½ to ¾ inch thick, patted dry

Salt and freshly ground black pepper

1. To make the marinade, combine the soy sauce, sweet bean sauce, mustard, fructose, oil, rosemary, and parsley in a small bowl or measuring cup and whisk to blend. Place the fillets in a nonreactive container, add the marinade, and turn to coat the fillets. Cover and refrigerate overnight.

2. Prepare a hot fire in the grill. Remove the fillets from the marinade and discard the marinade. Grill the fillets for 3 to 4 minutes on each side for rosy rare to medium rare (125° to 130° F). Remove the meat to a cutting board and allow to rest for 5 minutes.

3. Thickly slice on an angle and divide the slices among 4 plates. Spoon any accumulated juices over the slices and serve immediately.

Zone yield per recipe: 16 protein blocks, less than one carbohydrate block

Broiled Ostrich Burgers with Smoked Tomato Ketchup

4 SERVINGS Ground ostrich is so lean that it can easily dry out during cooking. A little added moisture can make ostrich more forgiving. If the moisture also happens to be loaded with flavor, so much the better—and that is surely the case with Smoked Tomato Ketchup (page 39). If you plan ahead when ripe tomatoes are bountiful, you can have it in your freezer ready to use. For variety, substitute Charred Tomato Ketchup (page 38).

NUTRITIONAL ANALYSIS PER SERVING: 188 CALORIES, 32 G PROTEIN, 6 G CARBOHYDRATE,
4 G FAT (1 G SATURATED), 90 MG CHOLESTEROL, 159 MG SODIUM, 1 G FIBER

1¼ pounds ground ostrich

½ cup Smoked Tomato Ketchup
   (page 39)

2 teaspoons extra virgin olive oil

   Salt and freshly ground
   black pepper

1. Place the ostrich in a bowl with ¼ cup of the ketchup and 1 teaspoon of the oil. Season generously with salt and pepper and combine well without overworking. Form into 4 patties.

2. Preheat the broiler. Brush the bottom of a nonstick broiler pan with the remaining 1 teaspoon oil. (You will not use the top of the pan). Place the burgers in the pan and broil 3 to 4 inches from the flame for about 4 minutes per side to medium rare (130° F). Do not overcook.

3. Serve immediately, with the remaining ketchup divided among the 4 plates.

Zone yield per recipe: 16 protein blocks, 2 carbohydrate blocks (1 tablespoon ketchup = 0 protein blocks, ¼ carbohydrate block)

Sautéed Ostrich Burgers with Smoked Tomato Ketchup *(Variation)* **4 SERVINGS**

NUTRITIONAL ANALYSIS PER SERVING: 197 CALORIES, 32 G PROTEIN, 6 G CARBOHYDRATE,
5 G FAT (1 G SATURATED), 90 MG CHOLESTEROL, 159 MG SODIUM, 1 G FIBER

1. Prepare the burgers as directed above. Instead of broiling the burgers, sauté the burgers in a skillet. Using ½ teaspoon oil for each, make a "footprint" for each patty. Place the patties in the oil and cook over medium-high heat for approximately 4 minutes per side. Serve with the remaining ketchup on the side.

Zone yield per recipe: 16 protein blocks, 2 carbohydrate blocks (1 tablespoon ketchup = 0 protein blocks, ¼ carbohydrate block)

Barbecued Ostrich Fillets 4 SERVINGS

One summer afternoon, I marinated filet mignons, pork tenderloins, veal chops, and ostrich fillets in this sauce and threw them all on the grill. Then my husband, two friends, and I conducted a taste test. The ostrich won by a length. Since ostrich contains less than 1 gram of fat per ounce, and the sauce contains no oil, you can save most of your fat allowance for your carbohydrates. | Most barbecue sauces and ketchups interfere with insulin control because they employ significant amounts of high-glycemic sweeteners. This low-glycemic version of the sauce relies on fructose instead of sugar. If you are not on a strict regimen, replace 1½ teaspoons soy sauce and 1-½ teaspoons of the fructose with 1-½ teaspoons molasses. As written, the sauce contains about 2 grams of carbohydrate per tablespoon.

NUTRITIONAL ANALYSIS PER SERVING: 198 CALORIES, 32 G PROTEIN, 12 G CARBOHYDRATE, 2 G FAT (0 G SATURATED), 90 MG CHOLESTEROL, 358 MG SODIUM, 2 G FIBER

Barbecue Sauce

1   tablespoon water

1½ teaspoons Worcestershire sauce

1½ teaspoons soy sauce

1½ teaspoons dry mustard

1½ teaspoons ground cumin

1½ teaspoons chili powder

   Pinch cayenne pepper or more to taste

¼   cup finely chopped onion

¼   cup Smoked Tomato Ketchup (page 39) or Charred Tomato Ketchup (page 38)

2   tablespoons malt vinegar

2   tablespoons strong brewed decaffeinated coffee

1½ tablespoons fructose

1   garlic clove, crushed

   Salt and freshly ground black pepper

1¼ pounds ostrich fillets, ½ to ¾ inch thick

1. To make the barbecue sauce, combine the water with the Worcestershire, soy sauce, mustard, cumin, chili powder, and cayenne. Whisk to dissolve the spices and transfer to a small nonreactive saucepan. Add the onion, ketchup, vinegar, coffee, fructose, and garlic and bring to a boil. Reduce the heat to low and simmer for 10 to 15 minutes, stirring frequently, until the sauce thickens to a ketchup-like consistency. Remove from the heat and cool to room temperature. Puree if desired. Add salt and pepper to taste. (The sauce can be made in advance and refrigerated for up to 1 week or frozen for up to 6 months.)

Barbecued Ostrich Fillets

Barbecued Ostrich Fillets (continued)

2. Place the fillets in a nonreactive container and add the sauce, turning the meat to coat on all sides. Cover and refrigerate overnight.

3. Remove the fillets from the container and transfer the remaining sauce to a small saucepan. If excess marinade clings to the meat, scrape it into the saucepan. Bring the marinade to a boil and simmer for 2 minutes, stirring often. Set aside.

4. Prepare a hot fire in the grill. Grill the fillets for 3 to 4 minutes per side for rosy rare to medium-rare (125° to 130° F). Do not overcook. Allow the meat to rest for 5 minutes.

5. Thickly slice the meat on an angle and divide the slices among 4 plates. Serve immediately, with 1 tablespoon of the sauce spooned on the side of each portion. Pass the remaining sauce at the table.

Zone yield per recipe: 16 protein blocks, 3 carbohydrate blocks (1 tablespoon sauce = 0 protein blocks, ¼ carbohydrate block)

Curried Ostrich Patties with Pignoli 4 SERVINGS

Increasingly available freshly ground ostrich meat is a happy discovery for health-conscious hamburger lovers. Ostrich contains much less fat than beef, 45 percent less cholesterol, and more iron. Its flavor falls somewhere between beef tenderloin and skinless duck breast or lamb. Because it is so lean, it cooks quickly and lends itself to fast, high-heat methods— broiling, grilling, sautéing, and stir-frying. It should be eaten rare to medium-rare at internal temperatures of 125° to 130° F.

NUTRITIONAL ANALYSIS PER SERVING: 194 CALORIES, 34 G PROTEIN, 2 G CARBOHYDRATE, 7 G FAT (1 G SATURATED), 90 MG CHOLESTEROL, 530 MG SODIUM, 1 G FIBER

1¼ pounds ground ostrich

¼ cup pine nuts, toasted

2 teaspoons curry powder

¾ teaspoon salt or to taste

Freshly ground black pepper

¼ cup ice water

1. In a small bowl, combine the ground ostrich, pine nuts, curry powder, salt, pepper to taste, and water. Mix gently but do not overwork. Shape into 4 patties, about 1½ inches thick. Refrigerate for 2 hours.

2. Preheat the broiler. Broil 3 to 4 inches from the flame for about 4 minutes per side, until nicely browned, to an internal temperature of 130° F for medium-rare. Do not overcook. Serve at once.

Zone yield per recipe: 16 protein blocks, less than one carbohydrate block

Carbohydrate Dishes

Dietary carbohydrate stimulates insulin secretion; the recipes in this section are designed to keep that secretion slow and steady rather than rapid and spiking. The benefits of this approach include lower average insulin levels and enhanced fat-burning capacity. As a bonus, the absence of insulin spikes delays the onset of hunger after meals and helps eliminate carbohydrate craving. | Carbohydrate dishes contain high-fiber vegetables, legumes, and fruits that support insulin control. The amount of carbohydrate you should eat depends on the macronutrient ratio you seek. In terms of Zone yields per recipe, 4 carbohydrate blocks provide approximately 36 grams. In combination with 28 grams of protein, this yields a protein to carbohydrate ratio of 3 to 4, the standard for 40/30/30 diets, such as the Zone. Gram counts per serving may be found in the nutritional analysis accompanying each recipe. | Small quantities of protein accompany the carbohydrate in fruits, vegetables, and legumes. Because fiber limits its absorption, the Zone yield per recipe ignores this plant-based protein. Zone yields do, however, include both the protein and carbohydrate contributions from dairy products (e.g., cheese, buttermilk, and yogurt). The standard nutritional analyses include the protein from all sources. | The intrinsic fat in plant-based foods rarely alters the fat content of carbohydrate dishes, but there are exceptions. Certain rich sources of healthy fat such as avocados, nuts, and olives contribute noticeable fat to recipes. The nutritional analyses reflect the fat from all sources. In general, total fat counts prove to be low, leaving room for some fat in the protein portion of one's meal. However, if you prefer even greater reductions, you may wish to satisfy your carbohydrate requirement with 1 or 2 servings of a carbohydrate recipe and then add fresh fruit (negligible fat) to make up the remainder. This will enable you to keep any meal's fat content *extremely* low.

Salads and Vegetables
In my high glycemic days of pasta, rice, and bread, I did not devote much time or attention to vegetables. They merely went along for the ride. Now I am a tireless hunter-gatherer in the produce department, targeting high-fiber carbohydrate sources in hope of new and interesting combinations.

My passion for high-fiber vegetables grew out of concerns about insulin levels. Without being absorbed by the body, *soluble* fiber slows down the conversion of carbohydrate to glucose and the release of that glucose into the bloodstream. By smoothing out the rise in blood sugar, it helps keep average insulin levels lower. *Insoluble* fiber (similarly not absorbed) adds bulk to meals and increases satiety. Together, soluble and insoluble fiber help control insulin levels and postpone the sensation of hunger.

But the value of vegetables extends well beyond fiber. An increasing body of medical evidence suggests that vegetables' storehouse of antioxidant vitamins (beta carotene, C, and E) and phytochemicals can protect us from various diseases. For example, tomatoes and cruciferous vegetables, which figure in many of the recipes in this chapter, appear to have anticarcinogenic effects. (Crucifers include mustard and collard greens, kale, broccoli, cauliflower, broccoflower, turnips, cabbage, radishes, brussels sprouts, and arugula.) The allium group (garlic, onions, leeks, scallions, and chives) is credited with fighting cancer, lowering cholesterol and blood pressure, and thinning blood. Mushrooms also display anticoagulant properties that protect coronary arteries. As a result, my refrigerator overflows with vegetables at all times: boiled, roasted, and smoked; alone and in prepared dishes.

When I turned toward vegetables and away from grain-based foods, I thought I would never use my pasta pot again. As it turns out, I use it now more than ever. My favorite salad combinations start with precooked vegetables. I like to do the precooking in batches large enough to see me through several days of meals. Although steaming vegetables preserves more vitamins and minerals than boiling, when volume counts I reach for the pasta pot—not the vegetable steamer. I fill the pot three-quarters full with water and bring it to a boil. Meanwhile, I load the pasta insert with vegetables, and lower it into the boiling water. After 3 or 4 minutes, when the vegetables are crisp-tender, I pull out the insert and turn the vegetables into an ice water bath to stop the cooking while the water in the pot continues boiling. Then a second batch of vegetables goes into the insert and I repeat the process. It's not unusual for me to do 5 or 6 different vegetables in a row using the same pot of boiling water. I might have one batch in the pot, one in the ice bath, one draining in a colander, one drying between two layers of kitchen towels, and two on the launching pad. The cooling and drying steps enhance taste, texture, and appearance while they lengthen refrigerator shelf-life. I find that making cooked vegetables ahead of time speeds meal preparation on busy week nights.

Lovers' Artichokes alla Romana (page 166), Minted Pea and Radish Salad (page 164) and Roasted Peppers with Anchovies and Capers (page 147)

Crudités with Roquefort Dip 4 TO 6 SERVINGS This easy appetizer suits insulin-

conscious dinner parties because it can be made ahead in double or triple quantities and served without any last-minute fussing. Although Roquefort cheese bears considerable fat, intense flavor justifies its inclusion. Meanwhile, nonfat yogurt and ricotta dramatically reduce overall fat content per serving. If you have any dressing left over, use it on salads or as a dip for steamed artichokes, green beans, or cauliflower.

NUTRITIONAL ANALYSIS PER SERVING: 156 CALORIES, 12 G PROTEIN, 16 G CARBOHYDRATE, 6 G FAT (3 G SATURATED), 18 MG CHOLESTEROL, 491 MG SODIUM, 3 G FIBER

Roquefort Dip

1   cup nonfat plain yogurt

½   cup nonfat ricotta cheese

3   tablespoons tarragon vinegar

2   teaspoons anchovy paste

1   garlic clove, crushed

3   ounces Roquefort cheese, crumbled

¼   cup minced flat-leaf parsley

    Salt and freshly ground
    black pepper

2   cups 3-inch peeled and seeded
    cucumber spears

2   cups 3-inch peeled celery sticks

2   cups 3-inch fennel sticks

2   cups 3-inch red, orange, and
    yellow bell pepper strips

1. To make the dip, combine the yogurt, ricotta, vinegar, anchovy paste, and garlic in a food processor and process until smooth. Add the Roquefort and pulse once or twice to break up the lumps, but do not puree. Transfer to a small bowl and fold in the parsley. Season to taste with salt and pepper. Store in the refrigerator for up to 12 hours in advance.

2. To serve, arrange the vegetables on a platter and the dressing in a bowl.

Zone yield per recipe: 6 protein blocks, 4 carbohydrate blocks (1 tablespoon dip = ⅐ protein block, ⅒ carbohydrate block)

Roasted Peppers with Anchovies and Capers

6 SERVINGS The secret to this appetizer lies in the treatment of the anchovies. To decrease their impressive fat content, rinse and dry them. Then, to restore their moisture, what better agent than the syrupy juice from your roasted peppers? Roll your anchovies in that and—presto!—they are juicy again and low in fat. (Pictured on page 145.)

NUTRITIONAL ANALYSIS PER SERVING: 92 CALORIES, 7 G PROTEIN, 16 G CARBOHYDRATE, 2 G FAT (0 G SATURATED), 7 MG CHOLESTEROL, 357 MG SODIUM, 7 G FIBER

3   *large red bell peppers*

3   *large yellow bell peppers*

12   *anchovy fillets*

1   *tablespoon capers, drained*

1. Roast the peppers by thoroughly charring the skins under the broiler. Transfer to a paper bag and allow to steam for 10 to 15 minutes to loosen the skins. Remove stems, skins, seeds, and membranes. Tear the peppers along the natural dividing lines into manageable lobes and place in a plastic container. The peppers will release their juice as they cool. Refrigerate until you are ready to serve. (The roasted peppers can be prepared to this point up to 48 hours in advance.)

2. Place the anchovy fillets in a sieve and rinse under cold running water. Pat dry between layers of paper towels. Reserving the pepper juice, remove the peppers from the container and set aside. Toss the anchovy fillets in the pepper juice to moisten.

3. Starting at one end of a platter large enough to hold the peppers, make 1 horizontal row of peppers, skinned side up. Lay a few anchovies over the peppers. Sprinkle with a few capers. Repeat with the remaining peppers, anchovies, and capers in partially overlapping rows. Serve at room temperature or slightly chilled.

Zone yield per recipe: Less than one protein block, 4 carbohydrate blocks

Salad of Bitter Leaves and Concord Grapes

4 SERVINGS Concord grapes, a gorgeous late summer treat, contain potassium as well as vitamins A, B6, and folate. Despite limited fiber content, their glycemic index ranks with that of an orange. If you notice a tiny seed here or there, simply ignore it. If necessary, halved seedless red or black grapes can be used instead of Concord grapes.

NUTRITIONAL ANALYSIS PER SERVING: 72 CALORIES, 2 G PROTEIN, 13 G CARBOHYDRATE, 2 G FAT (0 G SATURATED), 0 MG CHOLESTEROL, 30 MG SODIUM, 3 G FIBER

Dressing

1½ teaspoons extra virgin olive oil

1½ tablespoons balsamic vinegar

1½ tablespoons water

1½ teaspoons Dijon mustard

4 cups torn or chopped romaine lettuce

2 cups torn or chopped baby arugula

2 cups torn or chopped radicchio

2 cups chopped Belgian endive

Salt and freshly ground black pepper

2 cups Concord grapes

1. To make the dressing, combine the oil, vinegar, water and mustard in a small bowl or measuring cup. Whisk to blend.

2. Combine the lettuce, arugula, radicchio, and endive in a large bowl. Add the dressing and toss. Season with salt and pepper to taste.

3. Divide the greens among 4 plates and mound ½ cup of grapes on top of each. Serve immediately.

Zone yield per recipe: Less than one protein block, 4 carbohydrate blocks (1 tablespoon dressing = 0 protein blocks, ⅐ carbohydrate block)

Mixed Salad with Garlic Ranch Dressing

4 SERVINGS Since he was a tot, my son has loved the salad with ranch dressing at The Village Smokehouse in Brookline, Massachusetts. After many trials and errors, I hit upon a version that passed muster. The dressing can double as a delicious companion to an array of chilled cooked vegetables such as broccoli, cauliflower, asparagus, and green beans. It even works with poached chicken and fish.

NUTRITIONAL ANALYSIS PER SERVING: 80 CALORIES, 5 G PROTEIN, 15 G CARBOHYDRATE, 1 G FAT (0 G SATURATED), 1 MG CHOLESTEROL, 378 MG SODIUM, 5 G FIBER

Garlic Ranch Dressing

½ cup nonfat buttermilk

1 tablespoon low-fat mayonnaise

1 tablespoon Roasted Garlic Paste (page 24)

½ teaspoon salt or to taste

   Freshly ground black pepper

2 tablespoons minced flat-leaf parsley

2 tablespoons minced fresh chives (preferably garlic chives)

8 cups torn romaine lettuce

2 cups sliced cucumbers

1½ cups halved cherry tomatoes

½ cup thinly sliced red onion

1. To make the dressing, combine the buttermilk, mayonnaise, roasted garlic paste, salt, and pepper to taste in a small bowl or 2-cup measure and emulsify using a stick blender. (Alternatively, emulsify in a traditional blender and transfer to a bowl.) Stir in the parsley and chives. Adjust the seasoning with salt and pepper to taste. Refrigerate until you are ready to serve.

2. Combine the lettuce, cucumbers, tomatoes, and red onion in a large bowl. Toss well.

3. Divide the salad among 4 plates and drizzle 1 tablespoon of the dressing over each serving. Serve immediately, passing the extra dressing at the table.

Zone yield per recipe: 1 protein block, 4 carbohydrate blocks (1 tablespoon dressing = 0 protein blocks, ⅐ carbohydrate block)

Spinach Salad with Smoked Portobellos and Roquefort Dressing

4 SERVINGS Spinach salad offers a delightful opportunity to fortify your diet with fiber, vitamin A, iron, and magnesium. Unfortunately, it often carries a heavy load of saturated fat via bacon and cheese. In this version, smoked portobello mushrooms supply bacon's smoky undertones without adding any fat, while nonfat buttermilk and low-fat mayonnaise dilute the fat content of the Roquefort.

NUTRITIONAL ANALYSIS PER SERVING: 129 CALORIES, 11 G PROTEIN, 19 G CARBOHYDRATE, 4 G FAT (2 G SATURATED), 6 MG CHOLESTEROL, 487 MG SODIUM, 8 G FIBER

Roquefort Dressing

¼ cup nonfat buttermilk

1 ounce Roquefort cheese, crumbled

1 tablespoon low-fat mayonnaise

1 tablespoon white balsamic or white wine vinegar

2 tablespoons minced flat-leaf parsley

¼ teaspoon salt or to taste

Freshly ground black pepper

2 cups sliced Smoked Portobello Mushrooms (page 29), at room temperature or chilled

Salt and freshly ground black pepper

2 pounds fresh spinach, stemmed

2 cups halved cherry tomatoes

1. To make the dressing, combine the buttermilk, Roquefort, mayonnaise, and vinegar in a bowl or 2-cup measure and emulsify using a stick blender. (Alternatively, emulsify in a traditional blender.) Stir in the parsley and season to taste with salt and pepper.

2. Season the mushrooms with salt and pepper to taste. Divide the spinach, mushrooms, and tomatoes among 4 plates. Drizzle 1 tablespoon of the dressing over each salad and serve immediately, passing the extra dressing at the table.

Zone yield per recipe: 1 protein block, 4 carbohydrate blocks (1 tablespoon dressing = ⅒ protein block, ⅒ carbohydrate block)

Cucumber-Orange-Radish Salad   4 TO 6 SERVINGS   This Japanese-influenced salad

must be served cool and crisp. Salting the cucumbers will help preserve their crunch. If you wish to prepare the individual ingredients ahead, refrigerate them separately until you are ready to serve. If you assemble the salad in advance, it will become soggy. It goes especially well with grilled or broiled fish.

NUTRITIONAL ANALYSIS PER SERVING: 60 CALORIES, I G PROTEIN, 12 G CARBOHYDRATE,
I G FAT (0 G SATURATED), 0 MG CHOLESTEROL, 473 MG SODIUM, 3 G FIBER

---

2   *cups peeled, halved, and thinly sliced seedless cucumbers*

1   *teaspoon salt*

2   *oranges, peeled, quartered, and thinly sliced, with seeds removed*

1   *cup halved and thinly sliced red radishes*

1   *tablespoon unhulled sesame seeds, toasted*

Dressing

2   *tablespoons rice vinegar*

2   *teaspoons fructose*

    Salt

1. Place the cucumbers in a colander and toss with the salt. Drain for 20 minutes. Rinse well, drain, and spread out on paper towels in a single layer. Cover with another layer of paper towels, roll up, and gently squeeze.

2. To make the dressing, combine the vinegar, fructose, and salt to taste in a small bowl or measuring cup and whisk to dissolve the fructose.

3. Just before serving, combine the cucumber, orange, and radish slices in a bowl. Add the dressing, toss, adjust the seasoning, and garnish with the sesame seeds. Serve immediately.

Zone yield per recipe: Less than one protein block, 5 carbohydrate blocks (1 tablespoon dressing = 0 protein blocks, ½ carbohydrate block)

Curried Slaw with Fruit and Pistachios

6 SERVINGS Fresh fruit, cooked or raw, can take the place of chutney as a sweet accompaniment to meats. This slaw goes beautifully with Spiced Turkey Kebabs (page 94) and other dishes with an Indian flair. It also complements plain grilled pork and duck. The dressing is excellent with crudités, salads, and cold steamed vegetables, as well as poached chicken or fish. (Pictured on page 95.)

NUTRITIONAL ANALYSIS PER SERVING: 94 CALORIES, 3 G PROTEIN, 14 G CARBOHYDRATE, 4 G FAT (0 G SATURATED), 0 MG CHOLESTEROL, 265 MG SODIUM, 2 G FIBER

Dressing

½   cup fresh orange juice

½   cup nonfat plain yogurt

2   tablespoons low-fat mayonnaise

1   teaspoon grated orange zest

1   tablespoon chopped fresh mint

1   teaspoon curry powder

½   teaspoon salt or to taste

4   cups finely shredded green cabbage

¼   cup thinly sliced red onion

½   cup halved red grapes

¾   cup peeled, diced apple tossed with 1 teaspoon lemon juice

¼   cup shelled dry-roasted salted pistachios

   Salt and freshly ground black pepper

1. To make the dressing, bring the orange juice to a boil in a small saucepan. Reduce to a volume of 2 tablespoons. Remove from the heat and cool to room temperature. Reserve 1½ teaspoons. Set aside the remainder for another use.

2. Combine the orange syrup with the yogurt, mayonnaise, orange zest, mint, curry powder, and salt. Whisk to blend.

3. In a large bowl, combine the cabbage, onion, grapes, apple, and pistachios in a large bowl. Add the dressing and toss well to coat. Add salt and pepper to taste and serve immediately.

Zone yield per recipe: 1 protein block, 6 carbohydrate blocks (1 tablespoon dressing = 0 protein blocks, ⅐ carbohydrate block)

Fennel-Pepper Slaw with Ginger **4 SERVINGS** Grating ginger is a labor of love

requiring elbow grease and special equipment, but I recommend it anyway. With the help of a beautiful porcelain *oroshigane* (Japanese grater), you will obtain velvety grated ginger with pungent ginger juice, which particularly suit recipes in which the ginger is eaten raw. If you don't have this specialized gadget, you can use the small, rough-edged punched holes of a conventional box grater; stand it on a plate to catch the juice.

NUTRITIONAL ANALYSIS PER SERVING: 114 CALORIES, 4 G PROTEIN, 24 G CARBOHYDRATE,
2 G FAT (0 G SATURATED), 0 MG CHOLESTEROL, 830 MG SODIUM, 2 G FIBER

Dressing

¼ cup low-fat mayonnaise

¼ cup nonfat plain yogurt

2 teaspoons rice vinegar

2 teaspoons fructose

1 teaspoon grated fresh ginger with juice

1 teaspoon kosher salt or to taste

2 large fennel bulbs (about 8 ounces each), halved, cored, and thinly sliced

1 cup grated daikon radish

½ cup sliced red bell pepper

½ cup sliced yellow bell pepper

½ cup chopped scallions (1-inch lengths)

¼ cup coarsely chopped fennel fronds

1. To make the dressing, combine the mayonnaise, yogurt, vinegar, fructose, ginger, and salt in a small bowl or measuring cup. Whisk to blend. Refrigerate until you are ready to serve.

2. Combine the fennel, daikon, peppers, and scallions in a large bowl. Just before serving, pour the dressing over the vegetables and toss to coat. Garnish with fennel fronds. Serve immediately.

Zone yield per recipe: Less than one protein block, 8 carbohydrate blocks (1 tablespoon dressing = 0 protein blocks, ⅙ carbohydrate block)

Fresh Pineapple Slaw

4 TO 6 SERVINGS With pineapple available year-round, this fruited slaw can be made any time. One cautionary note: Fresh pineapple contains an enzyme powerful enough to tenderize meat, so you will not want to expose your slaw to it in advance. If you wish, prepare the individual ingredients ahead, but do not mix them together until you are ready to serve.

NUTRITIONAL ANALYSIS PER SERVING: 65 CALORIES, 2 G PROTEIN, 13 G CARBOHYDRATE, 1 G FAT (0 G SATURATED), 0 MG CHOLESTEROL, 364 MG SODIUM, 2 G FIBER

Dressing

¼ cup low-fat mayonnaise

¼ cup nonfat yogurt

2 teaspoons distilled white vinegar

2 teaspoons fructose

½ teaspoon salt or to taste

   Freshly ground black pepper

4 cups shredded green cabbage

1 cup diced fresh pineapple

½ cup julienned red bell pepper

1 tablespoon minced fresh chives

1. To make the dressing, combine the mayonnaise, yogurt, vinegar, fructose, salt, and pepper to taste in a small bowl or measuring cup. Whisk to blend. Refrigerate until you are ready to serve.

2. Combine the cabbage, pineapple, and pepper in a large bowl. Just before serving, add the dressing and toss to coat. Garnish with the chives. Serve immediately.

Zone yield per recipe: Less than one protein block, 6 carbohydrate blocks (1 tablespoon dressing = 0 protein blocks, 1/6 carbohydrate block)

Hot and Sweet Asian Slaw

6 SERVINGS This refreshing slaw tastes best cold and crisp. If you wish to do some advance preparation, make the dressing and cut the vegetables, but keep them separate until you're ready to eat. Then slice the pear, assemble the salad, toss with the dressing, and serve. If you wish to increase the percent of monounsaturated fat in the dressing, you can substitute peanut or canola oil for the toasted sesame oil, but you will give up significant flavor in doing so.

NUTRITIONAL ANALYSIS PER SERVING: 72 CALORIES, 2 G PROTEIN, 12 G CARBOHYDRATE, 3 G FAT (0 G SATURATED), 0 MG CHOLESTEROL, 211 MG SODIUM, 3 G FIBER

Hot and Sweet Asian Slaw (continued)

Dressing

2   teaspoons toasted sesame oil

1   teaspoon hot sesame oil

2   tablespoons rice vinegar

2   teaspoons fructose

1   teaspoon grated fresh ginger
    with juice

½   teaspoon salt or to taste

4   cups shredded napa cabbage

2   cups bean sprouts, rinsed and dried
    between layers of kitchen towels

½   cup red bell pepper strips
    (1½-inch lengths)

½   cup chopped scallions
    (1-inch lengths)

1   Asian pear (or any firm pear),
    cored, quartered, and thinly sliced

1. To make the dressing, combine the sesame oils, vinegar, fructose, ginger, and salt in a small bowl or measuring cup. Whisk to dissolve the fructose.

2. Just before serving, combine the cabbage, bean sprouts, peppers, scallions, and pear in a large bowl. Add the dressing and toss to coat. Serve immediately.

Zone yield per recipe: Less than one protein block, 4 carbohydrate blocks (1 tablespoon dressing = 0 protein blocks, ¼ carbohydrate block)

Red Grapefruit Slaw 4 TO 6 SERVINGS Grapefruit is a glycemic hero of the fruit world—helping, when present, to keep average blood sugar and insulin levels low. It is also a delightful and refreshing addition to cole slaw, especially in the dead of winter when grapefruits are at their peak. If you wish to prepare the slaw in advance, reserve the salt until the last possible moment. Otherwise, it will unleash its formidable osmotic power on your slaw and turn it into a watery mess. For variety, substitute orange sections for the grapefruit.

NUTRITIONAL ANALYSIS PER SERVING: 64 CALORIES, 1 G PROTEIN, 14 G CARBOHYDRATE, 1 G FAT (0 G SATURATED), 0 MG CHOLESTEROL, 356 MG SODIUM, 2 G FIBER

Dressing

¼   cup low-fat mayonnaise

3   tablespoons fresh grapefruit juice

1   to 2 teaspoons fructose

1   teaspoon grated grapefruit zest

½   teaspoon salt or to taste
    Freshly ground black pepper

4   cups shredded green cabbage

1   cup chopped ruby red grapefruit
    sections (¾-inch chunks)

½   cup thinly sliced red onion

2   tablespoons minced flat-leaf parsley

1. To make the dressing, combine the mayonnaise, grapefruit juice, fructose, zest, salt, and pepper in a small bowl or measuring cup.

Whisk to blend. Refrigerate until you are ready to serve.

2. In a large bowl, combine the cabbage, grapefruit sections, and onion in a bowl. Add the dressing and toss to coat. Garnish with the parsley and serve immediately.

Zone yield per recipe: Less than one protein block, 6 carbohydrate blocks (1 tablespoon dressing = 0 protein blocks, ⅛ carbohydrate block)

Sesame Slaw with Pea Pods

4 TO 6 SERVINGS The colors and crunchy texture of this salad take me back to 1973, to the Spiral Restaurant in Coral Gables, Florida. It was a tiny counterculture outpost known for smoothies and health food. They made the most delicious salads in Miami, with 10 kinds of sprouts, 6 kinds of seeds, and much more carbohydrate and fat than I've allowed here. This trimmed-down version is still loaded with fiber, beta carotene, potassium, and flavor.

NUTRITIONAL ANALYSIS PER SERVING: 150 CALORIES, 7 G PROTEIN, 12 G CARBOHYDRATE, 9 G FAT (0 G SATURATED), 0 MG CHOLESTEROL, 218 MG SODIUM, 3 G FIBER

1½ cups snow peas

2 cups shredded red cabbage

2 cups bean sprouts, rinsed and dried between layers of paper towels

1 cup grated daikon radish

1 tablespoon unhulled sesame seeds, toasted

Dressing

¼ cup tahini

3 tablespoons fresh orange juice

2 tablespoons brown rice vinegar

1 tablespoon Japanese soy sauce or to taste

1. Blanch the pea pods in boiling water for 1 to 2 minutes, transfer them to an ice water bath, and drain in a colander. For thorough drying, lay them out in a single layer on a kitchen towel, place another towel on top, and roll them up, squeezing them gently as you roll. Julienne the pea pods or leave whole.

2. To make the dressing, combine the tahini, orange juice, vinegar, and soy sauce in a small bowl or 2-cup measure and emulsify using a stick blender. (Alternatively, emulsify in a traditional blender.)

3. In a large bowl, combine the snow peas, cabbage, bean sprouts, and daikon radish. Pour the dressing over the vegetables and toss to coat. Garnish with sesame seeds. Serve immediately.

Zone yield per recipe: Less than one protein block, 5 carbohydrate blocks (1 tablespoon dressing = 0 protein blocks, ⅛ carbohydrate block)

Broccoflower Salad with Cashew Butter Dressing 6 SERVINGS

Cauliflower and broccoli stand among the most powerful supporters of insulin modulation. Roughly half their carbohydrate content comes from dietary fiber. This means slow conversion to glucose, slow release into the bloodstream, and a slow insulin response. Broccoflower, a cross between the two, has a somewhat milder flavor that cozies up nicely to this mellow dressing. If you can't find broccoflower, use broccoli or cauliflower instead. | To insure success, avoid overcooking your vegetables and dry them well before dressing. Also, make sure your cashew butter is 100 percent pure, without added safflower oil. If you feel concerned about the fat content of cashew butter, consider that 1 tablespoon contains only 8 grams of fat—about half the fat in a tablespoon of olive oil.

NUTRITIONAL ANALYSIS PER SERVING: 82 CALORIES, 6 G PROTEIN, 10 G CARBOHYDRATE, 3 G FAT (0 G SATURATED), 0 MG CHOLESTEROL, 245 MG SODIUM, 5 G FIBER

Cashew Butter Dressing

4 tablespoons nonfat buttermilk

2 tablespoons smooth roasted cashew butter

2 teaspoons cider vinegar

½ teaspoon salt or more to taste

Freshly ground black pepper

6 cups bite-size cooked broccoflower, at room temperature

¼ cup finely chopped red onion

2 tablespoons minced fresh chives

1. To make the dressing, combine the buttermilk, cashew butter, vinegar, salt, and pepper to taste in a small bowl or 2-cup measure. Emulsify using a stick blender. (Alternatively, emulsify ingredients in a traditional blender.)

2. In a large bowl, combine the broccoflower and onion. Pour the dressing over the vegetables and toss to coat. Garnish with the chives. Serve immediately.

Zone yield per recipe: Less than one protein block, 3 carbohydrate blocks (1 tablespoon dressing = 0 protein blocks, ⅒ carbohydrate block)

Broccoli Salad with Pickled Ginger

6 SERVINGS Like asparagus stems, broccoli stems should be peeled for full enjoyment. Cut across the spears below the florets where the thick, fibrous stem begins. Trim the end and cut the stem crosswise into manageable cylinders 2 to 3 inches long. Then, using a paring knife, remove the tough skin and the fibrous layer beneath it. (If you are impatient, you can use a few downward strokes with a chef's knife.) Prepared this way, the stem is sweet, delicate, and tender. I assure you, it is entirely worth the effort.

NUTRITIONAL ANALYSIS PER SERVING: 85 CALORIES, 5 G PROTEIN, 11 G CARBOHYDRATE, 4 G FAT (1 G SATURATED), 0 MG CHOLESTEROL, 386 MG SODIUM, 5 G FIBER

Dressing

2   tablespoons Japanese soy sauce

1   tablespoon chopped pickled ginger

1   tablespoon Pseudo-Mirin (page 37)

2   teaspoons toasted sesame oil

1   teaspoon hot sesame oil

6   cups bite-size cooked broccoli, chilled

⅓   cup chopped scallions (1-inch lengths)

1   tablespoon unhulled sesame seeds, toasted

1. To make the dressing, combine the soy sauce, ginger, Pseudo-Mirin, and sesame oils in a small bowl or measuring cup. Whisk to blend.

2. Combine the broccoli and scallions in a large bowl. Pour the dressing over the broccoli and toss to coat. Garnish with the sesame seeds. Serve at room temperature or chilled.

Zone yield per recipe: Less than one protein block, 4 carbohydrate blocks (1 tablespoon dressing = 0 protein blocks, ¼ carbohydrate block)

Brussels Sprout Salad with Tahini-Buttermilk Dressing

6 SERVINGS The underappreciated brussels sprout provides ample fiber, potassium, and vitamins A, C, and folate in a glycemically friendly little bud. Like other cruciferous vegetables, it also possesses anticarcinogenic properties. Its bad reputation must be due, at least in part, to widespread overcooking, which transforms it into a tasteless, gray blob. In my opinion, the cooking method of choice is steaming, and the goal is a crisp-tender sprout.

NUTRITIONAL ANALYSIS PER SERVING: 94 CALORIES, 5 G PROTEIN, 13 G CARBOHYDRATE, 4 G FAT (0 G SATURATED), 0 MG CHOLESTEROL, 232 MG SODIUM, 6 G FIBER

Tahini-Buttermilk Dressing

4 tablespoons nonfat buttermilk

2 tablespoons tahini

½ teaspoon salt or to taste

   Pinch cayenne pepper

5 cups steamed brussels sprout halves, chilled

2 scallions, chopped

2 teaspoons unhulled sesame seeds, toasted

1. To make the dressing, combine the buttermilk, tahini, salt, and cayenne in a small bowl or 2-cup measure and emulsify using a stick blender. (Alternatively, emulsify in a traditional blender.)

2. Place the brussels sprouts in a large bowl, pour the dressing over, and toss to coat. Garnish with the chopped scallions and sesame seeds.

Note: Knowing that the stem end is more compact than the rest, conscientious cooks cut an X in the bottom of each sprout to facilitate even cooking. Cutting sprouts in half lengthwise solves this problem with 1 cut instead of 2 and decreases cooking time as well. Steaming time depends on sprout size, which is highly variable. Average sprouts (1 inch in diameter) take about 6 minutes to steam to a crisp-tender stage. When they reach the desired state, toss them into an ice water bath to stop the cooking. Dry them thoroughly on kitchen towels and proceed with the recipe.

Zone yield per recipe: Less than one protein block, 5 carbohydrate blocks (1 tablespoon dressing = 0 protein blocks, ⅐ carbohydrate block)

Cauliflower-Green Bean Salad with Arame   6 TO 8 SERVINGS

Arame is a mild-tasting sea vegetable whose fiber content approaches 100 percent. It operates as a potent carbohydrate extender—contributing taste, texture, vitamins, and minerals, without glycemic consequences. Dried arame comes in packages and can be found in health food stores. It must be rehydrated before use.

NUTRITIONAL ANALYSIS PER SERVING: 81 CALORIES, 3 G PROTEIN, 11 G CARBOHYDRATE, 4 G FAT (0 G SATURATED), 0 MG CHOLESTEROL, 62 MG SODIUM, 6 G FIBER

---

1   cup dried arame (about 1 ounce)

1   tablespoon ume plum or red wine vinegar

4½ cups bite-size cooked cauliflower, chilled

2½ cups cooked green beans, chilled

    Salt and freshly ground black pepper

Dressing

2   teaspoons toasted sesame oil

1   teaspoon hot sesame oil

1   large garlic clove, minced

2   tablespoons ume plum or red wine vinegar

1   tablespoon tahini

1   tablespoon water

2   tablespoons minced scallions (white part only)

1. Soak the arame in water to cover for 10 minutes. Drain, rinse, and place in a saucepan with water to cover and 1 tablespoon vinegar. Simmer for 15 minutes. Drain and cool to room temperature.

2. To make the dressing, heat both oils in a small nonstick skillet over medium heat. Add the garlic and sauté for 1 minute. Remove from the heat and stir in the vinegar. Pour into a small bowl or 2-cup measure and cool to room temperature. Add the tahini and water to the cooled oil. Emulsify using a stick blender. (Alternatively, emulsify in a traditional blender and transfer to a small bowl or measuring cup.) Stir in the scallions.

3. In a large bowl, combine the cauliflower, green beans, and arame. Add the dressing and toss well to coat. Season to taste with salt and pepper. Serve immediately.

Zone yield per recipe: Less than one protein block, 3 carbohydrate blocks (1 tablespoon dressing = 0 protein blocks, 0 carbohydrate blocks)

Cauliflower-Green Bean Salad with Arame

Cauliflower-Tomato Salad with Almond Butter and Chives

6 SERVINGS Despite its rich taste and texture, almond butter contains significantly less fat than olive oil: 8 grams per tablespoon compared with 14. It blends well with creamy nonfat bases such as buttermilk, mayonnaise, and yogurt to produce an array of unusual salad dressings. The choice of acid (vinegar, lemon juice, or lime juice) and flavoring agents gives it an ethnic orientation. Soy sauce and rice vinegar, used in this recipe, obviously look toward Japan; but yogurt, cider vinegar, and curry powder could instantly direct the salad toward India. Instead of almond butter, try tahini or soynut, cashew, or peanut butter. Use green beans, broccoli, or asparagus rather than cauliflower. You could make a different variation every night for a month.

NUTRITIONAL ANALYSIS PER SERVING: 72 CALORIES, 3 G PROTEIN, 8 G CARBOHYDRATE,
4 G FAT (0 G SATURATED), 0 MG CHOLESTEROL, 201 MG SODIUM, 3 G FIBER

Dressing

4 tablespoons nonfat buttermilk

2 tablespoons smooth roasted almond butter

1 tablespoon Japanese soy sauce

1 tablespoon brown rice vinegar

Salt and freshly ground black pepper

4 cups bite-size cooked cauliflower, chilled

2 cups halved cherry tomatoes

¼ cup chopped fresh chives

1. To make the dressing, combine the buttermilk, almond butter, soy sauce, and vinegar in a small bowl or 2-cup measure. Emulsify using a stick blender. (Alternatively, emulsify in a traditional blender.) Season to taste with salt and pepper.

2. Combine the cauliflower and tomatoes in a large bowl, add the dressing, and toss to coat. Garnish with the chives. Serve immediately.

Zone yield per recipe: Less than one protein block, 3 carbohydrate blocks (1 tablespoon dressing = 0 protein blocks, ¹⁄₁₀ carbohydrate block)

Fresh Bean Salad with Parsley-Buttermilk Dressing 6 SERVINGS

When I was not insulin aware, I narrow-mindedly reserved buttermilk for biscuits and potato salad. Now I lavish it on low-glycemic salads of all kinds. Mixed with almond butter and minced smoked onions, it makes a terrific dressing for cold brussels sprouts; with cashew butter and cider vinegar, it gives a creamy tang to a salad of broccoli, cauliflower, and red onion. Here it cooperates with mayonnaise and white wine vinegar to dress green and wax beans.

NUTRITIONAL ANALYSIS PER SERVING: 54 CALORIES, 3 G PROTEIN, 11 G CARBOHYDRATE, 1 G FAT (0 G SATURATED), 1 MG CHOLESTEROL, 263 MG SODIUM, 3 G FIBER

Parsley-Buttermilk Dressing

6 tablespoons nonfat buttermilk

2 tablespoons low-fat mayonnaise

1 tablespoon white wine vinegar

½ teaspoon salt or to taste

Freshly ground black pepper

½ cup minced flat-leaf parsley

¼ cup finely chopped red onion

2½ cups cooked green beans, chilled

2½ cups cooked wax beans, chilled

1. To make the dressing, combine the buttermilk, mayonnaise, vinegar, salt, and pepper to taste in a small bowl or 2-cup measure cup. Emulsify using a stick blender. (Alternatively, emulsify in a traditional blender.) Stir in the parsley and red onion.

2. Combine the beans in a large bowl, add the dressing, and toss to coat. Adjust the seasoning and serve immediately.

Zone yield per recipe: Less than one protein block, 5 carbohydrate blocks (1 tablespoon dressing = 0 protein blocks, ⅒ carbohydrate block)

Green Beans with Lemon Oil Vinaigrette **6 SERVINGS** Green beans offer

fiber, potassium, and vitamin A in a delicious, versatile, low-density carbohydrate. They can be eaten at any temperature. If you transfer them from pot to ice bath to kitchen towel, lightly cooked green beans will keep well for nearly a week in the refrigerator. | Lemon oil appeared on the fancy food scene several years ago and has gained wide distribution in stores and catalogs. It contributes a mysterious brightness to sauces of all kinds without altering nutritional counts significantly. Be aware of its intensity, however; a little goes a long way.

NUTRITIONAL ANALYSIS PER SERVING: 68 CALORIES, 2 G PROTEIN, 10 G CARBOHYDRATE, 3 G FAT (0 G SATURATED), 0 MG CHOLESTEROL, 19 MG SODIUM, 4 G FIBER

Lemon Oil Vinaigrette

1   tablespoon extra virgin olive oil

1   tablespoon red wine vinegar

1   tablespoon mild Dijon mustard

¼   to ½ teaspoon lemon oil

Salt and freshly ground
black pepper

5   cups cooked green beans, chilled

½   cup quartered and thinly sliced
red onion

2   tablespoons minced flat-leaf parsley

2   tablespoons chopped fresh dill

1. To make the vinaigrette, combine the olive oil, vinegar, mustard, lemon oil, and salt and pepper to taste in a small bowl or 2-cup measure. Whisk to blend.

2. Combine the beans, onion, parsley, and dill in a large bowl. Pour the vinaigrette over the vegetables and toss well. Serve at room temperature or chilled.

Zone yield per recipe: Less than one protein block, 4 carbohydrate blocks (1 tablespoon vinaigrette = 0 protein blocks, 0 carbohydrate blocks)

Minted Pea and Radish Salad

6 SERVINGS Since peas with edible pods are less carbohydrate-dense (and higher in fiber) than English peas, they are more desirable for insulin-modulating diets. They are also beautiful, flavorful, and require little cooking. Dressed with a light Asian vinaigrette, they pair wonderfully with grilled meats and poultry. (Pictured on page 145.)

NUTRITIONAL ANALYSIS PER SERVING: 82 CALORIES, 4 G PROTEIN, 11 G CARBOHYDRATE, 3 G FAT (0 G SATURATED), 0 MG CHOLESTEROL, 180 MG SODIUM, 3 G FIBER

2½ cups snow peas

2½ cups sugar snap peas

½ cup sliced red radishes

Salt and freshly ground black pepper

¼ cup chopped fresh mint

Dressing

1 tablespoon light soy sauce

1 tablespoon toasted sesame oil

1 tablespoon rice vinegar

2 teaspoons fructose

1. Blanch the pea pods in boiling water for 1 to 2 minutes, transfer them to an ice water bath, and drain in a colander. For thorough drying, lay them out in a single layer on a kitchen towel, place another towel on top, and roll them up, squeezing them gently as you roll. Combine the pea pods and radish slices in a large bowl.

2. To make the dressing, combine the soy sauce, oil, vinegar, and fructose in a small bowl or measuring cup. Whisk to dissolve the fructose.

3. Pour the dressing over the vegetables and toss to coat. Season to taste with salt and pepper. Garnish with the mint. Serve at room temperature or chilled.

Zone yield per recipe: Less than one protein block, 5 carbohydrate blocks (1 tablespoon dressing = 0 protein blocks, ⅓ carbohydrate block)

Steamed Artichokes with Balsamic Vinaigrette 4 SERVINGS As a child,

my favorite "fancy" food was the lobster-stuffed artichoke at a Coconut Grove restaurant called The Country Store. Full of mayonnaise, heavy cream, and croutons, it was a heart attack on a plate. These artichokes are Spartan by comparison, but they make a delicious, high-fiber appetizer. You may wish to double the dressing for use on salads. It keeps indefinitely in the refrigerator.

NUTRITIONAL ANALYSIS PER SERVING: 238 CALORIES, 20 G PROTEIN, 42 G CARBOHYDRATE, 4 G FAT (0 G SATURATED), 0 MG CHOLESTEROL, 574 MG SODIUM, 28 G FIBER

1 lemon, halved

4 large artichokes

Balsamic Vinaigrette

3 tablespoons best-quality balsamic vinegar

3 tablespoons water

1 tablespoon extra virgin olive oil

1 tablespoon Dijon mustard

Salt and freshly ground black pepper

1. Fill a large bowl with cold water and squeeze the lemon into it. Throw the rind in as well. Cut off the top ½ inch each artichoke. Trim the stems. Snip off the sharp points from the leaves. Halve the artichokes vertically. Remove the choke with a paring or grapefruit knife. Rinse under running water and toss into the bowl of lemon water.

2. Place the artichokes in a steamer basket over 2 inches of boiling water. Steam for 15 to 20 minutes, until the hearts are tender when tested with a fork. Remove and immerse in a cold water bath to stop the cooking. Drain and allow to cool. Chill, if desired.

3. To make the vinaigrette, combine the vinegar, water, oil, and mustard in a small bowl or measuring cup, adding salt and pepper to taste. Whisk to blend.

4. To serve, place 2 artichoke halves on each plate. Drizzle each serving with 2 tablespoons vinaigrette. Serve at once.

Zone yield per recipe: Less than one protein block, 6 carbohydrate blocks (1 tablespoon vinaigrette = 0 protein blocks, ⅕ carbohydrate block)

Lovers' Artichokes alla Romana

2 TO 4 SERVINGS You must be driven by an almost insane passion—either for artichokes or for another human being—to tackle this recipe. Its Roman origin makes perfect sense given Rome's reputation as both paradise and purgatory of passion. To this day, a matron sits in the Mercato dei Fiori with her relentless paring knife, stripping irresistible artichokes for this dish. Only the choke stands between the impetuous Roman and his pleasure. Does our Puritan heritage, by contrast, require that we Americans labor before love? I don't know, but these artichokes are worth it. Wear rubber gloves to protect your hands while trimming the artichoke. Serve them as an appetizer. They deserve one's full attention. (Pictured on page 145.)

NUTRITIONAL ANALYSIS PER SERVING: 166 CALORIES, 9 G PROTEIN, 28 G CARBOHYDRATE, 5 G FAT (1 G SATURATED), 0 MG CHOLESTEROL, 616 MG SODIUM, 13 G FIBER

1 lemon

4 jumbo or 6 medium artichokes

1 tablespoon extra virgin olive oil

4 teaspoons minced garlic

¼ teaspoon red pepper flakes or to taste

1 cup water

½ teaspoon salt or to taste

Freshly ground black pepper

1. Fill a medium-size bowl with cold water and squeeze the lemon into it. Add the rinds. To trim an artichoke, snap off the green leaves by bending them backward until you reach the yellow leaves. The "bend" in the artichoke should now be visible. Holding the stem, slice off the top of the artichoke just below the "bend" and expose the choke. Slice off the stem. Holding the artichoke bottom in the palm of your hand, remove the choke using a grapefruit knife. Then, with a paring knife, trim off the leaf and stem stumps down to the white layer. With a horizontal (square-edged) vegetable peeler, smooth the entire surface, including the stem area. Transfer to the bowl of water and repeat with the remaining artichokes.

2. Heat the oil in a deep sauté pan or Dutch oven over medium heat and add the garlic and pepper flakes. Sauté for 1 minute. Remove from the heat and add ½ cup water and ½ teaspoon salt. Return to medium heat and add the artichoke bottoms, stem side down. Cover and cook for 7 minutes. Turn the artichokes over and add the remaining ½ cup water. Cover and cook for another 8 minutes. Remove the pan from the heat, but leave the artichokes in the covered pan for 15 minutes. Transfer the artichokes to a serving dish and set aside.

3. Bring the cooking liquid to a boil and reduce until syrupy. Cool to room temperature. Add salt, if needed, and pepper to taste.

4. Spoon the sauce over the artichokes and serve at room temperature.

Zone yield per recipe: Less than one protein block, 2 carbohydrate blocks

Roasted Garlic Asparagus

6 SERVINGS You may not relish peeling your asparagus, but if you force yourself to do it, you'll love the results. Peeled asparagus cook evenly and become silky, sweet, and wholly edible. In response to an instruction in one of Julia Child's books, I peeled them once and have not been able to eat them any other way since. Be sure to salt them before roasting. │ To keep raw asparagus fresh in your refrigerator, trim the stem ends and stand them upright in about ½ inch of water. Loosely drape a plastic bag over the tips. (Pictured on page 131.)

NUTRITIONAL ANALYSIS PER SERVING: 70 CALORIES, 5 G PROTEIN, 9 G CARBOHYDRATE, 3 G FAT (0 G SATURATED), 0 MG CHOLESTEROL, 24 MG SODIUM, 0 G FIBER

3   *pounds fresh asparagus,*
    stems peeled

1   *tablespoon roasted garlic oil*

    Salt

1. Preheat the oven to 450° F. Lay the asparagus flat on a nonstick jelly roll pan. (Do not crowd the asparagus. If they do not all fit in a single layer on one pan, plan to roast the asparagus in 2 batches, dividing the oil between them.) Drizzle with oil and toss well to coat. Salt generously.

2. Roast for 5 to 8 minutes, depending on the thickness of the spears, until crisp-tender. Serve immediately.

Zone yield per recipe: Less than one protein block, 4 carbohydrate blocks

Lemon-Ginger Broccoli

8 SERVINGS Of all the vegetables in the world, broccoli may stand as the health-seeker's most powerful ally. It packs an astonishing array of phytochemicals that appear to fight cancer and protect against heart disease. Isothiocyanates, flavonoids, carotenoids, organosulfides, and indoles head the list of credits belonging to broccoli; calcium, iron, vitamin C, folate, and fiber fill out its resume. Dressed with a little lemon, ginger, and soy sauce, it reveals culinary charms as well.

NUTRITIONAL ANALYSIS PER SERVING: 73 CALORIES, 5 G PROTEIN, 11 G CARBOHYDRATE, 2 G FAT (0 G SATURATED), 0 MG CHOLESTEROL, 555 MG SODIUM, 5 G FIBER

8   cups bite-size broccoli florets and peeled stems

Lemon-Ginger Sauce

¼   cup Japanese soy sauce

3   tablespoons fresh lemon juice

1   tablespoon fructose

1   tablespoon grated lemon zest

1   tablespoon grated fresh ginger

1½ teaspoons toasted sesame oil

1½ teaspoons hot sesame oil

    Freshly ground black pepper

1. Steam or boil the broccoli for 3 to 4 minutes until crisp-tender. Drain well in a colander and transfer to a large bowl.

2. To make the sauce, combine the soy sauce, lemon juice, fructose, lemon zest, ginger, sesame oils, and black pepper to taste in a small bowl or measuring cup. Whisk to blend.

3. Add the sauce to the broccoli and toss well. Serve hot, warm, or at room temperature.

Zone yield per recipe: Less than one protein block, 4 carbohydrate blocks (1 tablespoon sauce = 0 protein blocks, ¼ carbohydrate block)

Brussels Sprouts with Shallots and Mustard 4 TO 6 SERVINGS Brussels

sprouts share the health-enhancing attributes of the other cabbage family members, including a rich array of antioxidants, minerals, and vitamins. Cup for cup, they contain as much vitamin C as orange sections and as much dietary fiber as broccoli. In addition, they're convenient, versatile, and accommodating to a wide range of meat dishes. I have served this dish with veal chops, roast pork, and a Thanksgiving turkey. Make sure you use a mellow Dijon mustard, such as Maille brand, rather than a strong one like Grey Poupon.

NUTRITIONAL ANALYSIS PER SERVING: 92 CALORIES, 4 G PROTEIN, 14 G CARBOHYDRATE, 4 G FAT (1 G SATURATED), 0 MG CHOLESTEROL, 55 MG SODIUM, 6 G FIBER

4½ cups trimmed brussels sprout halves (about 1½ pounds)

1   tablespoon extra virgin olive oil

¼   cup thinly sliced shallots

1   teaspoon yellow mustard seeds

1½ tablespoons sherry vinegar

1½ tablespoons mild Dijon mustard

1½ tablespoons water

1   teaspoon fructose

    Salt and freshly ground black pepper

1. Steam the brussels sprouts in a basket over 2 inches of boiling water for 6 to 10 minutes, until crisp-tender. Transfer to an ice water bath, drain, and dry well on kitchen towels.

2. Heat the oil in a large nonstick skillet over medium-high heat. Add the shallots and mustard seeds and sauté until the shallots are golden, 2 to 3 minutes. Reduce the heat and add the vinegar, mustard, water, and fructose. Blend well. Add the brussels sprouts and toss to coat. Season generously with salt and pepper and transfer to a serving dish. Serve immediately.

Zone yield per recipe: Less than one protein block, 4 carbohydrate blocks

Spicy Stir-Fried Brussels Sprouts

4 TO 6 SERVINGS I devised this stir-fry in desperation several years ago when I discovered some long-forgotten brussels sprouts in my refrigerator. I needed the pungent Chinese sauce to mask their deterioration, but the combination was so successful that I have made it ever since with prime specimens. It has even become a staple of my Chinese Thanksgiving table. If you hate brussels sprouts, surely it is because you have not tasted this.

NUTRITIONAL ANALYSIS PER SERVING: 97 CALORIES, 4 G PROTEIN, 16 G CARBOHYDRATE, 4 G FAT (1 G SATURATED), 0 MG CHOLESTEROL, 442 MG SODIUM, 6 G FIBER

4½ cups trimmed brussels sprout halves (about 1½ pounds)

2 tablespoons soy sauce

1 tablespoon Shaoxing rice wine

2 teaspoons fructose

2 teaspoons peanut or canola oil

1 teaspoon toasted sesame oil

1 tablespoon minced garlic

1 tablespoon minced fresh ginger

1 teaspoon curry powder

¼ teaspoon hot red pepper flakes

1. Steam the brussels sprouts in a basket over 2 inches of boiling water for 6 to 10 minutes, until crisp-tender. Transfer to an ice water bath, drain, and dry well on kitchen towels.

2. Combine the soy sauce, rice wine, and fructose in a small bowl or measuring cup. Whisk to dissolve the fructose. Set aside.

3. Heat the oils in a nonstick wok or skillet over medium-high heat. Add the garlic, ginger, curry powder, and pepper flakes. Stir-fry for 10 seconds. Add the brussels sprouts and toss to coat. Add the soy sauce mixture, reduce the heat to low, and toss to combine. Stir-fry for 1 to 2 minutes. Transfer to a serving dish and serve immediately.

Zone yield per recipe: Less than one protein block, 5 carbohydrate blocks

Lemon-Scented Eggplant

6 SERVINGS Eggplant has a neutral personality that makes it an accommodating companion to many proteins and other carbohydrates. Although eggplant has the capacity to act as a sponge for fat, the roasting technique below requires almost none. For variety, add Tiny Tomato Jewels (page 35) just before serving.

NUTRITIONAL ANALYSIS PER SERVING: 60 CALORIES, 2 G PROTEIN, 9 G CARBOHYDRATE, 3 G FAT (0 G SATURATED), 0 MG CHOLESTEROL, 5 MG SODIUM, 4 G FIBER

---

6   cups cubed Roasted Eggplant (1-inch cubed) (page 30)

   Salt and freshly ground black pepper

1   tablespoon extra virgin olive oil

2   teaspoons fresh lemon juice

1   teaspoon grated lemon zest

2   tablespoons minced flat-leaf parsley

2   teaspoons minced fresh rosemary (optional)

1. Heat the oil in a large nonstick skillet over medium heat. Add the eggplant cubes and season with salt and pepper. Add the lemon juice, lemon zest, parsley, and rosemary, if using. Toss to combine. Serve hot, room temperature, or chilled.

Zone yield per recipe: Less than one protein block, 3 carbohydrate blocks

Hot Sesame Green Beans

6 SERVINGS High-temperature roasting in a nonstick pan intensifies flavor without significant added fat. When green beans are subjected to this treatment, they emerge crisp and sweet. Do not be concerned by their slightly shriveled appearance: This indicates water evaporation—in other words, concentrated flavor. Salting before roasting expedites the process and makes the beans even sweeter. (Pictured on page 119.)

NUTRITIONAL ANALYSIS PER SERVING: 59 CALORIES, 2 G PROTEIN, 9 G CARBOHYDRATE, 2 G FAT (0 G SATURATED), 0 MG CHOLESTEROL, 4 MG SODIUM, 4 G FIBER

1½ pounds green beans, trimmed

1   teaspoon toasted sesame oil

1   teaspoon hot sesame oil

   Salt to taste

2   teaspoons unhulled sesame seeds, toasted

1. Place the rack in the upper third of the oven and preheat to 450° F. Place the beans in a large nonstick jelly roll pan (they need not fit in a single layer) and drizzle with the oils. Season generously with salt and toss to coat.

2. Roast for 4 minutes, toss, and roast for 4 minutes longer. Transfer to a serving dish and garnish with the sesame seeds. Serve immediately.

Zone yield per recipe: Less than one protein block, 3 carbohydrate blocks

Hot Stir-Fried Green Beans 4 SERVINGS Because of their year-round availability and

rapid cooking, I find green beans almost indispensable. I always keep plain boiled ones on hand to throw into

salads and eat with dips. However, when life permits, I treat them more respectfully, as in the Chinese preparation

below. If you happen to have cooked green beans in your refrigerator, take the following short-cut: Heat the oil,

make the sauce, and add the beans at the end just to heat them through.

NUTRITIONAL ANALYSIS PER SERVING: 98 CALORIES, 3 G PROTEIN, 14 G CARBOHYDRATE,
4 G FAT (1 G SATURATED), 0 MG CHOLESTEROL, 560 MG SODIUM, 4 G FIBER

Sauce

1   *tablespoon bean sauce*

1   *tablespoon Shaoxing rice wine*

1   *tablespoon soy sauce*

1   *teaspoon fructose*

⅓ *cup chicken broth*

1   *tablespoon peanut or canola oil*

4   *cups trimmed green beans*

1   *tablespoon minced garlic*

1   *tablespoon minced fresh ginger*

2   *tablespoons minced scallions
    (white parts only)*

½ *teaspoon hot red pepper flakes*

1. To make the sauce, combine the bean sauce, rice wine, soy sauce, fructose, and chicken broth in a small bowl or measuring cup and whisk to dissolve the fructose. Set aside.

2. Heat the oil in a nonstick wok or large skillet over medium-high heat. Add the beans and stir-fry for 3 minutes. Add the garlic, ginger, scallions, and pepper flakes and stir-fry for another minute. Add the sauce mixture and stir-fry for 1 to 2 minutes. Serve immediately.

Zone yield per recipe: Less than one protein block, 4 carbohydrate blocks

Stir-Fried Mustard Greens 4 SERVINGS

Mustard greens speak for themselves—the simpler the preparation, the better. Their peppery sharpness flatters rich meats such as pork, veal, and duck. Nutritionally, they're efficient suppliers of vitamin A, bearing almost as much as an equivalent amount of cantaloupe. Mustard greens support insulin control via high fiber content and low carbohydrate density.

NUTRITIONAL ANALYSIS PER SERVING: 146 CALORIES, 4 G PROTEIN, 28 G CARBOHYDRATE, 4 G FAT (0 G SATURATED), 0 MG CHOLESTEROL, 294 MG SODIUM, 7 G FIBER

2 ripe pears, peeled, halved, and cored

1 tablespoon extra virgin olive oil

2 pounds mustard greens, stemmed and coarsely chopped

1 tablespoon balsamic vinegar

1 tablespoon soy sauce

Salt and freshly ground black pepper

1. Preheat the oven to 350° F. Spray a nonstick baking sheet with canola oil. Place the pear halves, cut side down, on the baking sheet. Roast for 20 to 30 minutes, until browned slightly and tender. Slice and set aside.

2. Heat the oil in a large nonstick skillet over medium-high heat. Add the greens by handfuls over several minutes, stir-frying to incorporate each batch. When all the greens are in the pot, add the vinegar and soy sauce. Continue stir-frying until the greens are wilted and tender, but remain bright green.

3. If only a little liquid has accumulated, season the greens with salt and pepper and transfer to a serving dish. If the greens are sitting in watery liquid, remove the greens to a serving dish with a slotted spoon and reduce the liquid until syrupy. Pour over the greens. Divide the greens among 4 plates, garnish with pear slices, and serve immediately.

Zone yield per recipe: Less than one protein block, 8 carbohydrate blocks

Spicy Greens with Roasted Tomatoes and Peppers **6 SERVINGS** This

lively Italian-style sauté requires some advance preparation in the form of roasted tomatoes and peppers. These ingredients create a superb dish. However, you may achieve a satisfactory result with canned plum tomatoes and fresh bell peppers if you sauté them with the garlic, parsley, and pepper flakes.

NUTRITIONAL ANALYSIS PER SERVING: 88 CALORIES, 4 G PROTEIN, 14 G CARBOHYDRATE, 3 G FAT (0 G SATURATED), 0 MG CHOLESTEROL, 52 MG SODIUM, 7 G FIBER

1   red bell pepper

1   yellow bell pepper

1   tablespoon extra virgin olive oil

1   tablespoon minced garlic

1   tablespoon minced flat-leaf parsley

*¼   teaspoon hot red pepper flakes or
     to taste*

1   head escarole, cut into 1-inch pieces

1   head chicory, cut into 1-inch pieces

*1   cup quartered Slow-Roasted Plum
     Tomatoes (page 34)*

*   Salt and freshly ground black
     pepper to taste*

1. Roast the peppers by thoroughly charring the skins under the broiler. Transfer to a paper bag and allow to steam for 10 to 15 minutes to loosen the skins. Remove stems, skins, seeds, and membranes. Julienne the flesh and set aside.

2. Heat the oil in a large nonstick skillet over medium heat. Add the garlic, parsley, and pepper flakes. Sauté for 1 minute. Add the greens by handfuls, tossing to incorporate each new batch, until they are all in the skillet. Cover and cook for 3 minutes until slightly wilted. Add the peppers (with any accumulated pepper juice) along with the tomatoes and toss to combine. Cook for another 1 to 2 minutes. Season generously with salt and pepper. Serve immediately.

Zone yield per recipe: Less than one protein block, 4 carbohydrate blocks

Spicy Greens with Roasted Tomatoes and Peppers

Mushroom Hash

4 SERVINGS This off-beat duxelles is not as dry or dense as the classic version, but the porcini and porcini oil give it greater intensity. It makes a luxurious bed for thick slices of lean beef (my husband's automatic choice) or veal, but it also complements roast chicken and rich-tasting fish such as Chilean sea bass. In addition, it makes a delicious stuffing for giant portobellos. If you're in an extravagant mood, sauté the mushrooms in olive rather than porcini oil and add a whiff of truffle oil (1 teaspoon) just before serving.

NUTRITIONAL ANALYSIS PER SERVING: 93 CALORIES, 4 G PROTEIN, 13 G CARBOHYDRATE, 4 G FAT (1 G SATURATED), 0 MG CHOLESTEROL, 10 MG SODIUM, 3 G FIBER

---

1 (⅓ ounce) package dried porcini mushrooms (about ⅓ cup)

1½ pounds assorted mushrooms (portobello, shiitake, oyster, etc.), trimmed

1 tablespoon extra virgin olive oil or porcini mushroom oil

2 tablespoons minced shallots

1 tablespoon minced garlic

2 tablespoons balsamic or sherry vinegar

⅛ teaspoon freshly grated nutmeg

Salt and freshly ground black pepper

2 to 3 tablespoons minced fresh chives

3 tablespoons minced flat-leaf parsley

1. Place the porcini in a measuring cup or bowl with 1 cup boiling water. Soak for 20 minutes and drain, discarding the soaking liquid or saving for another use. Rinse the mushrooms under cold running water, rubbing with your fingers to remove any grit. Pat dry on paper towels. Finely chop and set aside.

2. Trim the fresh mushroom caps as needed. Separate the stems from the caps, discarding the inedible stems. Combine in a food processor and pulse to chop finely, but do not puree.

3. Heat the oil in a large nonstick skillet over medium-high heat. Add the shallots and garlic and sauté 1 to 2 minutes, until tender.

Add the chopped fresh mushrooms and sauté for about 15 minutes, stirring occasionally, until they give up their liquid. Add the porcini. Stir in the vinegar and cook until most of the liquid evaporates. Remove from the heat. Add the nutmeg and season generously with salt and pepper. Stir in the chives and parsley. Serve immediately.

Zone yield per recipe: Less than one protein block, 4 carbohydrate blocks

Baked Pesto Portobellos 6 SERVINGS The nutritional profile of mushrooms includes

fiber, niacin, potassium, phosphorus, and copper. In addition, mushrooms appear to enhance the immune

and cardiovascular systems. Portobellos provide these benefits in a particularly delicious and satisfying way.

Choose firm ones with intact, closed caps that curve down toward the stem. Frayed caps that flare out suggest

diminished freshness.

NUTRITIONAL ANALYSIS PER SERVING: 133 CALORIES, 7 G PROTEIN, 17 G CARBOHYDRATE,
6 G FAT (1 G SATURATED), 1 MG CHOLESTEROL, 44 MG SODIUM, 4 G FIBER

---

3   teaspoons extra virgin olive oil

½   pound white mushrooms, diced

6   medium portobello mushrooms, stems peeled and diced, caps separated and left whole

Salt and freshly ground black pepper

½   cup tightly packed fresh basil leaves

2   tablespoons dry-roasted shelled pistachio nuts

2   tablespoons finely grated Parmesan cheese

¼   cup Roasted Garlic Paste (page 24)

1. Heat 1½ teaspoons of the olive oil in a nonstick skillet over medium-high heat. Add the diced mushrooms and cook, stirring frequently, until the mushrooms have given up their liquid and most of it has evaporated. Season with salt and pepper and transfer to a bowl. Cool to room temperature.

2. Combine the basil, pistachios, and 1 tablespoon of the Parmesan in a food processor and pulse to chop finely, but do not puree. Add the basil mixture to the chopped mushrooms along with the roasted garlic paste and blend well. Adjust the seasoning.

3. Place the rack in the upper third of the oven and preheat to 450° F. Spray a nonstick baking sheet with olive oil and place the portobello caps gill side up. Season with salt and pepper. Divide the pesto-mushroom mixture evenly among them, spreading it to cover the surface. Sprinkle each cap with ½ teaspoon Parmesan and drizzle with ¼ teaspoon olive oil.

4. Bake 10 for 15 minutes, until tender. Serve immediately.

Zone yield per recipe: Less than one protein block, 9 carbohydrate blocks

Sauté of Roasted Fennel and Tomatoes with Smoked Peppers

6 SERVINGS My husband loves fennel in any form, and I am always searching for new ways to present it. This colorful, deeply satisfying dish evolved out of my desire to please him and a pragmatic effort to use up some leftover roasted tomatoes and smoked peppers. Ironically, I fell in love with it myself and now I make this dish from scratch for its own sake. Since the tomatoes are time-intensive, prepare them in advance. I try to make all the vegetables ahead (they'll keep 4 to 5 days in the refrigerator) so that the sauté takes only 5 minutes.

NUTRITIONAL ANALYSIS PER SERVING: 141 CALORIES, 5 G PROTEIN, 25 G CARBOHYDRATE, 4 G FAT (1 G SATURATED), 0 MG CHOLESTEROL, 686 MG SODIUM, 4 G FIBER

---

4   medium fennel bulbs (about 1½ pounds), stalks trimmed

1   tablespoon extra virgin olive oil

1   tablespoon minced garlic

2   Smoked Bell Peppers (1 red, 1 yellow), julienned (page 32)

1   cup sliced Slow-Roasted Plum Tomatoes (page 34)

1   teaspoon salt or to taste

    Freshly ground black pepper

1. Preheat the oven to 450° F. Halve the fennel bulbs lengthwise and remove the cores. Place the cut sides of each bulb together and wrap each bulb tightly in a foil packet. Arrange the packets on a baking sheet and roast for approximately 30 minutes, until tender. When the fennel is cool enough to handle, remove from the packets, drain, and cut each half lengthwise into ⅓-inch slices. (Do not be concerned if the layers of the slices separate.)

2. Heat the oil in a large nonstick skillet over medium heat. Add the garlic and sauté for 1 to 2 minutes. Add the peppers and tomatoes and cook for 1 minute, tossing. Add the fennel, salt, and pepper to taste. Cook for 2 to 3 minutes, stirring to combine. Adjust the seasoning and serve immediately.

Zone yield per recipe: Less than one protein block, 8 carbohydrate blocks

Sauté of Roasted Fennel and Tomatoes with Smoked Peppers

Skillet Cherry Tomatoes

4 SERVINGS For years, sautéed cherry tomatoes have been a frequent accompaniment to grilled and roasted meats on my dinner table. In the old days, I would peel them and then toss them in melted butter. Occasionally, I even sprinkled them with sugar! Fortunately, the thin-skinned vine cherry tomatoes from Israel and Mexico that have entered our markets are so sweet that a quick turn, unpeeled, in good olive oil suffices for a delicious side dish. This bright and simple preparation complements fish, chicken, lamb, or beef. Choose the herb combination that fits the personality of your protein.

NUTRITIONAL ANALYSIS PER SERVING: 54 CALORIES, 2 G PROTEIN, 8 G CARBOHYDRATE, 2 G FAT (0 G SATURATED), 0 MG CHOLESTEROL, 18 MG SODIUM, 2 G FIBER

1½ teaspoons extra virgin olive oil

4 cups cherry tomatoes

2 to 3 tablespoons chopped assorted fresh herbs (flat-leaf parsley, rosemary, thyme, marjoram, oregano, tarragon, chives, chervil, mint)

Salt and freshly ground black pepper

1. Heat the oil in a large nonstick skillet over medium heat. Add the tomatoes and roll around for several minutes until they begin to crack. Remove from heat, toss with the herbs, and season generously with salt and pepper. Serve immediately.

Zone yield per recipe: Less than one protein block, 4 carbohydrate blocks

Glazed Sweet Bean Turnips 4 SERVINGS

Every Thanksgiving, I prepare a Chinese banquet and this dish always appears on the menu. It gratifies the desire for a sweet vegetable such as pumpkin, yams, or butternut squash without the attendant glycemic difficulties. In addition, its intensity makes it satisfying in small amounts. On days other than Thanksgiving, I serve it with pork, duck, and veal—all of which have the capacity to balance its savory richness.

NUTRITIONAL ANALYSIS PER SERVING: 107 CALORIES, 3 G PROTEIN, 15 G CARBOHYDRATE, 5 G FAT (1 G SATURATED), 0 MG CHOLESTEROL, 440 MG SODIUM, 4 G FIBER

1   *tablespoon peanut or canola oil*

1   *tablespoon minced garlic*

1   *tablespoon minced fresh ginger*

1½ *pounds purple-top turnips, peeled and cut into 1-inch chunks*

2   *tablespoons sweet bean sauce*

1   *tablespoon soy sauce*

1   *teaspoon fructose*

1   *cup chicken broth*

1. Heat the oil in a nonstick wok or skillet over medium-high heat. Add the garlic and ginger. Stir-fry for 10 seconds. Add the turnips and stir-fry for 1 minute. Add the sweet bean sauce, soy sauce, fructose, and chicken broth. Cover and cook for 10 minutes, until the turnips are tender. Uncover and reduce the sauce until syrupy, tossing the turnips until nicely glazed. Serve immediately.

Zone yield per recipe: Less than one protein block, 4 carbohydrate blocks

Glazed Sweet Bean Turnips

Turnip "Fries" 4 SERVINGS

Turnips belong to the same cruciferous family as cabbage, horseradish, and broccoli. The pungent odors of these plants protect them from predators. Interestingly, a growing body of scientific evidence points to protective effects in humans as well—specifically anticarcinogenic activity. Turnips can be as delicious as they are healthful, becoming tender and sweet when roasted at high temperatures. Salt them well before roasting to draw out any bitterness they may possess.

NUTRITIONAL ANALYSIS PER SERVING: 55 CALORIES, 1 G PROTEIN, 10 G CARBOHYDRATE, 2 G FAT (0 G SATURATED), 0 MG CHOLESTEROL, 98 MG SODIUM, 4 G FIBER

---

5 cups peeled and julienned purple-top turnips (⅓-inch by 2-inch sticks)

2 teaspoons peanut or canola oil

Salt

2 teaspoons malt vinegar (optional)

1. Place the rack in the upper third of the oven and preheat to 425° F. Place the turnips on a nonstick jelly roll pan or baking sheet. Drizzle with the oil and toss to coat. Spread out in a single layer. Salt generously.

2. Roast for about 30 minutes, turning several times, until nicely browned and tender. Serve immediately, sprinkled with the vinegar if desired.

Zone yield per recipe: Less than one protein block, 3 carbohydrate blocks

Broiled Zucchini with Double Basil **4 TO 6 SERVINGS** I live in Massachusetts

where winters are long and harsh. Zucchini and fresh basil, available year-round, keep the possibility of summer in mind, even when it is dark by mid-afternoon. In this recipe, the basil oil adds a mellow complexity to the brightness of the fresh herb. | Depending on the distribution of heat from your broiler, you may have to broil the zucchini in batches or move them around during cooking for even browning. (Pictured on page 83.)

NUTRITIONAL ANALYSIS PER SERVING: 59 CALORIES, 3 G PROTEIN, 8 G CARBOHYDRATE, 3 G FAT (0 G SATURATED), 0 MG CHOLESTEROL, 8 MG SODIUM, 3 G FIBER

3   *pounds medium zucchini, ends trimmed, halved lengthwise*

2   *to 3 teaspoons basil oil*

   Salt and freshly ground black pepper

¼   *to ⅓ cup coarsely chopped fresh basil*

1. Preheat the broiler. Arrange the zucchini halves on the broiler pan cut sides up. Brush very lightly with the oil. Season generously with salt and pepper.

2. Broil 4 inches from the flame until nicely browned, about 4 minutes. Turn, brush with the remaining oil, season with salt and pepper, and broil for 2 to 3 minutes longer. Remove to a platter. Sprinkle with the chopped basil. Serve hot, warm, or at room temperature.

Zone yield per recipe: Less than one protein block, 3 carbohydrate blocks

Summer Squash with Double Rosemary *(Variation)* **4 TO 6 SERVINGS**

NUTRITIONAL ANALYSIS PER SERVING: 75 CALORIES, 3 G PROTEIN, 12 G CARBOHYDRATE, 3 G FAT (0 G SATURATED), 0 MG CHOLESTEROL, 3MG SODIUM, 4 G FIBER

1. For variety, substitute summer squash for the zucchini and rosemary for basil. Use 2 to 3 teaspoons rosemary oil with 3 to 4 teaspoons chopped fresh rosemary.

Zone yield per recipe: Less than one protein block, 3 carbohydrate blocks

Beans and Lentils

I am ashamed to admit that I knew beans about beans when I lived on grains. But when I gave up pasta and rice, legumes suddenly looked intriguing. Curiosity led me to the glycemic index literature where the most favorable carbohydrates turned out to be beans! In one scientific study, a mere ½ cup of beans per day helped control blood sugar in diabetics. What could be better for insulin-modulating diets?

Beyond this, beans have a beneficial effect on blood lipids—decreasing triglyceride and cholesterol levels and increasing circulating HDL (good cholesterol). They also possess anticarcinogenic properties and contribute significant amounts of calcium and iron. Finally, they constitute the most potent natural source of soluble fiber, which increases satiety and aids in controlling blood sugar, insulin, and cholesterol levels.

My respect for the nutritional properties of beans drew me, as a cook, into their world of flavor and texture where I faced a choice between home-cooked and canned varieties. When I learned that the processing of canned beans increases glycemic index, I decided to cook my beans from scratch and discovered I strongly preferred their taste and texture.

Although cooking beans from scratch may seem too time-consuming, with a little planning, you can easily fit it into any busy life. I soak the beans overnight and cook them early the next morning. If I start cooking soaked beans when I get up at 6 A.M., they're done by the time I take my son to school. Then in the evening, I'm ready to make the final dish. I frequently make several types of beans at once when I have time and freeze them in 1-cup quantities until I need them.

Dried beans usually double in volume when cooked. Therefore, ½ cup dried beans should yield approximately 1 cup cooked. Cooked beans in cooking liquid will keep for several days in the refrigerator or for up to 6 months in the freezer.

Although a quick-soak method exists for dried beans, I do not recommend it. It drags out the actual cooking process and ends up being more trouble than it's worth. I believe in old-fashioned overnight soaking. Spread the dried beans in a single layer on a white kitchen towel. Remove any discolored beans or stones. Place in a strainer and rinse under cold running water. Transfer to a bowl large enough to hold water equal to 4 times the bean volume. Soak overnight.

The next morning, drain and rinse your beans. Transfer to a deep pot and add water equivalent to 4 times the bean volume. Add some or all of the following to the bean water: ½ celery stalk, ½ carrot, ½ onion, several peeled garlic cloves, several sprigs of flat-leaf parsley, several sprigs of thyme, 1 to 2 bay leaves. Bring to a boil and simmer, partially covered, until tender. Remove the aromatic vegetables and herbs. Salt to taste.

Lentils (and channa dal) do not require presoaking. Cooking times for lentils and dals vary with the type and sometimes even with brand. For best results, follow package directions.

Adzuki Beans with Cucumbers and Scallions (page 186)

Adzuki Beans with Cucumbers and Scallions 4 SERVINGS Small, reddish-

brown adzuki beans, *Phaseolus angularis,* most commonly appear in sweet red bean paste and Japanese confections. However, their mild flavor suits salads as well. If "adzuki" goes unrecognized where you shop, work your way through the following spellings and appellations until you find them: adsuki, aduki, asuki, azuki, chi dou, feijao, field pea, hong xiao dou, red oriental, or Tiensin red. By any name, they taste as sweet. (Pictured on page 185.)

NUTRITIONAL ANALYSIS PER SERVING: 148 CALORIES, 6 G PROTEIN, 21 G CARBOHYDRATE, 1 G FAT (0 G SATURATED), 0 MG CHOLESTEROL, 176 MG SODIUM, 4 G FIBER

½ cup dried adzuki beans, picked over, rinsed, and soaked overnight

4 cups water

½ cup sake or dry sherry

3 quarter-size slices fresh ginger, smashed

3 large garlic cloves, peeled and smashed

3 whole scallions, smashed

1 cup peeled, seeded, and diced English cucumber

¼ cup sliced scallions

Dressing

1 teaspoon sesame oil

2 teaspoons Japanese soy sauce

2 teaspoons rice vinegar

1 teaspoon fructose

¼ teaspoon wasabi powder or to taste

1. Drain and rinse the beans and transfer to a medium saucepan. Add the water, sake, ginger, garlic, and smashed scallions. Bring to a boil, reduce the heat, and simmer, partially covered, for 30 to 45 minutes, until tender but not mushy. Remove the ginger, garlic, and scallion pieces. Cool the beans to room temperature and refrigerate until you are ready to serve. (The beans can be made in advance and refrigerated for up to 3 days or frozen for up to 6 months.)

2. To make the dressing, combine the oil, soy sauce, vinegar, fructose, and wasabi powder in a small bowl or measuring cup. Whisk to blend.

3. Drain the beans well and combine with the cucumbers and scallions in a large bowl. Pour the dressing over the vegetables and toss to coat. Serve immediately.

Zone yield per recipe: Less than one protein block, 6 carbohydrate blocks

Black Bean Salad with Avocado

6 SERVINGS I grew up in Miami surrounded by people from Cuba and "The Islands." Black beans and rice, plantains, and cumin-scented chicken appeared often on our dinner table. When I was unaware of insulin's effects, I included rice in this salad, but it is equally delicious and lower in glycemic impact without it. (Pictured on page 77.)

NUTRITIONAL ANALYSIS PER SERVING: 124 CALORIES, 6 G PROTEIN, 19 G CARBOHYDRATE,
3 G FAT (1 G SATURATED), 0 MG CHOLESTEROL, 6 MG SODIUM, 7 G FIBERA

---

2   cups cooked and drained black beans

½   cup diced red bell pepper

½   cup diced yellow or green bell pepper

½   cup diced avocado

½   cup diced red onion

½   cup peeled and diced cucumber

½   teaspoon ground cumin or to taste

2   tablespoons minced flat-leaf parsley

1   tablespoon minced fresh oregano

1   to 2 tablespoons balsamic vinegar

1   tablespoon lime juice

    Tabasco sauce

    Salt and freshly ground black pepper

1. Combine all the ingredients in a bowl, adding Tabasco sauce and salt and pepper to taste. Toss well. Serve at room temperature or chilled.

Zone yield per recipe: Less than one protein block, 8 carbohydrate blocks

Warm Black Beans with a Smoky Sofrito

6 SERVINGS A Cuban friend taught me to make a sofrito when I was 10, and I made it her way for 30-odd years. Then I began my adventures in stovetop smoking and profoundly altered my approach. The classic Cuban version still occupies a place in my repertoire, but the following smoky variant has overtaken it as a routine starting point for sautés and stews of all kinds. Feel free to increase the spices and vinegar for a more intense experience.

NUTRITIONAL ANALYSIS PER SERVING: 136 CALORIES, 7 G PROTEIN, 22 G CARBOHYDRATE, 3 G FAT (0 G SATURATED), 0 MG CHOLESTEROL, 394 MG SODIUM, 8 G FIBER

1   tablespoon extra virgin olive oil

1   tablespoon minced garlic

¼   teaspoon hot red pepper flakes

1   cup coarsely chopped Smoked Onions (page 27)

1   cup coarsely chopped Smoked Bell Peppers (red and yellow) (page 32)

¼   teaspoon chili powder

¼   teaspoon ground cumin

¼   teaspoon dried oregano

2   cups cooked and drained black beans

1   teaspoon salt or to taste

2   teaspoons sherry or cider vinegar

    Freshly ground black pepper

1   tablespoon minced flat-leaf parsley

1. Heat the oil in a large nonstick skillet over medium-high heat. Add the garlic and red pepper flakes and sauté for 1 minute. Add the onions, peppers, chili powder, cumin, and oregano. Sauté for 1 minute. Add the beans and salt. Cook, stirring, for 2 minutes. Stir in the vinegar and black pepper to taste. Garnish with the parsley. Serve immediately.

Zone yield per recipe: Less than one protein block, 9 carbohydrate blocks

Black-Eyed Peas with Collard Greens and Smoked Garlic

4 SERVINGS Collard greens are low in carbohydrate density and high in vitamin A and fiber. As cruciferous vegetables, they share the phytochemical profile and anticarcinogenic properties of that amazing family of plants. Their traditional pairing with black-eyed peas usually gains depth from a ham hock. Here, smoked garlic and red wine intensify flavor without adding saturated fat. Brief cooking will keep the greens beautiful and delicious. Take care when you fold in the peas to avoid dislodging their delicate skins.

NUTRITIONAL ANALYSIS PER SERVING: 142 CALORIES, 5 G PROTEIN, 17 G CARBOHYDRATE, 4 G FAT (1 G SATURATED), 0 MG CHOLESTEROL, 121 MG SODIUM, 6 G FIBER

---

1 tablespoon extra virgin olive oil

2 bunches collard greens (about 1½ pounds), stemmed and coarsely chopped

½ cup chicken broth

½ cup red wine (preferably Merlot)

¾ cup cooked and drained black-eyed peas

4 large cloves Smoked Garlic (page 25), peeled and sliced lengthwise

Salt and freshly ground black pepper

1. Heat the oil in a large nonstick skillet or wok over medium-high heat. Add the greens, in batches if necessary, and stir-fry for 4 minutes. Add the broth and wine. Cover, reduce the heat, and simmer for 5 minutes. Gently fold in the peas and garlic slices and heat through.

2. To serve, remove the greens, beans, and garlic to a serving dish with a slotted spoon. Reduce the liquid remaining in the skillet until syrupy. Pour over the greens. Season generously with salt and pepper. Serve immediately.

Note: When you smoke the garlic cloves for this recipe, start checking tenderness after 15 minutes and remove them when they yield to a fork but remain firm enough to be sliced.

Zone yield per recipe: Less than one protein block, 4 carbohydrate blocks

Black-Eyed Pea Salad with Radishes and Cucumbers 4 SERVINGS

The westward migration of black-eyed peas apparently started in Asia and followed the African slave trade to our American South. Whatever the route, my friend Diana Bateman said, "Pure Texas," when she read this recipe—imagining the dusky peas, tangy buttermilk, crunchy sharp radishes, and cool cucumbers.

NUTRITIONAL ANALYSIS PER SERVING: 74 CALORIES, 4 G PROTEIN, 13 G CARBOHYDRATE,
1 G FAT (0 G SATURATED), 1 MG CHOLESTEROL, 383 MG SODIUM, 3 G FIBER

Dressing

¼   *cup nonfat buttermilk*

2   *tablespoons low-fat mayonnaise*

1   *tablespoon cider vinegar*

½   *teaspoon salt or to taste*

    Freshly ground black pepper

1   *cup cooked and drained black-eyed peas*

½   *cup diced red radishes*

½   *cup seeded and diced cucumbers (peeling is optional)*

2   *tablespoons minced flat-leaf parsley*

1. To make the dressing, combine the buttermilk, mayonnaise, vinegar, salt, and pepper to taste in a small bowl or measuring cup. Whisk to blend.

2. Combine the peas, radishes, and cucumbers in a medium-sized bowl. Add the dressing and toss to coat.

3. Adjust the seasoning and garnish with the parsley. Serve immediately.

Zone yield per recipe: Less than one protein block, 4 carbohydrate blocks (1 tablespoon dressing = 0 protein blocks, ¹⁄₁₀ carbohydrate block)

Black-Eyed Pea Salad with Radishes and Cucumbers served with grilled sirloin steak

Black-Eyed Peas and Collard Greens with White Truffle Oil

4 SERVINGS The best white truffle oil results from the immersion of white truffles in extra virgin olive oil. Brands differ in intensity and cost, increasing in tandem. After receiving some as a gift, I conducted a series of experiments and found that various combinations of beans and greens benefited from its pungent, woodsy influence. This discovery propelled me through the entire bottle!

NUTRITIONAL ANALYSIS PER SERVING: 106 CALORIES, 5 G PROTEIN, 15 G CARBOHYDRATE, 4 G FAT (0 G SATURATED), 1 MG CHOLESTEROL, 32 MG SODIUM, 6 G FIBER

2   *bunches collard greens (1½ pounds), stemmed and coarsely chopped*

2   *teaspoons extra virgin olive oil*

¼   *cup finely chopped onion*

1   *teaspoon minced garlic*

½   *cup brown chicken stock or chicken broth*

¾   *cup cooked black-eyed peas with ½ cup cooking liquid*

½   *to 1 teaspoon white truffle oil*

Salt and freshly ground black pepper

1. Bring a large pot of salted water to a boil and add the collards. Cook for 3 minutes, drain in a colander, and run under cold water to stop the cooking. Drain well.

2. Heat the olive oil in a large nonstick skillet over medium heat. Add the onion and sauté until translucent, 2 to 3 minutes. Add the garlic and cook for 1 minute longer. Add the greens, stock, and pea cooking liquid. Bring to a boil. Reduce the heat and add the peas and truffle oil. Simmer for 2 minutes and season generously with salt and pepper.

3. If desired, remove the collards and beans to a serving dish with a slotted spoon and reduce the liquid until syrupy. Pour over greens and peas and serve immediately.

Zone yield per recipe: Less than one protein block, 4 carbohydrate blocks

Cannellini Beans with Rosemary   **4 SERVINGS** Although home-cooked beans have

a low glycemic index, they do exhibit high carbohydrate density. In other words, a small quantity contains a large amount of carbohydrate. For example, ¼ cup cooked beans contains more carbohydrate than an entire head of iceberg lettuce. On the other hand, their high soluble fiber content makes them very filling. As a result, a serving is small, but satisfaction is great. (Pictured on page 135.)

NUTRITIONAL ANALYSIS PER SERVING: 139 CALORIES, 8 G PROTEIN, 22 G CARBOHYDRATE, 3 G FAT (0 G SATURATED), 0 MG CHOLESTEROL, 439 MG SODIUM, 6 G FIBER

(continued)

Cannellini Beans with Rosemary (continued)

2   cups cooked cannellini beans with ¼ cup cooking liquid

2   large cloves Roasted Garlic (page 24)

2   teaspoons extra virgin olive oil

2   teaspoons chopped fresh rosemary

¾   teaspoon salt or to taste

    Freshly ground black pepper

1. Combine ¼ cup of the beans, the ¼ cup cooking liquid, and the roasted garlic cloves in a blender. Puree until smooth.

2. Heat the oil in a small nonstick saucepan over medium-low heat. Add the rosemary and sauté for 1 to 2 minutes. Add the beans, bean puree, salt, and pepper to taste.

Cook for 2 minutes to heat through. Remove from the heat. Adjust the seasoning and serve immediately.

Zone yield per recipe: Less than one protein block, 7 carbohydrate blocks

Cannellini-Tomato Salad with Anchovies and Capers

4 TO 6 SERVINGS Anchovy fillets come packed in oil. To get around this problem, rinse them thoroughly in a sieve and pat them dry on paper towels. You'll significantly decrease their fat content without diminishing their flavor. The moisture from the tomatoes and dressing will revitalize them.

NUTRITIONAL ANALYSIS PER SERVING: 92 CALORIES, 6 G PROTEIN, 15 G CARBOHYDRATE, 2 G FAT (0 G SATURATED), 2 MG CHOLESTEROL, 112 MG SODIUM, 4 G FIBER

Dressing

1   tablespoon champagne or white wine vinegar or to taste

1   teaspoon extra virgin olive oil

2   teaspoons coarsely chopped anchovy fillets (rinsed and dried before chopping)

1½   teaspoons chopped capers

½   teaspoon grated lemon zest

1½   cups cooked and drained cannellini beans

1½   cups chopped fresh tomatoes

2   tablespoons minced flat-leaf parsley

    Salt and freshly ground black pepper

1. To make the dressing, combine the vinegar, oil, anchovies, capers, and lemon zest in a small bowl or measuring cup. Whisk to blend.

2. Combine the beans, tomatoes, and parsley in a bowl. Add the dressing and toss to coat. Adjust

the seasoning, adding salt and pepper to taste. Serve at room temperature or slightly chilled.

Zone yield per recipe: Less than one protein block, 6 carbohydrate blocks (1 tablespoon dressing = 0 protein blocks, 0 carbohydrate blocks)

Cannellini-Tomato Salad with Anchovies and Capers

Channa Dal with Smoked Tomatoes and Cauliflower 6 SERVINGS

Channa dal is a small, quick-cooking legume that resembles split yellow peas. Although I have been unable to locate definitive nutritional information on channa dal, I do have a strategy for estimating its carbohydrate content. Since the existing descriptive literature ties channa dal to lentils and split yellow peas, I would expect its carbohydrate content to reflect these affinities. Cooked lentils contain 7.5 grams of insulin-stimulating carbohydrate per 1/4 cup, while cooked split peas contain 9 grams per ¼ cup. A reasonable guess for cooked channa dal would be 8 grams of insulin-active carbohydrate per ¼ cup. Its mild flavor enables it to soak up intense flavors of other ingredients, such as the smoked tomatoes and curry powder in the following stew.

NUTRITIONAL ANALYSIS PER SERVING: 134 CALORIES, 6 G PROTEIN, 22 G CARBOHYDRATE, 3 G FAT (0 G SATURATED), 0 MG CHOLESTEROL, 416 MG SODIUM, 4 G FIBER

½ cup channa dal

2 cups water

½ cup chopped onion

2 teaspoons curry powder

1 tablespoon extra virgin olive oil

1 tablespoon minced garlic

1 tablespoon minced ginger

½ teaspoon black mustard seeds

2 cups peeled and diced Smoked Plum Tomatoes, (page 36)

4 cups bite-size cooked cauliflower

1 teaspoon kosher salt or to taste

¼ teaspoon cayenne pepper (optional)

Freshly ground black pepper

1. Combine the channa dal, water, onion, and curry powder in a medium saucepan. Bring to a boil. Reduce the heat and simmer, covered, for approximately 45 minutes, until the beans are soft and partially disintegrated. Do not drain.

2. Heat the oil in a large nonstick skillet over medium heat. Add the garlic, ginger, and mustards seeds and sauté for 1 minute. Add the tomatoes and cauliflower and toss to coat. Stir in the channa dal, salt, and cayenne, if using. Blend well and season to taste with black pepper. Serve immediately in shallow bowls.

Zone yield per recipe: Less than one protein block, 12 carbohydrate blocks

Channa Dal with Swiss Chard

4 SERVINGS A certain confusion surrounds channa dal. Is it a split yellow lentil or a yellow split pea? Despite this lack of clarity, authorities generally agree on its exceptionally low glycemic index, which has stimulated considerable interest among the insulin-conscious. Channa dal commonly serves as a thickening agent in soups, stews, and curries. This nutrient-rich dish reheats beautifully in the microwave the next day.

NUTRITIONAL ANALYSIS PER SERVING: 173 CALORIES, 8 G PROTEIN, 28 G CARBOHYDRATE, 4 G FAT (0 G SATURATED), 0 MG CHOLESTEROL, 839 MG SODIUM, 3 G FIBER

1   tablespoon extra virgin olive oil

½   cup finely chopped onion

1   tablespoon minced garlic

1   tablespoon minced fresh ginger

1   teaspoon ground cumin

1   teaspoon ground coriander

½   teaspoon ground turmeric

½   cup channa dal

1   cup chopped and drained fresh or canned tomatoes

2   cups water

1   bunch red or green Swiss chard (about 1 pound)

1   teaspoon salt or to taste

    Freshly ground black pepper

1. Heat the oil in a nonstick skillet over medium-high heat. Add the onion and sauté for 3 to 4 minutes, until golden, stirring occasionally. Reduce the heat to medium and add the garlic, ginger, cumin, coriander, and turmeric. Sauté, stirring, for 1 to 2 minutes. Add the channa dal, tomatoes, and water. Bring to a boil, reduce the heat, and simmer, covered, for 45 minutes, until the beans are soft and partially disintegrated.

2. While the stew is simmering, separate the chard stems from the leaves. Chop the stems into ½-inch lengths and the leaves into 1-inch pieces.

3. When the beans are done, add the chard stems, cover, and simmer for 5 minutes. Uncover and add the leaves by handfuls, stirring to incorporate them. After all the leaves are in the pot, simmer for 1 to 2 minutes until the chard is wilted, but still bright green. Add the salt and pepper to taste. Serve immediately in shallow bowls.

Zone yield per recipe: Less than one protein block, 10 carbohydrate blocks

Chickpea, Fennel, and Red Pepper Salad 3 TO 4 SERVINGS Home-cooked

chickpeas are definitely not fast food. To decrease your average time investment per chickpea recipe, cook large quantities at once. Then freeze the beans with cooking liquid to cover in 1-cup containers to be used as needed.

NUTRITIONAL ANALYSIS PER SERVING: 133 CALORIES, 6 G PROTEIN, 20 G CARBOHYDRATE, 4 G FAT (0 G SATURATED), 0 MG CHOLESTEROL, 71 MG SODIUM, 5 G FIBER

Dressing

1   teaspoon extra virgin olive oil

1   tablespoon red wine vinegar or to taste

1   tablespoon minced oil-cured black olives

1   teaspoon Dijon mustard

½   teaspoon grated orange zest

1   cup cooked and drained chickpeas

½   cup chopped fennel

½   cup chopped red bell pepper

2   tablespoons finely chopped red onion

2   tablespoons minced flat-leaf parsley

2   tablespoons coarsely chopped fennel fronds

   Salt and freshly ground black pepper

1. To make the dressing, combine the oil, vinegar, olives, mustard, and orange zest in a small bowl or measuring cup. Whisk to blend.

2. In a large bowl, combine the chickpeas, fennel, bell pepper, onion, parsley, and fennel fronds.

Add the dressing and toss to coat. Add salt and pepper to taste. Serve at room temperature or chilled.

Zone yield per recipe: Less than one protein block, 5 carbohydrate blocks (1 tablespoon dressing = 0 protein blocks, 0 carbohydrate blocks)

Chickpea, Fennel, and Red Pepper Salad served with grilled veal chop

Curried Chickpeas with Cabbage and Arame 6 SERVINGS The hearty

ingredients of this sauté—a cruciferous vegetable, a sea vegetable, and a legume—stick to the ribs. I make it when the air turns crisp and cool, but the grill remains operational for tandoori-style meat dishes. This combination provides an intense nutritional boost for sagging spirits and drowsy bodies when the days suddenly become short and dark.

NUTRITIONAL ANALYSIS PER SERVING: 172 CALORIES, 7 G PROTEIN, 28 G CARBOHYDRATE, 4 G FAT (1 G SATURATED), 0 MG CHOLESTEROL, 468 MG SODIUM, 10 G FIBER

1 ounce dried arame (about 1½ cups)

4 cups sliced green cabbage

1 tablespoon extra virgin olive oil

2 tablespoons minced garlic

2 teaspoons curry powder

2 cups chopped Smoked Plum Tomatoes (page 36)

1 teaspoon fructose

2 cups cooked and drained chickpeas

1 teaspoon salt or to taste

Freshly ground black pepper

1. Soak the arame in water to cover for 10 minutes. Drain, rinse, and transfer to a saucepan. Add water to cover. Bring to a boil, reduce the heat, and simmer for 15 minutes. Drain well and set aside.

2. Meanwhile, steam the cabbage over 2 inches of boiling water until crisp-tender, about 10 minutes. Drain well.

3. Heat the oil in a large nonstick skillet over medium heat. Add the garlic and curry powder and sauté for 1 minute. Add the arame, tomatoes, and fructose. Cook, stirring, for 1 minute. Add cabbage, chickpeas, salt, and pepper to taste. Cook, stirring, for another 2 minutes. Serve immediately.

Zone yield per recipe: Less than one protein block, 12 carbohydrate blocks

Salad of Chickpeas, Broccoli, and Cauliflower **6 SERVINGS** With my

weekly batch of boiled fresh vegetables in the refrigerator and a freezer full of home-cooked beans, I can face

a recipe like this with equanimity even on a busy week night. If you're starting from scratch, you can cook the

cauliflower and broccoli together to save time. The chickpeas and vegetables can be used warm, at room

temperature, or chilled.

NUTRITIONAL ANALYSIS PER SERVING: 102 CALORIES, 6 G PROTEIN, 14 G CARBOHYDRATE, 3 G FAT (0 G SATURATED), 1 MG CHOLESTEROL, 125 MG SODIUM, 5 G FIBER

Dressing

2 teaspoons extra virgin olive oil

2 tablespoons red wine vinegar or to taste

6 Kalamata olives, pitted and chopped

2 teaspoons anchovy paste

1 cup cooked and drained chickpeas

2 cups diced cooked broccoli

2 cup diced cooked cauliflower

½ cup chopped red onion

¼ cup minced flat-leaf parsley

   Salt and freshly ground black pepper

1. To make the dressing, combine the oil, vinegar, olives, and anchovy paste in a small bowl or measuring cup. Whisk to blend.

2. Combine the chickpeas, broccoli, cauliflower, onion, and parsley in a large bowl. Pour the dressing over the vegetables and toss well to coat.

Season generously with salt and pepper and add more vinegar, if desired. Serve immediately.

Zone yield per recipe: Less than one protein block, 6 carbohydrate blocks (1 tablespoon dressing = 0 protein blocks, 0 carbohydrate blocks)

Lentil-Stuffed Zucchini **4 SERVINGS** The size, color, and texture of white lentils make them ideal for this recipe, but you can use another variety if you cannot find them. Regardless of the type of lentil used, make sure you avoid overcooking or your beans will be pasty. The stuffing can be made a day ahead and refrigerated. Bring it to room temperature before use.

NUTRITIONAL ANALYSIS PER SERVING: 115 CALORIES, 6 G PROTEIN, 15 G CARBOHYDRATE, 5 G FAT (1G SATURATED), 0 MG CHOLESTEROL, 80 MG SODIUM, 1 G FIBER

Stuffing

1   teaspoon extra virgin olive oil

1   teaspoon minced garlic

1   teaspoon minced flat-leaf parsley

⅛   teaspoon red pepper flakes

1   tablespoon chopped oil-cured black olives

1   cup peeled, seeded, and chopped fresh plum tomatoes

¾   cup cooked and drained white lentils

    Salt and freshly ground black pepper

4   medium zucchini (about 1½ pounds), trimmed and halved lengthwise

    Salt and freshly ground black pepper

2   teaspoons extra virgin olive oil

1. To make the stuffing, heat the oil in a small skillet over medium heat. Add the garlic, parsley, and red pepper flakes and sauté for 2 minutes. Add the olives, tomatoes, lentils, and salt and pepper to taste. Simmer for 3 to 4 minutes. Remove from the heat and set aside.

2. Scoop out the pulp from the zucchini halves, leaving a ¼- to ⅓-inch shell. (Set the pulp aside for another use.) Bring a large pot of salted water to a boil and blanch the zucchini boats for 2 minutes. Drain and run under cold water to stop the cooking. Dry well on paper towels. Season the cut surface with salt and pepper.

3. Preheat the oven to 450° F. Spray a nonstick baking sheet with olive oil. Spoon about 3 rounded tablespoons of stuffing into each boat, place on the baking sheet, and drizzle each with ¼ teaspoon olive oil.

4. Bake for 15 minutes. Serve hot, warm, or at room temperature.

Zone yield per recipe: Less than one protein block, 4 carbohydrate blocks

Lentil Salad with Hijiki and Roasted Red Peppers 4 TO 6 SERVINGS

Hijiki (a.k.a. "hiziki") is a calcium-rich seagrass. With a dietary fiber content approaching 100 percent, its elegant black strands can dress up a plate of humble lentils without adding to their insulin effect. Hijiki comes dried in packages and must be rehydrated. In this recipe, it undergoes sequential soaking, sautéing, and simmering. | Du Puy lentils have the ideal consistency for this salad, but you can use brown lentils in a pinch. Make sure you do not overcook them or else your salad will be mushy.

NUTRITIONAL ANALYSIS PER SERVING: 221 CALORIES, 11 G PROTEIN, 37 G CARBOHYDRATE, 4 G FAT (0 G SATURATED), 0 MG CHOLESTEROL, 560 MG SODIUM, 15 G FIBER

1   ounce dried hijiki (about 1 cup)

1½ teaspoons extra virgin olive oil

1½ teaspoons minced garlic

1   cup water

1   tablespoon balsamic vinegar

4   large red bell peppers

2   cups cooked French green lentils (du Puy)

¼   cup minced shallots

¼   cup minced flat-leaf parsley

Dressing

2   tablespoons balsamic vinegar

1   tablespoon Dijon mustard

1   tablespoon Japanese soy sauce

2   teaspoons extra virgin olive oil

2   teaspoons fructose or maple syrup

½   teaspoon salt or to taste

    Freshly ground black pepper

1. Place the hijiki in a heatproof bowl or 1-quart measuring cup and add boiling water to cover. Soak for 15 minutes, drain, dry on paper towels, and chop into 1½-inch lengths.

2. Heat 1½ teaspoons oil in a nonstick skillet over medium heat. Add the garlic and sauté for 1 minute. Add the hijiki and sauté, stirring, for 5 minutes. Add the water and 1 tablespoon balsamic vinegar. Cover, reduce the heat, and simmer for 15 minutes. Remove from the heat and drain.

3. Roast the peppers by thoroughly charring the skins under the broiler. Transfer to a paper bag and allow to steam for 10 to 15 minutes to loosen the skins. Remove stems, skins, seeds, and membranes. Julienne the flesh and set aside.

4. To make the dressing, combine the vinegar, mustard, soy sauce, olive oil, fructose, and salt and pepper to taste. Whisk to blend.

5. In a bowl, combine the hijiki, roasted pepper strips, lentils, and shallots. Pour in the dressing and toss to coat. Adjust the seasoning. Garnish with the parsley. Serve warm, at room temperature, or chilled.

Zone yield per recipe: Less than one protein block, 12 carbohydrate blocks (1 tablespoon dressing = 0 protein blocks, ¼ carbohydrate block)

Stew of White Beans, Greens, and Smoked Tomatoes

6 SERVINGS If you have cooked cannellini beans in the freezer and leftover smoked tomatoes in the refrigerator, this dish is a breeze to make. It's the sort of stew I love to serve midwinter with broiled or roasted meats: Perky, hearty, and healthy.

NUTRITIONAL ANALYSIS PER SERVING: 184 CALORIES, 12 G PROTEIN, 26 G CARBOHYDRATE, 4 G FAT (1 G SATURATED), 0 MG CHOLESTEROL, 497 MG SODIUM, 10 G FIBER

---

1 tablespoon extra virgin olive oil

1 tablespoon minced garlic

1 tablespoon minced flat-leaf parsley

¼ to ½ teaspoon hot red pepper flakes

12 cups chopped mixed greens, such as Swiss chard, red kale, and escarole (1-inch pieces)

2 cups cooked and drained cannellini beans

1 cup diced Smoked Plum Tomatoes (page 36)

3½ cups chicken broth

Salt and freshly ground black pepper

1. Heat the oil in a large nonstick skillet over medium heat. Add the garlic, parsley, and red pepper flakes and sauté for 1 minute. Add the greens by handfuls, tossing to incorporate each new batch. When all the greens are in the skillet, add the beans, tomatoes, and broth. Bring to a boil, reduce the heat, and simmer for 15 minutes.

2. With a slotted spoon, remove the greens and beans to a serving dish. Reduce the liquid until syrupy. Season with salt and pepper. Add to the beans and greens. Adjust the seasoning and serve immediately in shallow bowls.

Zone yield per recipe: Less than one protein block, 10 carbohydrate blocks

Lentil Salad with Hijiki and Roasted Red Peppers served with pan roasted salmon

Fruits and Fruit Desserts

The history of Western painting celebrates the physical attributes of fruits—their iconic forms, sensuous colors and textures, and poignant transience. Modern science documents other virtues—particularly their nutritional profiles (including glycemic index) and impressive phytochemical concentrations.

Many fruits have a low or moderate glycemic index, indicating that their sweetness (primarily due to fructose) does not cause insulin spikes. Cherries and grapefruit rank lowest of any fruits on the current glycemic index list, with plums, strawberries, peaches, pears, apples, oranges, grapes, and kiwis not far behind.

Why should you include fruits in your diet? First, they supply critical vitamins and minerals: Oranges provide folate, potassium, and vitamin C. Berries contribute iron. Pineapple contains manganese, a trace mineral involved in enzyme activation. Almost all fruits supply boron, important for the maintenance of healthy bones. Fruits may not rival legumes or sea vegetables as sources of fiber, but apples, figs, grapefruit, oranges, peaches, and raspberries all contain significant amounts. Fiber, as you now know, contributes directly to insulin control. In addition, fruits contain phytochemicals, such as carotenoids and flavonoids, that display anticarcinogenic activity.

Human beings have always delighted in the taste of fruits, and now we have more reasons than ever to include them in our diets. The sweet flavor of plain fresh fruit makes it the best dessert for insulin modulation. When you want something a bit more interesting, the simple fruit desserts in this chapter can be integrated into a careful diet.

Plain fresh fruit can help you satisfy your carbohydrate requirement without adding any fat at all. In the following list of glycemically favorable fruits, each "serving" represents approximately 9 grams of absorbable carbohydrate (total carbohydrate minus dietary fiber) or 1 Zone carbohydrate block.

Glycemically Favorable Fruits:

⅔ cup sliced apple (3 ounces)

⅔ cup apricot halves (3.5 ounces)

¾ cup blackberries (4 ounces)

½ cup blueberries (3 ounces)

9 medium cherries (2.5 ounces)

½ grapefruit or ½ cup grapefruit sections (4 ounces)

⅔ cup grapes (3 ounces)

⅔ cup sliced nectarine (3.5 ounces)

½ cup orange sections (4 ounces)

⅔ cup sliced peach (4 ounces)

½ cup sliced pear (2.5 ounces)

½ cup sliced plum (3 ounces)

¾ cup raspberries (4 ounces)

1 cup strawberries (6 ounces)

Baked Fruit with Warm Blueberry Sauce (page 204)

Baked Fruit with Warm Blueberry Sauce 4 SERVINGS This gorgeous

dessert is pure comfort food. During the cruelest months, it fills my kitchen with sweet fruit perfumes and the

whisper of vanilla. (Pictured on page 203.)

NUTRITIONAL ANALYSIS PER SERVING: 87 CALORIES, 1 G PROTEIN, 19 G CARBOHYDRATE, 2 G FAT (0 G SATURATED), 0 MG CHOLESTEROL, 2 MG SODIUM, 3 G FIBER

Sauce

2   cups blueberries

1   tablespoon fructose

¼   teaspoon vanilla extract

1   teaspoon water

    Pinch ground cloves

    Pinch ground cinnamon

3   ripe nectarines or peaches or
    2 Yellow Delicious apples or ripe
    pears, peeled, pitted or cored, and
    cut into 6 wedges

1   teaspoon macadamia nut or
    canola oil

1. To make the sauce, combine the blueberries, fructose, vanilla, water, cloves, and cinnamon in a medium saucepan and bring to a boil. Reduce the heat and simmer for 10 to 15 minutes, stirring occasionally, until the berries break down. Pass through a fine mesh sieve into a bowl, vigorously working the berry mass with a wooden spoon. Scrape into the bowl any pulp adhering to the underside of the sieve. (Discard the residue inside the sieve.) If a thicker sauce is desired, return it to the saucepan and reduce to your preferred consistency. Set aside ½ cup sauce for the fruit and reserve the remainder for another purpose. (The sauce can be made in advance

and refrigerated for up to 1 week or frozen for up to 6 months. Reheat in the microwave before serving.)

2. Preheat the oven to 350° F. Brush a nonstick baking sheet with the oil. Place the fruit wedges flat side down and bake for approximately 15 minutes for nectarines or peaches or 20 minutes for apples or pears, until tender.

3. Serve warm with 2 tablespoons of sauce spooned over each serving. Pass the extra sauce at the table.

Zone yield per recipe: Less than one protein block, 6 carbohydrate blocks (1 tablespoon sauce = 0 protein blocks, ⅓ carbohydrate block)

Broiled Fruit Skewers **4 SERVINGS** Availability, cost, and protein companion determine my

choice of fruits for this recipe. I use apples and pears in winter; peaches, plums, and nectarines in summer; and

fresh pineapple whenever it's cheap. If you wish to brush the fruits with a little oil, I suggest peanut or macadamia

nut, but they cook perfectly well without it. Broiling them *au naturel* allows you to save your fat coupons for the

rest of your meal. Double skewer the fruit for easy turning. | Served warm or at room temperature, these fruits

complement grilled or roasted meats, especially turkey, pork, duck, and lamb. They particularly enhance protein

dishes with Indian flavors by serving as low-glycemic chutney surrogates. They are lovely additions to composed

salads and even work as dessert. Leftovers are delicious cold or reheated in the microwave. If you like, garnish them

with chopped fresh basil, mint, or tarragon. (Pictured on page 111.)

NUTRITIONAL ANALYSIS PER SERVING: 43 CALORIES, 0 G PROTEIN, 11 G CARBOHYDRATE, 0 G FAT (0 G SATURATED), 0 MG CHOLESTEROL, 0 MG SODIUM, 2 G FIBER

---

1 firm apple, tart (Granny Smith) or sweet (Fuji or Yellow Delicious), peeled, cored, and cut into 1- to 1½-inch chunks

1 firm, ripe pear, peeled, cored, and cut into 1- to 1-½-inch chunks

or

2 cups chopped fresh pineapple (1- to 1-½-inch chunks)

or

1 rounded cup chopped firm, ripe peaches or nectarines (1- to 1½-inch chunks)

1 rounded cup chopped firm, ripe plums (1- to 1½-inch chunks)

1. Preheat the broiler. Thread the fruits loosely on skewers. Broil for 3 to 4 minutes. Turn and broil for another 3 to 4 minutes, until tender. Serve warm, at room temperature, or chilled.

Zone yield per recipe: Less than one protein block, 4 carbohydrate blocks

Chilled Fruit with Cold Blueberry Sauce 4 SERVINGS

Kiwis and strawberries can come to the table in a state of compromise between plain and fancy: party dress, no sugary make-up. For variety, use the sauce on other chilled fruits—cooked or raw—including apples, pears, peaches, and nectarines. Leftover sauce can be used with sautéed chicken breasts.

NUTRITIONAL ANALYSIS PER SERVING: 67 CALORIES, I G PROTEIN, I6 G CARBOHYDRATE, I G FAT (0 G SATURATED), 0 MG CHOLESTEROL, 4 MG SODIUM, 4 G FIBER

Blueberry Sauce

2   cups blueberries

1   tablespoon fructose

1   tablespoon blueberry, raspberry, or black currant vinegar

1   tablespoon water

2   kiwis, peeled and sliced

2   cups hulled strawberries, halved if large

1. To make the sauce, combine the berries, fructose, vinegar, and water in a medium saucepan and bring to a boil. Reduce the heat and simmer for 10 to 15 minutes, stirring occasionally, until the berries break down. Pass through a fine mesh sieve into a bowl, vigorously working the berry mass with a wooden spoon. Scrape into the bowl any pulp adhering to the underside of the sieve. (Discard the residue inside the sieve.) If a thicker sauce is desired, return it to the saucepan and reduce to your preferred consistency. Allow the sauce to cool and refrigerate it until you are ready to serve. Set aside ½ cup of the sauce for the fruit. Reserve the remainder for future use. (The sauce will keep in the refrigerator for up to 1 week or in the freezer for up to 6 months.)

2. Distribute the kiwi slices and strawberries among 4 bowls. Drizzle each with 2 tablespoons of the sauce. Serve immediately.

Zone yield per recipe: Less than one protein block, 5 carbohydrate blocks (1 tablespoon sauce = 0 protein blocks, ⅓ carbohydrate block)

Peaches with Blackberry Sauce 6 SERVINGS

This simple dessert provides a refreshing, subtly sweet conclusion to a meal. For variety, substitute nectarines or ripe pears. The sauce also works with unpeeled, raw fruit. If you do not rule out a little melon once in a while, try it on cantaloupe or honeydew. It's out of this world! The sauce can be made in advance and refrigerated for up to 1 week or frozen for up to 6 months.

NUTRITIONAL ANALYSIS PER SERVING: 50 CALORIES, 1 G PROTEIN, 13 G CARBOHYDRATE, 0 G FAT (0 G SATURATED), 0 MG CHOLESTEROL, 0 MG SODIUM, 3 G FIBER

Blackberry Sauce

1½ cups blackberries

1   tablespoon black currant or
    raspberry vinegar

1   tablespoon water

2   teaspoons fructose

6   ripe peaches

1. To make the sauce, combine the berries, vinegar, water, and fructose in a small nonreactive saucepan. Bring to a boil, reduce the heat, and simmer, stirring occasionally, for about 15 minutes until berries break down. Pass through a fine mesh sieve into a bowl, working the berry mass vigorously with a wooden spoon. Scrape into the bowl any pulp clinging to the underside of the sieve. (Discard the residue inside the sieve.) Reserve ½ cup of the sauce to serve with the peaches. Chill, if serving cold. Set aside the remainder for another use. (The sauce can be refrigerated for up to 1 week or frozen for up to 6 months.)

2. Preheat the oven to 425° F. Blanch the peaches in boiling water for 10 seconds and peel. Cut each into 6 wedges. Spray a nonstick baking sheet with canola oil and arrange the peach wedges flat side down. Bake for 10 minutes or until tender. Serve warm or cold, drizzled with the sauce.

Zone yield per recipe: Less than one protein block, 6 carbohydrate blocks (1 tablespoon sauce = 0 protein blocks, ⅙ carbohydrate block)

Roasted Pears with Gorgonzola

4 SERVINGS Fromage blanc is a fresh nonfat French-style soft cheese with a fluffy, light texture. Gorgonzola is a voluptuous, pungent, blue-veined Italian cheese that contains too much saturated fat for regular straight-up consumption. Their union enhances the flavor of one and the lipid profile of the other, and makes a special treat of simple roasted pears.

NUTRITIONAL ANALYSIS PER SERVING: 83 CALORIES, 3 G PROTEIN, 13 G CARBOHYDRATE, 2 G FAT (1 G SATURATED), 5 MG CHOLESTEROL, 112 MG SODIUM, 2 G FIBER

---

2 ripe pears, peeled, halved, and cored

1 ounce Gorgonzola (no rind)

2 tablespoons fromage blanc or nonfat ricotta

1 teaspoon cognac

1. Preheat the oven to 350° F. Spray a nonstick baking sheet with canola oil and place the pears cut side down. Roast for 20 to 30 minutes, until tender.

2. Meanwhile, combine the Gorgonzola, fromage blanc, and cognac in a small bowl and blend well.

3. To serve, divide the pears among 4 plates. Garnish each serving with a dollop of the cheese mixture. Serve immediately.

Zone yield per recipe: 1 protein block, 4 carbohydrate blocks

Fresh Figs with Virtual Mascarpone

4 SERVINGS Mascarpone is an Italian cream cheese made from cow's milk that rivals whipped cream as an accompaniment to fruits and berries. Unfortunately, 2 tablespoons contain 13 grams of fat, 10 grams of which are saturated. A little fromage blanc can lessen mascarpone's nutritional disadvantages without obliterating its sweet, rich taste. This dessert takes only 5 minutes to prepare. If you have more than 5 minutes, halve the figs and use a pastry bag to decorate the cut sides with the mascarpone mixture.

NUTRITIONAL ANALYSIS PER SERVING: 75 CALORIES, 2 G PROTEIN, 10 G CARBOHYDRATE, 3 G FAT (2 G SATURATED), 9 MG CHOLESTEROL, 18 MG SODIUM, 2 G FIBER

---

2 tablespoons mascarpone

2 tablespoons fromage blanc or nonfat ricotta

4 fresh ripe figs, quartered

½ teaspoon grated orange zest

1. Combine the mascarpone and fromage blanc in a small bowl and blend well.

2. Divide the figs among 4 plates and place a dollop of the cheese mixture on each serving. Sprinkle with a pinch of orange zest and serve at once.

Zone yield per recipe: 1 protein block, 4 carbohydrate blocks

Fresh Figs with Virtual Mascarpone

Acknowledgments

Although writing may be a solitary activity, cookbook writing requires a whole squadron of participants. The sheer quantity of chopping, trimming, washing, and drying—not to mention tasting—would overwhelm any individual. I would like to thank the critical contributors without whom I could never have managed this effort.

When this book was just a mess in my kitchen, my assistant, Isabel Rivera, stood by my side—cheerfully mincing, peeling, and organizing. When I had two stovetop smokers going full blast and four roasts in the oven, she made sure I did not forget to pick up my son after school. She kept her eagle eye on my inventory, charting the ever-changing levels of essential ingredients. Her unflappable and tireless support kept this project moving forward. My debt to her is tremendous, and I can never repay it.

Next in gratitude deserved are my husband and parents, who ate on command for an entire summer. They faced pork roast with black beans for breakfast and smoked snapper with mustard sauce for snacks. If mealtime arrived and I left no instructions, they tracked me down by phone so they could complete the day's tasting assignments. If that's not devotion, I don't know what is.

I also appreciated the tolerance of my son, Sam, who said, "Mom, I know your food is good. I just don't like it." He contentedly lived on "take-out" for 6 months and did his homework entirely on his own.

Valued friends, Susan Austrian, Diana Bateman, and Melinda Marble gave me three thumbs up right from the beginning. Their enthusiasm, encouragement, and trust helped me through many moments of intense fatigue and doubt.

My tutelary spirit—the brilliant, sophisticated, and marvelously insatiable Peter Benjamin—took this project completely seriously when there was no rational reason for doing so. A pleasure to know and feed, he filled my heart (and guest room) with his benevolence on many occasions. I could not have completed this project without him.

I am also deeply indebted to my three guides through the forbidding underworld of publishing:

Rollene Saal, Jay Cantor, and Miriam Altschuler. They used their considerable powers to further my journey, shining their special lights on the path and helping to clear it of obstacles.

I credit publisher James Connolly of Bay Books with the foresight (and palate) to have approached me with this project after a single unscheduled meal at my house one wintry night. His belief in my abilities gave me the confidence to face my first blank page.

My sister and brother, Barbara Garrett and David Friedson, cheered me all the way to the finish line and used their creative talents and personal influence to energize the business of getting this book published. They know the enormous need they filled and the deep gratitude I feel.

On the supply side, certain people magically intervened to help me along the way. I would like to thank Norma Gillaspie of the Cottonwood Cafe, Jim Neal of Fusion Foods, Chris Malone of C.M. International, Victoria Abbott Riccardi, and Ben and Josh Nathan. They greeted my off-beat intrusions enthusiastically and responded with generous support.

I thank the gentlemen of Newton Centre's famous John Dewar & Co., Inc. for their openness to new experiences and new friends. Harry Wedge, store manager, and Ken O'Reilly, *artiste,* raise the discipline of meat-cutting to the highest level. Ken is a veritable hero of the protein world: He never met a roast he could not trim to zero visible fat.

In addition, Bread and Circus Whole Foods Market, the Newton Store, was a constant source of inspiration and aid. This remarkable store reflects a passion and respect for food matching my own. I consider it my outside office and I love "working" there. The following individuals made specific contributions in kindness, knowledge, skill, and energetic service:

> *Joe Brennan, Meat Cutter*
> *Orlando Delgado, Front End*
> *Bob Delorey, Clerk*
> *Doug Ellis, Meat Manager*
> *Borys Gojnycz, Fish Cutter*
> *Larry Mihaloplos, Front End*
> *Ken Pimental, Meat Cutter*
> *Eric Piper, Cheese Team Leader*
> *Kirby Sullivan, Assistant Produce Team Leader*
> *Maria Vasquez, Cashier*
> *Anthony Yung, Meat Department Head Clerk*

Informative, steady, and kind, editors Jain Lemos and Andrea Chesman taught me well and helped me to be clear and consistent for my own good. Master photographer Tim Turner and Chef/Stylist Lynn Gagné took protein/carbohydrate ratios in stride, then deftly brought my food to life with unerring taste and art. Designer Madeleine Corson and ace photographer Rick Friedman also made distinct contributions to this book. I deeply value our collaboration.

Finally, I would like to thank Dr. Barry Sears, whose courage and persistent genius made the Zone available to everyone. His contribution enhanced my own health and life and that of my entire family. The force of his ideas created an intellectual clearing in which this book could appear.

INDEX